READING AND THE HISTORY OF RACE IN THE RENAISSANCE

Elizabeth Spiller studies how early modern attitudes toward race were connected to assumptions about the relationship between the act of reading and the nature of physical identity. As reading was understood to happen in and to the body, what you read could change who you were. In a culture in which learning about the world and its human boundaries came increasingly through reading, one place where histories of race and histories of books intersect is in the minds and bodies of readers. Bringing together ethnic studies, book history, and historical phenomenology, this book provides a detailed case study of printed romances and works by Montalvo, Heliodorus, Amyot, Ariosto, Tasso, Cervantes, Munday, Burton, Sidney, and Wroth. *Reading and the History of Race* traces ways in which print culture, and the reading practices it encouraged, contributed to shifting understandings of racial and ethnic identity.

ELIZABETH SPILLER is Professor of English and Director of the History of Text Technologies Program, Florida State University. She is the author of *Science, Reading and Renaissance Literature* (Cambridge, 2004), and editor of the two-volume *Seventeenth-Century English Recipe Books* (2008). She has been awarded fellowships from the NEH, the Fulbright, and the Mellon foundations, and her article "Situating Prospero's Art: Shakespeare and the Making of Early Modern Knowledge," which appeared in *South Central Review*, was awarded the Kirby Prize by the SCMLA for the best article of 2009. Her work has been published in such journals as *Renaissance Quarterly*, *Studies in English Literature*, *Modern Language Quarterly*, and *Renaissance Drama*.

READING AND THE HISTORY OF RACE IN THE RENAISSANCE

ELIZABETH SPILLER

CAMBRIDGE
UNIVERSITY PRESS

University Printing House, Cambridge CB2 8BS, United Kingdom

Cambridge University Press is part of the University of Cambridge.

It furthers the University's mission by disseminating knowledge in the pursuit of education, learning and research at the highest international levels of excellence.

www.cambridge.org
Information on this title: www.cambridge.org/9781107463370

© Elizabeth Spiller 2011

First published 2011
First paperback edition 2014

A catalogue record for this publication is available from the British Library

Library of Congress Cataloguing in Publication data
Spiller, Elizabeth.
Reading and the history of race in the Renaissance / Elizabeth Spiller.
p.   cm.
Includes bibliographical references and index.
ISBN 978-1-107-00735-2 (hardback)
1. Race awareness–Europe–History–16th century.   2. Books and reading–Europe–History–16th century.   3. Race awareness in literature.   4. Europe–Intellectual life–16th century.   I. Title.
HT1507.S75 2011
305.80094'09024–dc22
2011008030

ISBN 978-1-107-00735-2 Hardback
ISBN 978-1-107-46337-0 Paperback

Cambridge University Press has no responsibility for the persistence or accuracy of URLs for external or third-party internet websites referred to in this publication, and does not guarantee that any content on such websites is, or will remain, accurate or appropriate.

For Tim,
and in memory of
Robert Spiller
(1930–2009)

Contents

Acknowledgements

Like early modern romances, this book often seemed to spread out across a long plain, taking many turns in its plots. Over the course of imagining and writing this book, I have incurred many debts, personal and intellectual. Barbara Lewalski, Alan Shepard, and Roland Greene all supported this project from the outset and I appreciate their generous and unwavering support. Portions of this book have been presented at conference sessions and invited talks at MLA, RSA, SAA, Arizona State University, Trinity University, and Vanderbilt University: my thanks to Lynn Enterline, Heidi Brayman Hackel, Leah Marcus, Steve Mentz, Willis Saloman, Kathryn Schwarz, Ayanna Thompson, and Mary Floyd-Wilson for hosting and organizing those events. I had an opportunity to lead a seminar on "Figure, Form, and Color: Race and Genre in Early Modern Literature" at the 2008 Shakespeare Association of America: I learned a great deal from all of the participants in that seminar, some of which I hope informed my thinking in this book. Bruce Boehrer, Mary Thomas Crane, Katherine Crawford, Jonathan Crewe, Peter Erickson, Marjorie Garber, Carla Mazzio, Elizabeth Scala, Laurie Shannon, Kathryn Schwarz, Gary Taylor, Doug Trevor, Henry Turner, and Will West shared their thoughts and expertise, providing encouragement at key moments and listening patiently to my long accounts of even longer plots. I began thinking about this book while working on race and romance in Shakespeare's *Merchant of Venice*: that essay did not make it into this book, but I would like to thank Jeff Masten and Wendy Wall for encouraging my thinking on these topics. I also appreciate the vibrant intellectual community of English Department and the History of Text Technologies program at Florida State University: my colleagues and friends have helped shape this book in a hundred ways for which I am truly grateful.

This book was supported by a Fellowship from the National Endowment for the Humanities. I am very grateful to the NEH for this generous support which allowed me to spend the kind of time reading these romances that they had demanded from their original readers. Any views, findings, conclusions, or recommendations expressed in this book do not necessarily reflect those of the National Endowment for the Humanities. I spent time reading both Wroth and Heliodorus at the Newberry Library and thank the Newberry for the short-term fellowship that made that possible.

Last and first, my family deserves all my thanks. From Matthew and Samantha, I have seen new versions of romance – and the new technologies of reading that go with them – as they unfold on the computer screen in anime fan fiction; Tim has been the model reader of and for this book on the history of reading. My love and thanks to each of them.

Introduction: print culture, the humoral reader, and the racialized body

He that goeth in the Sonne, shalbe Sonne burnt, although he thinke
not of it. So they that will read this, or such like Bookes, shall in the
ende, bee as the Bookes are.
                    Thomas Wilson, *The Arte of Rhetorique* (1560)[1]

Oft turning others' leaves, to see if thence would flow
Some fresh and fruitful showers upon my sunburnt brain.
                    Philip Sidney, "Astrophil and Stella" (c. 1581)[2]

This is a book about early modern book history and race. Thus far, book
history and critical race studies have been two very different scholarly
activities. Scholarship in the history of the book has given us a rich
account of the materiality of early modern texts. The concept of the "soci-
ology of the text" has encouraged us to follow the material life-cycle of
texts through the process that began with the making of ink and paper
and ended with the printing, sale, and binding of volumes that readers
then annotated with their own pens and ink, often beginning a new process of production and consumption. While this approach has produced
an exciting and influential body of scholarship, book history has had less
to say about the history of human identity that such texts record and
create. In particular, book history has not focused on cultural categories
such as race primarily because scholarship has assumed a divide between
the form of books (their material state, which is part of book history) and
their content (which is generally not).

Yet, it is not simply books that had a material existence and history.
Readers also had their own physical existence. This point has not been
sufficiently understood or emphasized. Reading was something that early
modern readers knew to happen in and to the body. In a pre-Cartesian
world, reading was an embodied act: it was not prior or extrinsic to subject formation but instead was an important aspect of day-to-day lived
experience. Thus, reading was not understood to be a limitedly mental activity that primarily concerned the mind and soul; it was not a

mechanical process involving what Hobbes would later call the "strings" of the human machine or a chemical reaction produced by neurons.[3] Rather, reading was closely tied to the body: it involved not just the eyes and the ventricles of the brain, but the blood, vital spirits, and humors of the body. The act of reading could change what you thought; it could also change who you were, physically as well as emotionally. At a time when more readers were learning about the world and its human boundaries through their experiences as readers, racial identity was often a text-based practice. As I will suggest throughout this book, one place where histories of race and histories of books intersect is thus in the bodies of readers.

As scholars have made clear, the history of race in the early modern period involves overlapping and often competing concepts of religion, nation, and ethnicity. The Inquisition, New World voyages and settlements, the breakdown of Galenic humoralism, European interactions with the Ottoman and Marmeluk empires, renewed contact with Ethiopia, the rise of a "scientific" racialism, and the development of plantations and the slave trade: these historic events profoundly informed changing European attitudes toward race and identity. In ways that neither traditional book history nor critical race studies have fully recognized, the invention of the printing press was a key event in the early modern history of race.

Between the late fourteenth century and the mid-seventeenth century, the meaning of race changed from expressing relationships of kinship and genealogy to emphasizing differences of skin color and physical appearance. Summarizing the complexities of these multiple understandings of identity and ethnicity, Ania Loomba identifies this as a period of transition in which multiple definitions of ethnicity, or ethnos more generally, narrow down to produce what becomes a comparatively monolithic modern definition of race: she thus argues that the late sixteenth and early seventeenth centuries constituted "the last period in history where ethnic identities could be understood as fluid, or, as the first moment of the emergence of modern notions of race."[4] Focusing on printed romances from the Fall of Constantinople to early articulations of phenotype racialism in the seventeenth century, *Reading and the History of Race in the Renaissance* traces some of the ways in which print culture, and the reading practices it encouraged, contributed to that shift.

In coming to understand the competing philosophical, theological, economic, and ideological traditions of the early modern period that contribute in different ways to produce what became a modern version of race, scholars such as Margo Hendricks, Patricia Parker, Peter Erickson, Kim

Hall, and Mary Floyd-Wilson have been right to argue that we cannot just retrofit our contemporary conceptions of race onto early modern understandings of it. Race, as both a term and a concept, does not always extend comfortably from early modern to post-modern understandings of identity and ethnicity.[5] Recent scholarship has gone a long way to avoid anachronistic understandings of the content of race and its precursors, but another central goal of this book is to suggest that during this period it is not just the content of race that changed, but also the practices of reading that both created and allow us to understand that content. As important as our need to historicize the history and pre-history to race, we also have to be careful not to problematize just race, as if race were merely a type of content that can be classified as this and not that. We also have to address the practices through which we say we know what constitutes race, what race is and means.

One of the most important of those practices for us as critics is that of reading: our ability to apprehend early modern assumptions about race and its precursors is achieved almost entirely through written texts and documents. In many respects, though our assumptions about reading are as anachronistic and as potentially problematic as are those about race. In much the same way that race is constructed and not a natural phenomenon, neither is reading. If pre-Cartesian readers understood reading to be a distinctively corporeal act, this means that they did not just read about bodies and the world in which those bodies existed. In fact, they read about bodies *in and through their own bodies*. Changes in early modern assumptions about the body changed the act of reading; conversely, the act of reading also fundamentally shaped early modern experiences of identity and the body. We have been able to recover different components of the pre-racial quality to early modern thinking about identity. For instance, Geraldine Heng suggests that race is a discursive practice; Mary Floyd-Wilson has argued that regional humoralism constituted the dominant mode for making ethnic distinctions; Gary Taylor has problematized the historic moment at which it became possible for European men to understand themselves as white.[6] Such acts of critical recovery, though, have been achieved only through our own acts of reading in our tacitly mechanized, racialized bodies. Rather than relying upon reading as a seemingly transparent tool for understanding the past, I hope to show how reading was often the material process through which early modern forms of ethnic and racial identity were created.

Literary discussions of the history of racial identity in the early modern period have understandably gravitated toward thinking about how race functions on stage, particularly in the works of Shakespeare. Scholarship on the cultural history of race in early modern culture, at least in English, has focused overwhelmingly on dramatic works.[7] More significantly, scholars have also approached the subject from a theoretical perspective that might be loosely described as "performances of identity" or even "performances of race." This emphasis on understanding both the representation and the historical practice of race in dramatic terms began with G. K. Hunter's provocative "Othello and Colour Prejudice," which was given as a lecture to the British Academy in 1967.[8] Rejecting the claims of Coleridge, and others, who had insisted that Othello was in some way not black, Hunter argued that Othello's color was both real and significant to our understanding of the play.[9] Hunter's essay was, as Andrew Hadfield has noted, "the first serious attempt to understand Elizabethan attitudes toward race."[10] Although scholars have challenged several of Hunter's claims, his essay has been constitutive of the field of critical race studies that has emerged in Renaissance scholarship because he claimed race as a valid object of study by arguing that race was central to both performance and audience reception.[11] For Hunter, it was only possible to move toward a historical understanding of race by way of performance.

Subsequent scholarship has continued this initial emphasis on understanding the history of early modern representations of race through histrionic mimesis. For some critics, race has provided a way to reassess the mimetic assumptions of early modern culture.[12] Dympna Callaghan thus regards Shakespeare's representations of race as integrally connected to larger cultural concerns about the nature of mimesis. Speaking both of theater and of representation more generally, Callaghan argues that "many of Shakespeare's contemporaries did not share our faith in representation … [and] feared the encroachments mimetic representation made upon the real."[13] Blackface and boy actors meant that historically both Othello and Desdemona were played by light-skinned males, by "white men," a performance fact that means that, on stage, "there are, indeed, no authentic 'others' – raced or gendered – of any kind, only their representation."[14] The absence of Africans and all women from the Renaissance stage works as both a kind of pre-condition that makes drama itself possible ("all representation is predicated upon the absence of the thing represented") and a cultural marker that both groups were understood to be incapable of mimesis.[15] In this context, the performance of race on the early modern stage provides a limit case for understanding early modern attitudes toward mimesis.

Other critics have taken performance models from the stage and used them as critical tools for understanding early modern experiences and practices of racial and ethnic identity in terms of various forms of lived imitation. From this critical perspective, the most powerful and culturally significant "performances of race" may well not have appeared on stage at all. In her landmark *Mimesis and Empire*, Barbara Fuchs, for example, draws on the work of Homi Bhabha and Michael Taussig to articulate a model for explaining identity and difference in terms of "cultural mimesis." From this critical perspective, identity and difference can be best understood by putting more pressure on the notion of identity, rather than just difference. For Fuchs, "identity" is inherently a mimetic one, a "sameness" that includes lived experiences that are achieved through the aesthetic practices of "identification, mimicry, and reproduction."[16] Fuchs focuses almost exclusively on non-dramatic texts (romances, religious texts, epics, and historical documents), but, in a way that recognizes the heuristic power of these theoretical models for understanding identity, she nonetheless frames her work with two examples of public performances and uses a performative model of identity to chart the non-dramatic texts that are at the center of her work. The history of difference as it impacted European notions of *imperium* thus involves understanding lived encounters that involve both performance (embodied simulation) and reception (the audiences, both political and cultural, to those simulations). Fuchs' project stands in some ways in sharp contrast to Callaghan's: whereas Callaghan emphasizes the way in which representations of race, and mimesis in general, are achieved out of a fundamental absence (Othello and Desdemona played by "white" men), Fuchs stresses the inherent fragility of the boundary between imitator and imitated (in festivals staged in Peru, Indians play the parts of Moors, while the Spanish play themselves).[17]

Drama has provided both the primary subject and the dominant theoretical model for early modern studies as a whole and critical work on race in the early modern era has consequently focused largely on drama. Stephen Greenblatt's *Renaissance Self-Fashioning* arguably set many of the terms for this dramatic inflection to the histories of cultural identity that have dominated Renaissance studies. Jacob Burckhardt's *The Civilization of the Renaissance in Italy* had provided a history of how the interconnected rise of the modern state and individual was achieved through various forms of art. In modifying the critical tradition that came through Burckhardt and his successors, Greenblatt's *Renaissance Self-Fashioning* replaced Burckhardt's "Renaissance Man" with a more fluid, contingent, and contestational model of the early modern "self." Although Greenblatt borrowed his theoretical language from structural anthropology (and thus, for instance, exchanged Burckhardt's view of both man and state as a "work of art" with Clifford Geertz's idea of the "cultural artifact"), his overall model distinguished itself from earlier scholarship primarily by pursuing an understanding of identity not just as an art, but as an ongoing cultural performance and practice.[18]

It may seem counter-intuitive to include Greenblatt, let alone Burckhardt, as a frame to an account of the history of early modern racial studies. Burckhardt's *Civilization* and Greenblatt's *Renaissance Self-Fashioning* are centrally stories, albeit substantially different ones, about the "rise of the individual." They, and the critical trajectory that connects their work, share an interest in pursuing the singular, and thus construct a certain kind of individual as at once exceptional and universal. In that respect, such versions of the Renaissance run directly counter to the kinds of questions that have been at the heart of recent scholarship on race and ethnicity, but these kinds of arguments about individual identity are nonetheless not innocent from implied claims about racial identity. Writing in 1860, Burckhardt saw Renaissance Man emerging against the backdrop of a medieval collectivity in which "man was only conscious of himself as a member of a race, people, party, family, or corporation – only through some general category."[19] With Greenblatt's early modern self, that structure is less teleological but is still achieved in ways that are inherently contestational: "self-fashioning is achieved in relation to something perceived as alien, strange, or hostile. This threatening Other … must be discovered in order to be attacked and destroyed."[20] Greenblatt's comments closely followed upon and echoed Edward Said's depiction of the West's engagement with the East as a form of theatrical spectacle. For Said, the theater provided a foundational metaphor for the display and spectacle of cross-cultural encounters: "The idea of representation is a theatrical one: the Orient is the stage on which the whole East is confined."[21]

This emphasis on identity as a form of performance, both individual and collective, has intensified in recent scholarship on race and ethnicity, which has benefited from the theoretical models of performativity that structure both post-colonial studies and feminist theory. Surveying "ethnographic" (Richard Schechner, Michael Taussig), "radical constructivist" (Judith Butler), and "oppositional" (Homi Bhabha) models of performativity, Susan Stanford Friedman notes that these approaches all articulate versions of a shared understanding that "the production of identity – individual and collective – involves performative imitation at the borders of difference."[22] These ways of thinking about identity in terms of performance and performativity have done little to correct a critical tendency to bring conversations about authenticity that are part of our own moment back to early modern literature and culture. In what is perhaps the best phenomenological and cognitive, rather than ideological, argument for performance-based models, Mary Crane notes that such models contain a persistent anti-theatrical strand, a feeling that theatricality and performance depend on the "deceptive, hollow, and illusory nature of the theatrical, even as it conjures the real into being."[23] Crane thus instead draws on cognitive studies which suggest that knowledge and experience emerge not through mental representation of an "already existing and stable external reality" but through a lived enactment in which "our embodied brains and our material environment reciprocally create that reality and give it meaning." Because theatrical performance "involves both a physical reality of embodied enactment and a secondary level of representation that emerges from it," Crane suggests that the theater provides a particularly powerful instance, both more intense and more self-conscious, of our lived experiences in which we *create* representations to understand the world.[24] More generally, a performative approach to thinking about early modern racial identity – whether along the lines implied by Taussig or Bhabha or Crane – is valuable because it enriches our critical ability to think about the nature of the encounters (what Friedman describes as the difference in-between rather than the difference between) that make up the cultural history of race.

Our knowledge of both identity and difference, though, did not simply emerge out of encounters, either actual or embodied. Indeed, it is arguable that the notion of encounter, which figures so centrally in performative models of racial identity, may involve an anachronistic notion of embodiment and thus implicitly posit the skin as a boundary between self and other in ways that are a by-product of the rethinking of the body that racial discourse itself helped produce. Such models may to this extent limit our ability to understand what "encounters" may have meant or what may have happened when the body in question was in some sense experienced in epistemologically different terms. Certainly, identity is not always a performance, and thus dramatic and histrionic models for understanding race cannot answer some questions.

Let us instead imagine a contemporary production of *The Merchant of Venice*. Let us also, for the sake of speculation, imagine that Shakespeare himself played the part of the Prince of Morocco, entering under the stage direction "a tawny Moor, all in white," and taking the part to plead that Portia "mislike me not for my complexion, / The shadowed liverie of the burnished sun" (2.1.1–2).[25] From a material and performative point of view, Shakespeare the actor is made tawny by the use of burnt cork or perhaps tallow;[26] the character he plays is imagined to have been "burnished" by the sun in ways that may reflect traditional geo-humoral medical thinking about how the sun brought the burned-away residue of black bile to the surface of the skin. Certainly, the burnishing of Morocco is as iconic as the King of Sparta's shield, with its image of "a black Ethiop reaching at the sun," in *Pericles* (2.2.20): the "blackening" of an actor within the theater seems to mimic cultural understandings of the "blackening" of human skin. In this context, the scene with Portia, which has been prefaced by a wholesale dismissal of other possible suitors on ethnic, national, and geographic grounds, thus becomes a quintessential image of an encounter with otherness.

Yet, Shakespeare's experience of otherness did not begin with cork; it did not even begin with lived encounters that gave shape to characters such as Morocco, Othello, Caliban, or Cleopatra. Rather, Shakespeare began as a reader. Like most early modern writers, his understanding of otherness began primarily on the page, and probably began through his common grammar school experiences in Stratford-upon-Avon, rather than as a practicing playwright living in the comparatively cosmopolitan mercantile, political, and court environments in and around London. That is, to understand early modern experiences of the creation of racial difference we should also focus on Shakespeare, the reader, rather than on just Shakespeare, the playwright-actor, or Morocco, the dramatic character.

Shakespeare's depiction (both in the play text and perhaps on stage) of the Prince of Morocco is likely to have emerged out of his reading of texts such as Richard Eden's translation of Peter Martyr's *Decades of the New Worlde or West India* (1555), which included an influential essay, "Of the colour of Indians," the first published use of the term "tawny" to refer to human complexion in the way in which Shakespeare uses it in this play.[27] Shakespeare's reading then becomes interesting precisely to the extent that it provides more than just a sourcebook of exotic details and useful plot devices, a set of contents that Shakespeare is imagined to borrow and reshape into characters such as the Prince of Morocco. That kind of account implicitly assumes some kind of exceptionalist transcendence in which Shakespeare changes what he reads, not the reverse, and it is through his ability to do that that he is in turn able to change us when we read. I would instead suggest that we need to see how reading, that of Shakespeare and others, developed over the preceding four generations of print culture into an increasingly dominant cultural practice that became a key component of social and intellectual identity. Resisting the temptations of limited biographical understandings of Shakespeare's works, Robert S. Miola argues that "Shakespeare created much of his art from his reading."[28] Here, I would simply note that we should at the same time also try to avoid seeing too sharp an opposition between reading and lived experience. For early modern readers, in particular, reading itself was a lived experience in ways that arose out of their understanding of the nature of the body and of how reading happened both *within and to* that body.

When we consider Shakespeare's depiction of the tawny Morocco as a consequence in some way of his reading, then, it might be useful to think about Thomas Wilson's evocative comments, cited in my epigraph, about the physical effects of reading. Wilson provides a way to recognize that the "burnishing" of the Prince of Morocco may come not so much from the sun or theatrical make-up, but rather from the transformative power of reading. In his *Arte of Rhetorique*, Wilson warned his own readers: "He that goeth in the Sonne, shalbe Sonne burnt, although he thinke not of it. So they that will read this, or such like Bookes, shall in the ende bee as the Bookes are." For a culture that remembered that "Ethiope" was etymologically linked to "burnt skin" and wanted to find explanations for the cause and meaning of differences in skin color, sunburn was a powerful cultural trope for concerns about identity and its apparent instability.[29] In making an analogy between reading books and becoming sunburnt, Wilson expresses the widespread perception that reading was a powerful and often dangerous activity. Reading was something you did, but it was also something that happened to you. It changed what you felt, how you thought, and who you were. Reading marked you. What Wilson and other early modern readers suggest, contemporary scholars working on cognition and the history of reading confirm: reading changes who we are, producing new forms of identity in ways that cross from the intellectual and the emotional to the corporeal.

With this approach to reading as a lived experience in mind, *Reading and the History of Race in the Renaissance* turns from questions about the performance of race to think about what Margo Hendricks has called "the epistemology of race" and does so by looking at how early modern understandings of racial identity in part emerged out of, and were expressed by way of, text-based reading practices.[30] This project focuses primarily on English and European printed romances from the late fifteenth through mid-seventeenth centuries. As I will suggest, Renaissance romance was strongly influenced by printing technologies, which enabled the production and circulation of texts and images (a rapid succession of continuations, translations, adaptations, epitomes, illustrated sequences and painting cycles derived from those texts) in ways that were consistent with both the narrative form and the ideological assumptions of the genre. Romance also provides a particularly good genre as a kind of case study for thinking about how reading contributed to early modern identity practices: as both contemporary readers and subsequent scholars have noted, romance promoted intense forms of reading. These forms of reading, as we shall see, emerge out of a generic interest in articulating identity as a social category, genealogical in nature and visual in form, in ways that were consistent with historic concerns about the meaning of identity within visual culture.

The beginning points for this study are, in the largest sense, the aftermath of the Fall of Constantinople and the invention of the printing press. These iconic moments have traditionally been understood to mark the end of the medieval period and beginning of the Renaissance.[31] The Fall of Constantinople and the invention of the printing press were also, as I will suggest, determining events in both the literary history of romance and the cultural history of race. My endpoint is the mid-seventeenth century, a moment when the fluidity to identity that Loomba points to has largely been replaced by a much more fixed, more recognizably modern, model of identity and when the romances that swept through Europe and England had largely ended. As a genre, romance relies on very different models of identity than drama and thus offers an overlooked literary form for understanding the historic emergence of our own assumptions about race and identity. Within printed romance, in particular, identity emerges within the conventions of reading, as a form of looking, perceiving, and identifying, rather than within those of dramatic performance, of personation and impersonation.

From a narrative and textual perspective (this includes narrative structures, ideological and social assumptions, textual production and dissemination), early modern romance was inherently compatible with and flourished within the visual and technological cultures of print. Indeed, early modern romance seems to pursue nostalgic forms of genealogy while also construing identity in ways that anticipate the advent of phenotype racialism. The advent of print culture provided a powerful and perhaps surprising catalyst for the genre of romance from the late fifteenth through mid-sixteenth centuries. In her important study of medieval romance, Geraldine Heng contends that "medieval romance becomes a medium that conduces with exceptional facility to the creation of races, and the production of a prioritizing discourse of essential differences among peoples."[32] Heng astutely emphasizes that race is most usefully understood as a discursive practice in the sense that the making of race involves "the sudden entrance of specific groups of humans *into* race, through acts of identification and naming."[33]

Like their medieval predecessors, early modern romances are also fundamentally concerned with acts of identification and naming that seek to create this kind of "taxonomy of essential differences" to which Heng points.[34] Although romance was long regarded as a retrograde and ideologically escapist genre, recent critics have begun to realize how romance is a genre in which, as Benedict Robinson has argued, "difference is explored in its most radical forms."[35] As we shall see, printing and the visual culture associated with it challenged the central act of genealogical identification around which romance was traditionally organized: that is, the narrative assumption that otherwise ineffable qualities are physically manifest in those that possess them. In the context of a commitment to virtue that is essentially fixed, romances generally do not tell stories about the development or transformation of character; instead, they show its identification within a world of visible symbols. In medieval romances such as *The King of Tars*, for instance, readers are assured of the true conversion of the Sultan of Damascus because, at the moment of his baptism, his skin changes from dark to fair, but that narrative will no longer be possible by the sixteenth century.

Early modern romances respond strongly to racial and ethnic differences that challenge this model of transparent identity (the fair are fair) and its related commitment to an understanding of race as genealogical connection (universal Christian aristocracy). Indeed, even when romance is not "about" race, its underlying structure accommodates itself to the shift by which race, which once functioned as a concept for establishing blood-based kinship relationships between people, instead became a way of using skin color to differentiate among what seemed to be categories and kinds of peoples. Post-Virgilian epic was able to ground itself in various forms of national identity that allowed it to displace the identities, appearances, and qualities it would reject onto its enemies (dark skinned, effeminized, un-Roman, for instance). Difference presents a more fundamental problem for romance. Within the universal Christendom of romance, one's opponent is, as Fredric Jameson notes, always some version of oneself. The black knight who is still black after he removes his helmet, or after he converts, threatens this narrative of universal and visibly manifest virtue. These challenges figure in classical and medieval romances (*Aethiopika*, *Guy of Warwick*, *The King of Tars*, and *Parzival*, among others), but they become prominent among the group of romances that appear in the aftermath of the Fall of Constantinople at a cultural moment that is defined by the rise of printed vernacular romances.

The narrative structure of romance was also intensified by the technological possibilities of print culture. Elizabeth Eisenstein instances the early printing of existing chivalric romances as evidence of the inherent conservativism of early print culture.[36] Early printed romances do evoke and adapt Greek and medieval romances and these earlier works themselves often continued to circulate in manuscript, but Renaissance romance as a whole is a distinctive product of early modern print culture. The publication history of the most well known and widely read of these romances, *Amadis*, provides a useful example of how both existing and new romances were in some ways the product, in material terms, of the technological possibilities of print.[37] Portions of this cycle were originally written, probably by multiple authors, sometime before 1379.[38] The *Amadis* that most readers knew, though, was a product of printing. The first narratives were substantially reworked, presumably by Garci Rodríguez de Montalvo; they were published sometime in the 1490s. The first extant edition, containing the first four books of the cycle, was published in Saragossa in 1508. Between 1508 and 1586, there were nineteen separate editions, published mostly in Seville and Saragossa, but Spanish editions were also published in a number of smaller Spanish publishing markets as well as in both Rome (1519) and Venice (1533). Romance cycles like *Amadis*, which were structured around the ability of publishers to produce new volumes as quickly as offspring could be imagined by their authors and translators, were written with the possibilities of printing in mind. The first continuations in the series, written by a whole series of new authors, began appearing in print in 1510. After 1503, Seville held important overseas trade monopolies, and copies of these editions (1511, 1526, 1531, 1535, 1539, 1547, and 1551) were in part printed expressly for shipment to the New World.[39]

By 1546 when the Spanish cycle had ended at twelve volumes, which by then included about a hundred distinct publications, Italian publishers had put out translations of the first four books, and Nicolas de Herberay des Essarts had almost finished his immensely influential translation of the cycle, releasing *Le Septiesme livre d'Amadis de Gaule*, the last of the French translations of the *Amadis* volumes to appear before the death of François

I. The French versions of *Amadis* provide an example of the rapid material transformations that romances underwent in the hands of early modern translators and printers and, by extension, readers. The Herberay translations, which were initially published in Paris by Denis Janot, became the property of Estienne Groulleau in 1548, the year after Groulleau also began publishing the anti-Amadisian romance, *L'Histoire Aethiopique de Heliodorus*. In rapid succession, Groulleau put out folio, octavo, and sextodecimo editions; he also almost certainly commissioned the lucrative epitome, *Trésor des livres d'Amadis* (1559), which excerpted letters from the romance for readers and which appeared in almost two dozen editions and several vernacular translations. Italian, German, Dutch, and English translations, by way of both the Spanish originals and the French versions, appear through the close of the sixteenth century.

The *Amadis* cycle and other romances circulated through European early modern book markets and were transported to American destinations quickly and fluidly. Their narrative and textual forms changed rapidly and, in contrast to theological, political and scientific writing, they were transmitted almost entirely in the vernacular.[40] Indeed, in some cases, romances carried the vernacular with them: in his remarkably detailed *Itinerary* (1617) of his travels through Germany, the Low Countries, and across Northern Europe, Fynes Moryson describes his purchases at the Lübecke bookshops where he "bought the fourteenth Booke of *Amadis de Gaule* in the Dutch tongue, to practise the same: for these Bookes are most eloquently translated into the Dutch, and fit to teach familiar language, and for this Booke I paid eighteene lubeckes shillings, and for the binding foure; and for a Map of *Europe* to guide me in my journey, I paide fourteene lubecke shillings."[41] As we shall see, romances like *Amadis* generally crossed national and geographical boundaries through the agency of translators, printers, and booksellers; in Moryson, though, we have an example of a traveler who in a way used *Amadis* to cross a border himself. Moryson's Dutch translation of the fourteenth edition of *Amadis* goes hand in hand with his new map of Europe for reasons that were at once practical and ideological. Lady Mary Wroth used maps, and indeed overlaid both biblical and pre-Fall of Constantinople maps onto contemporary maps of Europe in constructing her fictions, while Philip Sidney saw his *Arcadia* as an imagined rewriting of what Fulke Greville would later refer to as his "Map of Europe."[42] Printing clearly made romances both popular and portable. More importantly, as they were written by authors like Wroth and Sidney and as they were subsequently read by readers like Moryson, printed romances spread across Europe and into the New

World in a geographic diffusion that was consistent with the commit-ment to pan-European aristocracy and universal Christendom that these romances asked its readers to imagine.

Printing was also largely responsible for the particular reading prac-tices that came to be characteristic of Renaissance romance. Because romances arise out of concern about genealogy and kinship, they are structured in ways that tend to make their readers responsible for creating in social terms the relationships they imagine. As a number of scholars have noted, romance as a genre tends to both theorize and thematize the practice of reading.[43] Barry Ife cogently suggests that "the private reading of vernacular prose fiction in the early part of the sixteenth century was a new experience for most people and one which was highly distrusted by many authorities," and it was out of this resistance that romance, as the dominant and most controversial form of contemporary secular litera-ture, *integrated into its fictions* what Ife describes as "a practical defense of reading."[44] Ife and other critics have tended to regard the process of read-ing that romance initiated as "primarily psychological."[45] It is nonetheless worth thinking about the material and corporeal consequences to reading as perhaps most central to understanding how romance contributed to changing understandings of identity.

The high incidence of marginalia, the dominance of the vernacular, the large numbers of editions, continuations, adaptations and epitomes are, as I see it, consequences of the intersection between the model of identity that romance as a genre advocates and the possibilities of print technol-ogy as a media. More particularly, this negotiation of readers' identities in visible terms happens at the intersection between the text and the act of reading. Romance achieved its cultural dominance by adapting models of identity that defined characters within its fictions into a theory of reading that readers could take away from the page and bring back to their lives. The practice of making category distinctions among different kinds of people based on visual identification is at the heart of what romance, as a social genre, teachers its readers through the experiences of its fiction. Reading is more than a metaphor for how romance constructs identity and, by extension, how early modern culture learned to "identify" cat-egories such as race.

In her classic study of contemporary romance genre fiction, *Reading the Romance*, Janice Radway argues that with contemporary romance read-ing goes beyond entertainment or escape: it instead comes close to being a way of living, one that provides its readers with a key form of personal identity.[46] When Cervantes imagines that Quixote goes mad through reading romances, he mocks what was a strongly felt sense that the act of reading romances could indeed construct, or more probably disrupt, one's identity. For the contemporary readers that Radway examines, the identity that romance produces tends to be an individual one. As with Radway's case study, early modern romances are also as much ways of living as they are of reading, but what they articulate are collective and social identities and it is for this reason that they become relevant for understanding the role of printed texts in the articulation of new models of categorical identity.

Renaissance romance established a practice of reading that also comprised a theory of identity for those who read and in a way lived its fictions. In an influential argument about the need to undertake study that would produce a "history of reading," Robert Darnton called for scholars to integrate textual analysis with empirical historical research: this "dual strategy" would, he hoped, "make it possible to compare the implicit readers of the texts with the actual readers of the past and, by building on such comparisons, to develop a history as well as a theory" of reading. Building on Darnton's call, my goal in *Reading and the History of Race in the Renaissance* is to understand how the practices of reading that these romances articulated intersected with how they understood various forms of racial and pre-racial identity. Doing so makes it possible not just to understand individual texts or the practices of reading that they helped create, but also to think about how at least one early modern form of thinking about, creating, and practicing what became "racial identity" emerged from *what were essentially text-based practices*. For romance and the world it imagined, practices of looking (at the heart of what proto-racialism suggested in making skin color and physical appearance an identity category) were integrally connected to practices of reading.

In turning attention to how definitions of race and related forms of category identity may have emerged out of printed texts, I am in part interested in what is essentially a historic question: how did people learn about, and experience, the differences that became race? One current kind of answer to this question has involved trying to get more precise data about how many black Africans, for example, may have lived in a city like London in the 1590s.[47] This line of inquiry is entirely consistent with the encounter model of identity and is necessarily important when race is thought about from a performative perspective: the more black Africans in London – or perhaps the fewer, given the question of structuring absence – then the more powerfully those human experiences shape and are shaped by cultural and aesthetic representations. Yet the introduction of printing also meant that the sixteenth century was the historic moment at which more people were getting their information about the world and their place in it through written texts and paper images than had ever done so before.

As Lucien Febvre famously put it, the "age of the ear" was giving way to the "age of the eye."[48] Readers of Richard Eden's version of Martyr's *Decades*, for instance, were asked to think about the many colors of mankind, in all their shades and "dyvers sortes":

sum men are whyte after dyvers sortes of whyteness: yelowe after dyvers maners of yelowe: and blacke after dyvers sorts of blacknesse: and howe from whyte they go to yelowe by discolourynge to browne and redde: and to black by ashe coloure, and murrey sumwhat lyghter then blacke: and tawnye lyke unto the west Indians which are all togyther in general eyther purple, or tawny like unto sodden quynces, or of the coloure of chestnuttes or olyves.[49]

Most of those readers, though, were more likely to encounter this full spectrum of human color on the printed page, either described in words or depicted in illustrations, than they were in person. Carlo Ginzberg's miller Menocchio clearly encountered the new worlds that got him into trouble with the Inquisition largely through his activities as a reader: in 1599 he writes of having been "sorely troubled" by having "read that book of Mandeville about many kinds of races and different laws."[50] Although Menocchio's reading habits were probably unusual, more people read the fictions of Mandeville or the only slightly less fabulous travel accounts collected by writers such as Eden, Samuel Purchas, and Richard Hakluyt than actually traveled to India, Peru, or Ethiopia. Europeans were more likely to see the shadings of human complexion in what Valerie Traub has called the "cartographic bodies" that formed the borders and adorned the title pages of the atlases and maps published by Gerard Mercator, Peter Heylyn, William Blaeu, and John Speed than they were likely to see (or do any more than just see) the full range of those complexions on either the streets of London or the seas of the Mediterranean.[51]

In numbers and geographic dispersal, the publication and distribution histories of romance cycles such as *Amadis* were strangely parallel to those of travel narratives and new atlases. Theaters like the Globe certainly extended the possibilities of embodied encounters with other peoples, but, ultimately, more people in more places read or heard romances such as *Amadis* and *Don Quixote* than saw *The Merchant of Venice*, or the lost Cervantine romance, *The History of Cardenio*, on stage.[52] Thus, for instance, the extensive bookseller's catalogue that was published for the estate of Robert Greville, Baron Brooke (d. 1676), in 1678 contains very little of the drama and poetry of the period that captures our persistent critical interest: two editions of the plays of Beaumont and Fletcher, editions of the poems of John Donne (1633), Thomas Carew (1642), and Edmund Waller (1664), and nothing by Shakespeare. Instead, the vernacular sections of this library are full of works of ethnography, geography, and history: Pierre d'Avity's *Estates, empires, and principallities of the world* (1615), George Sandys' *Travels* (1621), multiple copies of the most important voyage narratives such as Richard Hakluyt's *Principall Navigations* (1599), Thomas Gage's *Survey of the West-India's* (1648), Samuel Purchas' *Purchas his Pilgrim* (1617, 1625, 1626), and Will Cast's *Short Discourse of the Coast and Continent of America* (1644?), Thomas Herbert's *Travels into Persia: A relation of some years travaile … into Afrique and the Greater Asia …* (1634), the *Travels, Voyages and Adventures of Ferdinand Mendez Pinto* (1653), *L'Histoire naturelle et generalle des Indes* (1556), and Nicolas Sanson's *L'Amerique en plusieurs cartes et en divers Traitres de Geographie et d'Histoire*, among others.

A contemporary reader may well have made sense of these geographic and ethnographic texts through the intellectual framework of Galenism set out in the humorally inflected moral and medical philosophy of Pierre Charron's *Of Wisdom*, Thomas Reynolds' *Treatise of the Passions* (1640), or Thomas Wright's *Passions of the Minde* (1621), editions of all of which appear in the Brooke catalogue. Alongside this collection of works that sought to describe the lands, peoples, and history of the other parts of the world, perhaps equally importantly, though, are a fairly extensive collection of romances: a Munday *Amadis de Gaule* (1619); the Harington *Orlando* (1634); *Palmerin of England* (1609/1610); *Don Quixote*, in both quarto and folio editions; *A Mirrour of Knighthood* (1598); Pierre-Daniel Huet's *Treatise of Romances* (1672); several copies of Heliodorus' *Aethiopika* (1633); John Barclay's *Argenis* (1624); and the second part of Honoré d'Urfé's *L'Astrée* (1610), among others.[53] The collection of books represented in this catalogue was likely put together over a period of time and may never have been read by a single reader, but we do see here a grouping of texts that suggests an intermingling of the discourses of romance and ethnography that is in keeping with a sense that these works offered readers different but allied answers to contemporary interest in imagining the world and its boundaries through texts.

As scholars since Elizabeth Eisenstein have made clear, print culture changed what people could know of their world and past. Indeed, as Eisenstein suggested, print made it possible for European culture to reconceptualize the geotemporal dimensions of the world itself.[54] As a result, print culture – and the new forms of reading that it encouraged – changed people's ability to imagine the worlds that they could not see and altered their perceptions of those that they could.

If printing was at the center of a new "age of the eye," so was the emergence of racialized conceptions of the body. Critics have warned against the problem of seeing color too soon, of anticipating in the sixteenth and early seventeenth centuries a color divide that does not solidify until at least the end of the seventeenth and perhaps not until the eighteenth century.[55] We may read too much into earlier attitudes toward skin color, complexion, and race when we read back through the perspective implied by later events. The printing press did not invent the racism that emerged from the Renaissance. Yet both presses and racism are in allied ways a consequence of the rise of a visual culture in early modern Europe that Michael Baxandall, Eisenstein, Alfred Crosby, and others have defined as a kind of cognitive transformation of space and time, things both visible and invisible, into a newly constant, homogeneous, mathematically boundable world. To the extent that visual culture produced new technologies, attitudes toward the notion of categories, or understandings of how we might see the world, then the way in which readers experienced identity is a good place to understand that visual culture.

In making these arguments, I am suggesting that, in ways that scholarship has not recognized, reading contributed to the emergence of ethnic models of identity in the early modern period. If that is right, then it also becomes important to ask what is the nature of the body that read. What happened when Shakespeare, or a thousand more anonymous readers, read the essay "Of Colour" in Peter Martyr's *Decades*? To ask this is to ask more than one question. One wants to know how what people read, or saw, in printed books changed how they understood identity. But it is also important to think about how assumptions about the nature of the body and human identity may have shaped how reading happened or, at least, was experienced as happening.

It is in trying to think through both sides of this question that I have paired my opening epigraphs from Thomas Wilson and Philip Sidney. While Wilson warns his readers that reading might transform their bodies as certainly as a sunburn altered the appearance of their skin, Philip Sidney's Astrophil laments that his "sunburnt brain" seems to have damaged not just his powers of poetic invention but even his ability to read ("oft turning others leaves," but finding no answers there). Certainly, these are necessarily difficult questions to answer. Here, I would stress that there is no fixed frame, no single variable. Reading is an identity practice that is inherently tied to the body, and, as such, the practice of reading was changing at the same time that its content was also changing.

As scholars working in the history of reading have made clear, reading may sometimes seem evanescent or invisible, but it is an inherently material practice.[56] The very idea that there is such a thing as a "history" to reading is predicated on the insight that reading itself begins as a material practice. As Robert Darnton has pointed out, book history as a whole first began to take its modern form in the late nineteenth century when analytic bibliography arose out of "the study of books as material objects."[57] Within that larger field, the history of reading takes as its starting point the assumption that reading has a history and that history can be understood through the material traces it leaves.

Scholarship in the history of reading has tended to track those traces as they appear in and on the texts that readers read, with most work falling into two general categories. The first concentrates on the study of exemplary readers, material traces of whose reading practices can be discerned through the details of their commonplace books, their library collections and catalogues, and their marginalia and *adversaria*.[58] Anthony Grafton and Lisa Jardine have thus provided a history of Gabriel Harvey's reading – and rereading – of Livy over a twenty-year period. For them, Harvey's annotations and the model of humanistic *imitatio* as a whole imply a *practice* of reading, one both active and directed toward guiding and prompting readers toward particular actions.[59] William Sherman likewise has pursued the elusive John Dee through his fabled library at Mortlake, paying particular attention to Dee's "adversaria," the marginal annotations that mark Dee's encounters with the thousands of volumes in his library.[60]

The second approach focuses on what Roger Chartier has called "object studies": here, the material history of reading attaches to the text as a physical object that may take different forms as it is used and read, passing through multiple hands and changing formats, over the course of time.[61] A particularly powerful example of this type of scholarship is Heidi Brayman Hackel's reconstruction of reading practices that emerged from her examination of 151 copies, from more than two dozen archives, of early modern folio editions of Sidney's *Arcadia*.[62] Brayman Hackel selected the *Arcadia* as a study text in part because of the unusually high incidence of markings in the different editions of this romance (in an astounding 70 percent of surviving copies, which is practically unheard of for any text but especially for a work of fiction), but her larger interest is using this graphic history of readers' responses to Sidney's text as a way to document the activities of more anonymous (and more usual) readers.[63] Taking as a starting point the assumption that "for all its elusiveness, reading is always a material practice," Brayman Hackel is committed to documenting the experiences of those readers whose traces are most likely to have disappeared from other historical records but "whose entry into the print marketplace provoked debate and changed the definition of literacy in early modern England."[64] Perhaps the most exceptional example of this type of scholarship has combined both these approaches: over a twenty-five-year odyssey across much of Eastern and Western Europe, America, and Asia, the historian of science Owen Gingerich pursued one of the world's great iconic texts, Copernicus' *De Revolutionibis*, as it was read and often copiously annotated by a remarkable group of exemplary readers (a list of luminaries that includes Galileo Galilei, Thomas Digges, John Dee, Tycho Brahe, Christopher Clavius, Johannes Kepler, and Geraldus Mercator, among others).[65]

The results from such studies have been exciting, perhaps in part because they tease a history out of what librarians, conservationists, and book collectors had once seen largely as unfortunate flaws and physical defects.[66] Leah Price is probably right to caution that there may be no necessary correlation between what readers did with and to texts and what those texts did to their readers precisely because reading is often a self-consuming act: "The greater a reader's engagement with the text, the less likely he or she is to pause long enough to leave a record: if an uncut page signals withdrawal, a blank margin just as often betrays an absorption too rapt for note taking. Can a book mark us if we mark it?"[67] The history of reading has, nonetheless, in some part emerged out of what had been a study of wear. It is in that respect a practice that, at its logical extreme, may function to make reading material by studying the process by which readers impose their own materiality (marks, marginalia, wear spots, even fingerprints) on texts that they are literally destroying as they read them. As Roger Stoddard eloquently puts it, the vitality of readers emerges against that of the books they read: "wear is the eradicator of vital signs. The squeeze and rub of fingers stain and wear away ink and color, fraying paper thin, breaking fibers, and loosening leaves from bindings. Rough hands sunder books, and over time even gentle hands will pull books apart."[68]

When the wear in the text becomes the basis for the history of reading, that means that the materiality of reading is understood to inhere largely in the text, and the history of reading becomes a history of what readers do to books. Here, I am interested in also thinking about what books might do to readers, and not simply emotionally but physically. In particular, in thinking about reading as an identity practice, we need to remember that the materiality of reading inheres not just in the text that is read but in the body that reads. That is, the body is as much the material site of reading as is the text itself. Understanding what people did with texts involves understanding the bodies with which and through which they read those texts.

This assumption drives the methodology of this book. First, as this theoretical position should make clear, this book is not primarily an account of "real" readers. In each of the chapters that follow, I provide details about the editions, textual formats, printing history, circulation and dispersal of the different romances that I discuss. I do so in part out of the recognition that these components of the material states of texts helped determine the possibilities for both historical acts of reading and, perhaps less directly, for the theories about reading that came to be associated with romance. I also identify, document, and discuss some cases involving individual readers. As we have seen, the travel diary and itinerary of Fynes Moryson, discussing his reading of a Dutch-language edition of *Amadis de Gaule*, and booksellers' catalogues and library inventories, such as the 1678 catalogue for the estate of Robert Greville, Baron Brooke (d. 1676), provide evidence of those who owned and may have read romances, and suggest conclusions about the physical and intellectual contexts within which they probably did so. In Chapter 4, at greater detail, I likewise examine the recorded responses from readers like Sir Edward Denny, Baron of Waltham, and George Manners, Earl of Rutland, as well as Wroth's own activities as a re-reader as evidenced in her marginal annotations to her personal copy of the published *Urania*, now at the University of Pennsylvania, and the material evidence of the bi-folio that was removed by an early reader, perhaps William Herbert, from the holograph copy of the second part of the *Urania* at the Newberry Library. On the whole, though, this project does not undertake to reiterate the meticulous archival work of historians of reading such as Brayman Hackel and Sherman, but should instead be understood as standing in a complementary relationship to these projects that have done so much to recover the history of early modern reading practices.

Likewise, while I include and assess evidence about the kinds and categories of readers who may have read romances, this book is not primarily concerned with the field of literacy studies or with related sociological forms of literary history. Certainly, it is clearly valid and valuable to work to determine, in categories, kinds, and numbers, who actually read romances or, equally, those who may not have done so. Recent scholarship by Helen Hackett, Lori Humphrey Newcomb, Juliet Fleming, and Jacqueline Pearson, among others, has done much to provide better evidence about what Hackett has characterized as the otherwise "frustratingly illusive" question of who read romances, while also reminding us why this question has remained difficult to answer.[69]

Here, though, my discussion may provide insight into what it is about romances themselves that seems to prompt, even demand, that we ask these questions about who read them and how they were read. That is, throughout this study I am less interested in what readers tell us about romances than in what romances tell us about readers – about the acts of reading and the practices of identity to which this genre was understood to be allied. With that in mind, in the next section of this introduction I will outline the physiological components that, through at least the mid-seventeenth century, were typically understood to define reading. Here, I will pay particular attention to the different medical and philosophical assumptions that tied reading to the body and to identity. The language that early modern humanists, physicians, philosophers, translators and authors used to describe reading provides a crucial vocabulary for understanding how reading may have been experienced and conceptualized in the early modern period. As such, these statements suggest ways for approaching the study of reading as a lived experience. From this perspective, reading becomes a form of physical sensation and one that can be understood in terms of historical phenomenology.[70] In part, this emphasis on historical phenomenology provides a potentially helpful way to bring questions of identity to scholarship in the history of the book: as Bruce R. Smith has recently argued, historical phenomenology stands as a tacit "critique of the objectifying imperative that has come to govern textual studies."[71] Indeed, as we shall see, early modern readers in many respects anticipate the turn to material history that has come to define recent work in the history of reading; throughout, we shall also see how closely the material reality to reading is also linked to the fluidity of identity that defined this period.

More generally, this approach depends on the recognition that, as Adrian Johns has suggested, reading exists in and emerges out of a "physiology." To understand the historical dimensions to reading we need to pay fuller attention, in Johns' terms, to what early modern readers "thought actually occurred at the decisive moment of face-to-face confrontation between reader and read."[72] My goal is thus not to describe how reading really happened (or the "real" readers to which it happened); I likewise take care to avoid imposing our conceptual (or scientific) understandings of reading back onto early modern readers. Rather, my interest is in taking these statements as markers of a different lived experience of reading. In these accounts, I pay attention to moments when critics – as well as apologists – discuss romance as a genre that posed particular problems for readers. We will also see how romance came to be associated with and often to stand in more generally for the dangers and threats that all forms of reading were thought to present to would-be readers. Within the central chapters of the book, I will then build on this Introduction's theoretical and historical account of the phenomenology of reading by looking at how writers and translators of early modern printed romances integrated these questions and concerns about the relationships among reading, identity, and the body into the texts – the narrative structures and strategies, the construction of character, and the thematic concerns – of their fictions. The assumptions that structured the sixteenth- and early seventeenth-century critiques of romance became, as we shall see, part of the way that romances in turn imagined and constructed identity for both their characters and their readers.

Reading happened in the body largely because, for early modern readers, the body within which reading happened was a humoral one. Through the mid-seventeenth century, Galenic humoralism provided the dominant philosophical tradition through which the act of reading was understood, explained, and probably experienced. (By the mid-seventeenth century, mechanistic and dualistic philosophical traditions become important in shaping accounts of reading practices; in contrast to the humoralism that dominates sixteenth-century accounts, these traditions tended to see reading as a primarily imaginative, mental, or emotional, activity rather than as a fully somatic one and they thus produce notably different accounts of what happened to readers as they read.)[73] To the extent that humoralism was a pervasive and often unselfconscious way of experiencing the body, humoralism necessarily shaped forms of representation because one could not step outside it. Humoralism conceived of human temperament and complexion in terms of the balance within the body of four fluids – blood, phlegm, black bile, and yellow bile – that were tied to both the four elements and the products of the stages in human digestion.[74] Humoral theory linked the passions of the mind to both the humors of the body and the matter of the physical world as a whole; the humors manifested themselves in both the temper and the complexions of men. The humoral body provided intuitive and satisfying material explanations

for the experience of human emotion and passion. Humoralism also notably provided perhaps "the dominant mode of ethnic distinctions in the
late sixteenth and early seventeenth centuries."[75] As Michael Schoenfeldt
has argued, the humoral model of the body is less accurate at diagnosing and treating physical ailments than is the model of the body that we
have inherited from the Cartesian, mechanistic, and Paracelsian shifts of
the seventeenth century, but the Galenic body provided a language that
more fully captured the lived experience of the body; the experiences of
the Galenic body were thus arguably more fully a part of any representations that arose out of that body than have been subsequent physiologies.
Galenism certainly dominated early modern culture and did so in large
part because it was capacious enough to incorporate a wide range of phenomena into itself.[76]

Reading was one of those phenomena. Galen and his successors agreed
that the humoral balance of the body could be altered through six kinds of
external forces, the non-naturals (air, food and drink, sleep and wakeful-
ness, motion and rest, filling and evacuation, and accidents or passions of
the mind). As Philippe de Mornay, seigneur du Plessis-Marly, explained, the
non-naturals were things that, while "no parts at all, or members of the
body," were nonetheless necessary for the maintenance of life.[77] While
reading was clearly not integral to the preservation of life in the way that
breathing or food and drink were, Renaissance readers of Galen regarded
reading as something that was likely to disrupt the humoral balance of the
body, and they added reading to their list of non-naturals.[78]

Humoral physiology provided a materialist model for understanding the experience and significance of emotion. In this context, reading
was important because it was associated with the production of passion.
Sixteenth-century moralists and physicians like Mornay, Andreas du
Laurens, and Thomas Wright relied upon Galenism as a physiological
model for understanding the relationship between the immaterial soul
and the physical world as they were connected to one another within and
through the human body. For Wright, for instance, passions inhabit the
body and thus mediate between the immaterial (things of the soul) and
the material (things of the senses): "bordering upon reason and sense,"
passions are produced within the body, but they also create "some alteration of the body."[79] The soul was understood to experience the world
entirely through the senses, which were in turn physically connected to
the three ventricles of the brain. The front component of the brain, the
sensus communis, was warm, moist, and soft; it was here that sense perceptions were collected as they came into the body.[80] The central ventricle,

the most temperate part of the brain, was the site of reason and imagination, where ideas and perceptions were compared and scrutinized, while the last ventricle, cool, dry, and hard, provided a place in which ideas and sense perceptions could be collected and stored for later use.

While all sense perceptions could produce passions within the brain, reading was potentially particularly powerful and thus closely scrutinized because it was understood to affect the faculties associated with all three ventricles of the brain.[81] In speaking of Wright's influential account of the connection between the passions of the mind and the humors of the body, Katharine Craik thus explains that this kind of "theory of passionate cognition is also a theory of reading for some of the most problematic negotiations between the passions and the imagination are sparked off by encounters with books."[82]

Reading was logically connected, among the non-naturals, to the category of "passions of the mind," but the affect that reading had on the physical body was probably most often explained through comparisons to acts of eating and drinking. These comparisons are commonplace and thus provide a marker of the real physical consequences that were understood to attend improper or unsupervised acts of reading. In his *Essayes* (1597), Francis Bacon advised would-be readers, only in part ironically, that "Some bookes are to bee tasted, others to bee swallowed, and some few to bee chewed and digested: That is, some bookes are to be read only in partes; others to be read, but cursorily, and some few to be read wholly and with diligence and attention."[83] In the *Leviathan* (1651), Thomas Hobbes, by contrast, presented books not as sustenance but as a potential poison: one of the greatest dangers to civil government, he suggested, came from readers of Greek and Roman histories who lack "the Antidote of solid Reason" that could inoculate them against "receiving a strong, and delightfull impression, of the great exploits of warre."[84] In his moral regime, *Vertues Commonwealthe* (1603), Henry Crosse repeated the commonly accepted wisdom that virtue was "nourished by good tutors, reading good Bookes, and exercise," but bad books were "unsauoury and vituperable," "full of strong venom, tempered with sweete honey."[85] Juan Luis Vives devoted the fifth chapter of his *Education of a Christian Woman* (1524) to separating good books from bad. In adapting Jerome's theological instructions to print culture, Vives also modified Galen's model of the body: romances like *Amadis* are "a pestilence" and the woman who reads them "drinks poison into her breast."[86] In good books, however, "she will find without question in authors worth reading more ingenuity, more abundance, greater and surer pleasure – in brief, a most pleasant food for the soul."[87]

Was reading a poison, a pestilence, or a kind of pleasant food? In Galenic physic, a single substance might be variably food or medicine, depending on the humoral character of the patient. The body absorbed like substances into itself, digesting and concocting them into sustenance. Unlike substances could not be absorbed by the body and, functioning as either physic or poison, they thus absorbed the body to themselves. Books were likewise regarded as at once both sustenance and poison in ways that might depend on both the genre or category of book and the humoral character of the reader. In a profound counter-argument to the prevailing mechanistic models of matter that become increasingly dominant in the seventeenth century, John Milton in *Areopagitica* (1643) thus draws on these distinctions in arguing that different books will affect people differently. Glossing "to the pure, all things are pure," Milton insists "books are as meats and viands are ... Wholesome meats to a vitiated stomach differ little or nothing from unwholesome, and best books to a naughty mind are not unapplicable to occasions of evil. Bad meats will scarce breed good nourishment in the healthiest concoction."[88] As both Vives and Milton suggest, the content of books seemed to enter the body physically, changing its balance, and creating unhealthy and even dangerous passions.

Although Vives is using the term "poison" in a figurative sense and as the basis of a comparative, it is important to recognize that he does not understand the humoral imbalance that might be caused by reading to be any less real than that caused by physical poisons. Galenic dietaries that warned those of a melancholic disposition to avoid excessive study that might further "dry" out the complexion and midwives' manuals that urged that pregnant women be prevented from reading too much or too passionately were concerned about what were understood to be very real physical consequences to reading.[89] Milton certainly took this possibility seriously: "extraordinary temperat in his Diet," Milton came to believe that his blindness was caused either by a humoral excess that originated in his spleen, as a result of which, as he explained to Leonard Philaras, "permanent vapours seem to have settled upon my entire forehead and temples which press and oppress my eyes with a sort of heavy sleepiness," or by excessive reading.[90] For Milton, poor digestion and excessive reading were alike in that either might produce a humoral imbalance and build-up of badly concocted humoral fluids that collected over the eye; these fluids, he suspected, were the origin of his blindness.

As Sean McDowell has argued, in speaking of the humoral inflection to early modern thinking more generally, early modern accounts of the body and felt experience use a vocabulary that is at once "more precise" and "less metaphorical" than we tend to expect it to be.[91] It is in this context, as Schoenfeldt notes, that "reading was as much a moral and physiological phenomenon as it was a mental activity" and metaphors of ingestion and digestion became "*a very literal metaphor* for the proper act of reading."[92] In a physical sense, the passions that reading romances like *Amadis* incited were substantially identical to those caused by poisons and plagues. Humanist projects for controlling reading in this period should thus be understood as fundamentally related to more familiar projects that sought to exert control over the humanist body through diet: both were aimed at subduing passion and achieving reason within the humoral body.[93]

Within the framework of Galenic physiology, reading was understood to be a somatic experience that had physical, rather than just mental, consequences. Wright, for instance, argues that the passions of the mind were almost inseparable from the humors of the body. He thus notes that "there is no passion very vehement, but that it altereth extremely some of the humors of the body"; as a result, any "affections in the mind could alter the humors of our bodies, causing some passion or alteration in them."[94] In his *Touchstone of Complexions* (1576), Lemnius Levinus likewise argues that human temperament does not exist solely in the "inward mind of man," but "even in the outward shew, shape and behavior of the bodie ... in the countenance, which is the Image of the minde, in the eyes ... in the colour, linamentes, proportion and feature of the whole body."[95] Like other physical sensations, the matter of the books that we read in some way enters our bodies, through our eyes, and perhaps our ears and sense of touch. Books incite passions that animate our vital spirits – heating, as we shall see, the central ventricle of our brain – but they also transform mental temperament and, as importantly, change physical complexion. Thomas Wilson suggested that reading the wrong kind of books was much like staying out in the sun and becoming sunburnt. His analogy was one that his readers would have understood intuitively: as Craik suggests, the passions incited by the experience of reading books "inscribed themselves upon men's facial expressions, posture, carriage, gestures, and general deportment, as well as in the color, temperature, and texture of their skin."[96]

Whatever the physical consequences to reading in general, romance as a genre was closely associated to this idea that the act of reading might change the complexions of readers, potentially transforming the color, temperature, and texture of their skins, and it did so in a humorally specific way. As I will suggest both here in the Introduction and in the chapters that follow, romance as a genre had traditionally been concerned with affirmations of blood kinship and universal Christian identity within a narrative structure that was premised primarily on the fixed and visibly manifest nature of identity; the reading experiences that came to be associated with romance, though, instead sited romance at the fractures of early modern notions of identity. In part, this link followed from the dubious content of romances but, more importantly, it was also a result of the formal features that defined the genre, especially in its printed forms, and that were understood to have a powerful impact on those who read them. To the extent that romance itself had a complexion, early modern critics would probably have classified it as melancholic and most likely as an unnatural or pathological form of melancholy. Romances were thought to be likely to inflame readers, overheating their brains and burning away good blood, until they were left with the scorched black blood and the dark complexion of melancholy. In keeping with the therapeutic model of Galenism, this association also derived from the fact that romances were stereotypically associated with the kinds of readers who were understood to be weak enough to be drawn to read them.

There are not, to my knowledge, accounts of readers whose skin actually became dark as a result of reading *Amadis* or *Tristan*. Yet, contemporary attacks on romance – and, as we shall see, romances themselves – suggested that this and other physical transformations might be a possibility. I am interested here in the reasons that, within a physiology that extends from the burnished skin of Egyptians and Ethiopians to the sunburnt brains of lovers and the romance readers who read about them, such transformations were understood to be possible.[97] More generally and more importantly, romance as a genre came to stand in for the possible hazards to physical identity that reading as a whole seemed to pose. In some genres, as critics have suggested, humoralism often provided a way for readers to affirm – or reaffirm – various forms of geographic, ethnic, and religious identity. English dietaries, for instance, tended to reassure (white, male, upper-class English) readers that through proper acts of living and reading they might preserve and protect their identities.[98] Romance has, by contrast, remained comparatively neglected in the otherwise extensive recent scholarship on the discourses of humoralism. Nonetheless, romance was a genre that early modern moralists, philosophers, and physicians themselves paid attention to precisely because it seemed to bring out the fluidity of identity, its fragility and apparent boundlessness. Lemnius Levinus complained that complexions were "easelye one into an other transmuted"; romance as a genre only seemed to exacerbate this more general problem.[99]

It is worth noting here that, ordinarily, in the context of discourses of humoralism, one might expect to see substantial differences that would vary geographically. That is, writers from Spain, Italy, or other humorally more temperate regions might be likely to feel that romances were safer for the more naturally temperate readers of their regions. Such a perception would thus parallel the idea that some foods were thought to be better suited to the bodily humors of eaters of different geographic regions. While some categories of readers were thought to be particularly susceptible to romance, I have found no explicit evidence that suggests that romances were understood to be humorally compatible for people from *any* geographic region or complective type.[100] The absence of this kind of geographically specific discourse is notable: partly, this may arise from the sense that adust melancholy, the humor most consistently linked to the reading of romances, was not itself a naturally occurring humor; a humoral corruption that could be created when *any* of the humors was burnt away by a strong passion, adust melancholy was not native to any particular place or people.[101] More generally, this absence is also likely connected to precisely this sense that the act of reading romances was likely to unmake identity – rather than create or reaffirm it, as dietaries hoped with other genres.

In much the same way that different foods had different complexions, so were different kinds and categories of books associated with different humors, thus tempering the body in different ways. While some secular genres such as history and epic were sometimes accepted as morally tempering, romance was generally depicted as dangerous and damaging to readers. Among the most influential of the many sixteenth-century critical attacks on romance were Juan Luis Vives' 1524 condemnation of the romances of Amadís, Esplandián, Florisando, Tirant and Tristán as particularly dangerous books to read; Jacques Amyot's 1547 preface to his translation of Heliodorus, which tried to replace the "fevers" that might be produced by Amadisian romance with the epistemological reading that Heliodorian romance promised; and François de La Noue's condemnation of romances in his *Discours politiques et militaires* (1587).[102] Slightly less detailed but also influential discussions of the consequences to reading romances appear in the works of Montaigne, Pierre Charron, Pedro Malón de Chaide, Tasso, Stephen Gossen, and Robert Burton, among others. These attacks were widely read and cited by subsequent writers; they set the terms for early modern critical discussions of the consequences to reading romance, and their assessments arguably helped shape the lived experiences of the many who nonetheless did read romances despite this considerable body of advice to the contrary.[103]

These attacks follow from a humoral model of reading that assumes that romances, as much as romance readers, have a certain humoral complexion that is integral to both their content and form. Romances differed from other less dangerous forms of reading material because of the formal qualities that, in turn, defined their humoral complexion. The initial problem with romance was of course its subject matter: romances depicted the violence of love and war, the quests of desire and combat, across its pages in ways that seemed likely to incite strong passions in the minds of readers. Secular romances, while not on the Index, depicted various forms of religious conversion and other kinds of "passions" that might also be dangerous to readers.[104] Vives thus immediately rejects romances because they "kyndle and styr up covetousness, inflame angre, & all beastly and filthy desyre."

The danger, though, was not simply a matter of exposure to the subject matter of romance. Passion itself was not necessarily a bad thing and perhaps less dangerous in a textual than in a lived form: certainly, those who tried simply to repress their passions, rather than trying to regulate them properly, were likely to find that poorly concocted fluids would build up in their bodies and their "poores [would] become soft and delicate."[105] Indeed, the pleasure that so many readers found in romance would seem to confirm to one of Thomas Wright's central premises for good health. As he explains:

Pleasure and delight, if it be moderate … bringeth health, and they helpe marvellously the digestion of blood, so that thereby the heart engendreth great abundance, and most purified spirites, which … also clear the braine, and consequently, the understanding: For although while the passion endureth, it blindeth alittle the indifferent judgment, yet after that it is past, it rendereth the braine better disposed and apter to represent whatsoever occureth for speculation. From good concoction, expulsion of superfluities, and abundance of spirites proceedeth a good colour, a cleare countenance and an universall health of the bodie.[106]

Pleasure was generally desirable to the extent that it caused the heart to produce well-concocted blood and vital spirits; these cleared the brain of excessive superfluities, improving both the quality of sense perception and estimative judgments about those sense perceptions.

Romances may have produced pleasure in readers, but they did not produce the type of passion that was likely to expel superfluities or lead to good color and a clear countenance. Romances were immoderate in their very form: they were too long and they usually got even longer in the sequels: the first four books of *Amadis* ran to 298 folio pages in the 1508 edition; by 1533, the sixth book alone was close to 400 pages, just as Ariosto's *Orlando* is considerably longer than Boiardo's. The passions that readers experienced were likely to be prolonged for as long as the fiction lasted; these same passions were then likely to be renewed whenever a new volume appeared in print. In textual terms, romances presented readers with something which was at once a distant object and a source of desire and yet remained, in its textual form an (ever) present image of that desire. From a physiological perspective, the emotions of desire and pleasure that reading incited would heat readers' vital spirits, and the best and most fully concocted blood would go to the brain.[107]

When this state of textually induced passion continued too long – when page after page was filled with further depictions of the loves of Oriana and Amadis, in texts at once endless and yet recurring – humoral theories of reading suggested that the brain was likely to overheat. As the images from the page came into the *sensus communis*, they then stimulated the warm, moist, but still temperate central ventricle of the brain which housed the estimative faculty. When the same image or same kind of image kept recurring, these images were thought to be likely to overheat this part of the brain, causing it to burn up and dry out.[108] Too great or prolonged a passion sent too many vital spirits to the brain, drawing the purest and most fully concocted blood away from the heart while also overheating the brain: as Wright explains, "the heart being continually environed with great aboundaunce of spirites, becommeth too hote and inflamed."[109] In those who are healthy, images and the passions they produce "doe speedily passe away, not making any abode," but in those who are melancholic "the humour which is drie and earthie … suffereth not it selfe easily to be blotted out."[110] If not quickly expelled, such inflammation would overheat the brain, producing the black "burned blood" of adust melancholy.[111] In those who are "melancholie through adustion," explains Juan Huarte, the heat of this humor "drieth & hardneth the brain."[112]

The dangers of overheating were considerable: emphasizing that the brain must be kept consistently "refreshed and moistened" to retain its complexion, Mornay thus notes that, once the brain becomes hot, if it *continue long in that heat*, it becommeth blacke, and seething strongly, dries up and burnes" (my emphasis), leading to madness, desperation, and even death.[113] It is this physiological process leading to adust melancholy that the Spanish mystic Pedro Malón de Chaide describes in *La conversión de Magdelena* (1588): *Amadis* and other romances, he complains, "spread their deadly poison through the veins of the heart, until it takes hold of the quickest and purest part of the soul, where with *furious ardour* it dries up and desiccates the greenest and most flourishing part of our activities" (my emphasis).[114]

As these comments suggest, the dangers of reading arose in part from the extent to which the texts of romance were understood to incite passion. The danger was also, however, a feature of the way that reading itself was a form of visual sense perception and thus was subject to the diseases and afflictions of vision more generally. The degree to which the dangers of romance were understood to be caused by specifically *textual* features of these works can thus be seen as one of the only positive examples that is ever advanced in favor of reading romances. Adust melancholy was partly about over-concocted blood, but it was also specifically understood as an ophthalmological disease. It is in this context that the physician Andreas du Laurens treats adust melancholy as a humoral disease of the brain and of the eye, presenting his account "Of the diseases of Melancholy" as a sequel to his larger ophthalmological work in his *Discourse of the Preservation of Sight* (1597). In discussing du Laurens' work, Marion Wells calls attention to the visual character of the disease as it was understood in the Renaissance: "the fixity of the now unnaturally cold imaginative faculty activates *the perseverative focus on the image* (or more technically, the 'phantasm') of the beloved that *becomes the constitutive feature of the disease*" (my emphasis).[115]

Yet, as personal physician to Henri IV, du Laurens himself is reported to have arisen every morning to read *Amadis de Gaule* aloud to the king.[116] He did so not because he failed to anticipate the possible physical dangers to such texts: rather, reading aloud was accepted as a form of pneumatic therapy and was, in that sense, medicinally comparable to taking baths or eating foods that would "send up pleasant vapours unto the braine."[117] Such activities as reciting poetry or hearing books read aloud would stimulate the *pneuma* and bring with it the moist humors that might restore the desiccated brain of melancholics.[118] While it thus might have been physically dangerous or damaging for the king himself to read *Amadis*, since doing so was likely to dry out his complexion and overheat his humors, hearing the same histories and romances read aloud could moisten his brain and complexion and revitalize his health.

These kinds of accounts of what might happen to those who *read* romances sound suspiciously like a version of the "furious ardour" that seems so often to afflict the characters *within* the romances themselves. Richard Braitwaite, for instance, suggests a close and commonplace affinity between the madnesses of the lovers within romances and the readers of those romances: "Some wee have heard, that in reading the strange adventures of *Orlando Furioso*, and conveying the very impression of his amorous passion to themselves, would presently imitate his distraction, run starke naked … wholly turned savage and untractable, to personate that Knight more lively."[119] Braitwaite's construction is notably ambiguous here. On the one hand, the terms "imitate" and "personate" suggest that such readers may simply be engaging in a form of play-acting, consciously and willfully seeking to transform themselves into versions of their favorite fictional characters. Yet, at the same time, his sense that the act of reading conveys "the very impression" of Orlando's passion to readers also captures recognition that the forms of texts, and the characters they delineated, might imprint themselves on the eyes and minds of readers.

Partly this kind of textual effect, the permeability between fiction and lived experience, is one that romance as a genre tended to encourage. Here, though, there are important medical and philosophical congruities that informed both the depictions of love-sickness that are so prominent within the genre and the prevailing concern about the dangers that readers faced in reading examples of this genre. From a medical perspective, love-sickness (*amor hereos*) was understood to be a malign humoral imbalance that arose when an image (presumably that of the beloved) led to a malfunctioning of the would-be lover's brain. Visual images came into the body in the *sensus communis*, sited in the normally warm and moist first ventricle of the brain. Such sense perceptions would normally then be transferred to the central ventricle, the hottest part of the brain, which was the site of reason and imagination, while the last ventricle, cool and dry, provided a place in which ideas and sense perceptions could be collected and stored for later use.[120] In those who suffered from love-melancholy, though, these transfers between ventricles did not happen: instead, the "estimative faculty" of the second ventricle seemed to focus intensively and persistently on the image of the beloved, drawing heat and moisture from the other parts of the brain and body.[121] When the body responded to a visual image in this manner, it caused profound and dangerous changes in humoral balance and physical complexion. As a practicing physician, Ficino was preoccupied with this type of melancholy and, through his interest, this widely accepted medical understanding of love-sickness informed literary depictions of *amor hereos* within early modern romance.[122]

The furor that lovers feel, though, is notably comparable to the physical and emotional dangers that may afflict readers. The reason that descriptions of what happens to readers so closely parallel the descriptions of the love that romance characters suffer is that reading was thought to produce on the brains of readers an impact physiologically similar to that produced on the brains of benighted lovers by the images of love. Romance came to stand as a particularly powerful example of the possible consequences to reading precisely because these long, arguably repetitive, and certainly emotionally intense texts involved their readers in precisely the physiological acts that were most likely to disrupt the healthy functioning of the brain.

It is these medical assumptions that Miguel de Cervantes transforms into a typically metatextual narrative conceit when he describes how, for Quixote, "with too little sleep and too much reading his brains dried up."[123] Cervantes slyly reworks and extends upon the tradition of the "furioso" melancholic knights that he inherits from Montalvo and Ariosto in setting up the premise of his fiction. It is not reading *about* love and errantry that, in some misguided act of *imitatio*, transforms this once respectable hidalgo into a lover and knight. Rather, as Cervantes construes it, it is *in the act of reading itself* that, however unwittingly, Quixote most closely emulates his fictional heroes. Quixote is thus most like Amadis and Orlando when he is still at home, sitting in his library, reading. That is, reading dries out Quixote's brain just as love was understood to dry out the brains of those lovers, like Amadis and Orlando, who suffer from *amor hereos*. Orlando becomes enamored by the image of Angelica and, as we shall see, this changes his emotional state and, with that, his physical complexion; Quixote for his part becomes transformed by the image of the words on the page. A fictional rendering of the corporeal nature of reading, this transformation may explain his "more than moderately dark" complexion (669) as much as it does his madness, since both the physical and the emotional are integrally related components of Quixote's complexion as a reader.[124]

While Cervantes uses this episode to frame his relationship to his literary predecessors, he is also relying on common medical assumptions that guided assessments of reading. Scholars and others who studied too much were understood to be afflicted by divine furor and became subject to so-called "genial" melancholy as a result. Malón de Chaide's comments suggest that readers of romance, by contrast, were more likely to acquire adust or atrabilis melancholy, the corrupted, over-concocted form of melancholy in which the humors are burnt off. Such melancholics, who were "enemies to the Sun," were thus left with the cold, dry temperament and the "black" complexion that was otherwise understood to be produced when the sun drew black bile to the surface of the skin.[125] From this physiological context, then, the physical consequences to reading might indeed produce precisely the kind of "sunburn" that Wilson warns his would-be readers against. As both the medical theory and lived practice seemed to suggest, reading romances could leave readers with cold, dry bodies. Reading romances might easily cause susceptible readers to overheat and then dry out, in ways that changed the physical complexions and the humoral balance of readers.

Romance was most strongly affiliated with a humoral understanding of the body and its passions in the ways that it was agreed to affect particular kinds of readers more strongly than others. Vives famously warned of the vulnerability that women in particular had to romance. From 1506 through at least 1597, Spanish authorities likewise attempted to prevent their native subjects in the New World from reading romances. These decrees express the same kind of concern for the susceptibility of the indigenous Americans that Vives had for young women. In 1531, for instance, a decree from Queen Isabella attempts to redress this problem:

many books of fiction in the vernacular which are unrelated to religion such as Amadís and others of this sort go to the Indies; since this is bad practice for the Indians and something with which it is not well for them to be concerned or read, I command you, therefore, from this time henceforth neither to permit nor allow any person at all to take any books of fiction and of secular matters there, but only those relating to the Christian religion and morality upon which the above-mentioned Indies *may practice the art of reading* [my emphasis].[126]

Women and native barbarians were not the only readers who were thought to be at risk when they practiced the "art of reading" from romance. In his *Politicke and Militarie Discourses* (1588), François de La Noue worries that the young are likely to be adversely affected by the "poison" and "pollution" of reading romances. The Benedictine translator of *A Treasure of comfortable meditations* (1624) thus complains that English Catholics have been falsely accused of "translating, and printinge of divers lewed legends of knights errant, as Amadis, Palmerin, and the like" because reading romances could sway Protestant readers when religious texts could not.[127] These writers identify not just moral or spiritual weaknesses in these different categories of readers; rather, their comments also reflect a sense that romances are most likely to affect readers in ways that emerge out of the physical dispositions and humoral identities that were the primary components through which gender, body type, and geographic origin were understood.

Like diet and physic, reading was something that could indeed change your complexion, marking you as surely as the sun did and for related reasons. At the historic moment when humoralism was beginning to be supplanted by other philosophical and ethnographical models of the body, the genre of romance comes to stand in for a relationship between reading and the body. Romance as a genre came to emblematize cultural assumptions that reading was an extension of the humoral body, but one that did not affirm identity so much as imagine, at its most literal, the possible transformation of that body into something else. For both humanists and moral philosophers, in particular, the body that read was a humoral body. To the extent that humanist reaction against romance was responsible for framing the ways in which writers, translators, and publishers presented their work, this attention to the humoral passions that were understood to be associated with the act of reading romances had a strong impact on how early modern romances were constructed and understood. In the case of the *Urania*, as we shall see in Chapter 4, there are fundamental differences between the printed and manuscript volumes of Lady Mary Wroth's romance that are a by-product of changes in the cultural meaning of humoralism. The shift from Galenic humoralism to proto-racialism changes how Lady Mary Wroth understands the melancholy that defines her central character; that shift also changes how she conceives of the practices and possibilities of reading through which that character might be understood.

Yet, while humoralism provided the dominant physiological model through which critics of romance understood the problems of reading romance, it is important not to overstate the cohesiveness of this discourse. Other romances articulated or depended upon assumptions about reading that emerged out of other understandings of the relationship between the body and the identities that could be attached to it. This kind of multiplicity – in understandings of the body and in the adaptation of cultural forms for expressing those understandings – should be expected in a historically transitional moment. For instance, in Chapter 2, we will see how romances like Heliodorus' *Aethiopika* rely upon Aristotelian notions about the relationship between matter and form. Because these assumptions were understood to apply to both man and art, early modern readers thus used Aristotelian models of the body to frame the model of reading that they drew out of Heliodorus' *Aethiopika*. In Chapters 1 and 3, we will likewise be looking at how theological and political conflict over the identity of *conversos* involved not just certain assumptions about the nature of Jewish and Moorish bodies, but also allied beliefs about the forms of reading that were thought to inhere in those bodies. As these examples will suggest, various forms of reading that developed around romance were associated with different understandings of the body.

The common denominator across all these cases, though, is that the body that read was a pre-racial body. From the perspective of the history of natural philosophy and science, a dominantly humoral understanding of the body gave way in the seventeenth century to a mechanistic body. From the perspective of Galenic medicine, the humoral body was also challenged by a Paracelsian model of the body and disease. But, of course, during this same period, the humoral body was also being supplanted by an increasingly or at least differently racialized body. Early modern readers studied Eden's translations of *The Decades*, looked at William Blaeu's maps of Europe, Africa, and the world, and read the errant romances of *Amadis*, *The King of Tars*, the *Aethiopika*, and *Tirant lo Blanc*. They did so in ways that are no longer truly accessible to us not simply because such readers understood the world differently, but because they experienced their own bodies differently. The same complexities that are part of what makes it hard to determine where the boundaries are between representations of different racial, religious, ethnic, and geographical identity also apply to readers. We thus need to find ways to recognize that readers read out of the epistemological framework of their own bodies, a framework in which a changing understanding of the nature and content of identity can never be entirely separable from their own, inherently corporeal, acts of reading.

In this introduction, I have tried to outline a phenomenology of reading and have used early modern accounts of reading to do so. Although I have provided some details from individual readers, my primary sources here have included the works of natural philosophers, physicians, and humanists who tried to offer guidance – or warnings – about the emotional and often physical dangers that they saw in reading and in romances in particular. In many respects, these early modern sources anticipate many of the material features of reading that have come to dominate recent scholarship in the history of the book. These attacks and apologies for romance were responses to the remarkable popularity of the printed romances that swept across sixteenth-century Europe; they in turn structured how readers read romances and how romances themselves constructed the identities of both their characters and their would-be readers. Within the central chapters of this book, I will turn to the romances themselves to understand what they tell us about the act of reading and the forms of identity that it might create.

Chapter 1, "Genealogy and race after the Fall of Constantinople: From *The King of Tars* to *Tirant lo Blanc* and *Amadis of Gaul*," introduces these questions by examining how new racial theories associated with changing church policies on the status of conversion challenged romance's traditional commitment to genealogy as a central form of identity. This chapter is in part a response to a critical concern (Hunter, Lupton, and others) that religion rather than race is the dominant category of identity in this period. Here, I take up the most historically important instance in which religion and race are not distinct but rather are interrelated cultural categories: that is, how, in Spain, from about 1400 on, the definition of what it meant to be Jewish shifted from being a question of faith to being one of behavior and appearance, and finally one of birth. Changes in the understanding of religious identity produced new forms of racial identity.

Beginning with this historical argument (Netanyahu and others), I then trace how peninsular romances of the late fifteenth century, especially *Tirant lo Blanc* and the important fifth volume of the *Amadis* cycle, critique traditional romance by participating in a shift to descent-based models of religious identity. After the reconquest, peaceful conversion replaced imperial possession as a way of achieving what had been the goals of the Crusades. Romances such as *Tirant* and *Las sergas de Esplandián* introduce new stories about the winning of Muslim souls and lands, but they do so by imposing on these narratives new and theologically suspect models of racial identity that were the product primarily of domestic reactions against *conversos*. In doing so, these earliest of the printed romances move away from the genre's central claim to be able to provide fixed, legible identities that extended from the characters within the fiction to the readers of those fictions.

Chapter 2, "The matter and form of race," considers how questions about identity that would seem to apply to kinds and categories of peoples (classificatory questions about "purity," "adulteration," and, to use a later term, "miscegenation") were transposed onto early modern critical debates about generic categorization. Here, I look at Jacques Amyot's influential 1547 preface to his translation of Heliodorus' *Aethiopika* to show how Aristotelian physics and matter/form theory, in particular, inflected early the modern reception of Aristotle's poetics. Aristotelian physics provided an account of the relationships between matter and form; these relationships, in turn, defined how Aristotle understood poetic genre. A

chrono range

third-century Greek romance that tells the story of what happens after a black woman gives birth to a white child as a result of looking at a painting of the goddess Andromeda, the *Aethiopika* challenges both Aristotle's physics and his poetics. Amyot, in turn, re-introduced Heliodorus to European readers as a new form of romance. Tracking the responses to Amyot's Heliodorus from early modern writers, translators, and painters, I show how the Renaissance rejected Heliodorus' neo-Aristotelian model of reading and did so on racial grounds.

In Chapter 3, "The conversion of the reader," I turn to consider how the questions raised in Chapter 1 come to be answered by later readers and writers. Here, I am interested in the ways in which conversion may fulfill the religious aspirations of romance but also defeats its generic assumptions: the converted knight can bring victory but may also threaten the premise that virtue is or can be made visible. This chapter begins by going back to several early and mid-century responses to Montalvo: Ariosto's rewriting in *Orlando Furioso* (1516) of the madness of Amadis/Beltenebros in that of Orlando; Nicolas de Herberay's translations of the *Amadis* and *Esplandián* volumes (1540–44); and Antony Munday's defense of romance and his tacit critiques of Montalvo in his crypto-Catholic English translations of Books 7 and 9 (1514, 1530). How romances represent racial difference is important not simply for its own sake but because of romance's commitment to creating social identities for its readers. These concerns are at the heart of how readers respond to the new model of visual identity that emerged out of Montalvo's engagement with racialism.

This chapter thus ends with the greatest reader and theorizer of *Amadis* and of Renaissance romance as a whole, Cervantes' Don Quixote. Here, following Barbara Fuchs, I reassess the critical claim that Cervantes' hero is a knight of faith because he believes in what others cannot see. Don Quixote sees the world differently, not simply as a knight of faith but as a fictive *converso*. Whereas Sancho always identifies himself as "an Old Christian," Quixote has been converted to being a chivalric Christian knight. Other romances carefully place their converts on the edges of the narrative world, but Cervantes tells his story from this perspective. In keeping with historic denigrations of the literalness of Jewish reading practices, Don Quixote splits appearance from reality and, with it, romance as a genre.

Chapter 4, "Reading and racial melancholy in *The Urania*," provides a historicist reading of Pamphilia's "black" melancholy in Mary Wroth's printed prose romance *The Countess of Montgomery's Urania* (1621) and its unpublished manuscript continuation. This chapter stands as a logical historical endpoint because, in the differences between the two parts of Wroth's romance, we see how the emergence of modern racialism leads to a breakdown in traditional romance identity. Expanding upon Mary Floyd-Wilson's arguments about the intersection of humoral complexion and racial identity, I argue that Wroth introduces humoral models into her development of romance character and uses a racially and geographically marked version of melancholy typically associated with Egyptians, Ethiopians, and other Africans to depict her central fictional alter ego, Pamphilia.

As an autobiographical and literarily self-conscious fiction, the *Urania* is in part a record of Wroth's experiences as a reader. This record is evident in Wroth's citations and borrowing from earlier romances; it is also at the heart of her depiction of her fictional alter ego, Pamphilia. As a black melancholic who is impassioned but constant, Pamphilia stands in the *Urania* as a challenge to the arguments that Vives, La Noue, Amyot, Malón de Chaide, and others made about the physical consequences to reading romances. In the manuscript continuation of the romance, this humoral model of identity is complicated by Wroth's response to Burton's appropriation of melancholy and emerging racialist understandings of complexion. This change in what complexion means is coincident with a change in how reading works for Wroth. Part 1 establishes a model of reading as a deciphering of codes and visible symbols. As the well-known historical reception of Part 1 by court readers made clear, Wroth's assumptions about what kinds of identity could be made legible to would-be readers were unfounded. Part 2 engages in a more obscure, private mode of writing, apparent within both the narrative structure and the manuscript state of this volume, in which the new and visually oriented racialism means that identity itself is for Wroth no longer legible.

From Montalvo to Wroth, the ways that we learned, as a culture, to read identity – ours and others' – persist in a longer history of reading identity that this book seeks to document.

CHAPTER I

Genealogy and race after the Fall of Constantinople: from The King of Tars to Tirant lo Blanc and Amadis of Gaul

In his influential rereading of Northrup Frye and Erich Auerbach's accounts of the structure of identification that defines romance, Fredric Jameson argues that the genre is structured as much by difference as it is by recognition and identification. For Jameson:

Romance in its original strong form may then be understood as an imaginary "solution" to this real contradiction, a symbolic answer to the perplexing question of how my enemy can be thought of as being *evil* (that is, as other than myself and marked by some absolute difference) when what is responsible for his being so characterized is quite simply the *identity* of his own conduct with mine.[1]

As Jameson stresses, romance is predicated upon a commitment to the twin beliefs that the identity of the enemy is visibly "marked by some absolute difference" and yet that your identity is nonetheless ultimately indistinguishable from theirs. The seeming fixity and absoluteness of identity that characterizes romance also paradoxically demands a correlative fluidity of identity that stands against and alongside that fixity. Within romance, you need to be able to recognize the other less because of his utter difference than because his identity is some version of yours. In the material form of this demand for visible difference, the "black knight" is the enemy only so long as he wears his armor; when he puts that off and reveals his name, the knight who was the enemy becomes a version of the knight himself and must do so for both the social and moral structure of romance to work.

The question of identity is important because romance so often functioned, particularly in its medieval versions, as a genealogical document that was designed to assert lineage and kinship within a patriarchal world.[2] In the strong romances that Jameson has in mind, forms of physical appearance (from physical features and beauty to birthmarks and armor) provide evidence of an identity that is rooted in blood and kinship. Recognition scenes – which often turn on the unveiling of a scar or birthmark (Charikleia's black band, Odysseus' scar, the birthmarks of Esplandián and Amadis of Greece) – are the narrative expression of this generic commitment to the premise that identity is fixed (by birth and blood) and visibly manifest (within the social world that must recognize that identity). Within the narrative, these marks of birth and blood reveal the identity of the characters. Equally importantly, they also serve to affirm the identity of the true and noble reader as much as that of the characters within the fiction. As R. Howard Bloch notes in speaking of Chrétien de Troys' *Perceval*, romances connect social status to acts of proper reading: "the process of narration binds the status of nobility to a determined mode of understanding. To fail to read as Chrétien prescribes (literally 'pre-writes') is to lack the nobility which is as much a part of the book as it is an attribute of the book's princely patron."[3]

Jameson's model begs the question of what happens when the black knight is still "black" after he removes his helmet. What happens, that is, when difference does not collapse into the sameness of identity? This question becomes urgent in the printed romances that circulated across Europe in the sixteenth and early seventeenth centuries, and it is one that will have consequences for how romances could be read. Renaissance romances will be transformed not so much by the appearance of ethnically diverse characters – which are central to the genre from the outset – but by the introduction of new models of identity that challenged the genre's assumptions that identity was both fixed (established by birth) and manifest (affirmed by social practice). These challenges begin with the introduction of new forms of religious conversation narratives into the genre in the Spanish and Portugese peninsular romances of the late fifteenth and early sixteenth centuries. This chapter will examine two of the earliest and most influential of these romances from after the Fall of Constantinople: Joanet Martorell's *Tirant lo Blanc* (1490) and Garci Rodríguez de Montalvo's *The Labors of the Very Brave Knight Esplandián* (pub. 1510). Chapters 2, 3, and 4 will then turn to consider how these changes in the narrative structure of romance – its governing assumptions about religious identity and genealogical appearance – changed the models of reading that came to be associated with the genre.

Before turning to the printed romances, I would like to begin with the fourteenth-century middle English romance, *The King of Tars*, which in a concise manner illustrates how this generic dynamic between identity and difference functions in the kind of "strong" romances that Jameson has in mind. *The King of Tars* tells the story of the miraculous conversion of the pagan Sultan of Damascus after his marriage to the Christian daughter of the King of Tars. The details of the story derive from a number of historical chronicles, particularly those associated with the falsely claimed conversion of Ghazzan, the Mongol Khan of the Persians (b. 1271).[4] *The King of Tars* exists in three fourteenth-century manuscripts, most notably in the Auchinleck manuscript, but the popularity of the underlying narrative is also suggested by the widespread persistence of components of this story in both earlier and later chronicle literature.[5] *The King of Tars* provides a preliminary answer to this concern that persists, in one form or another, in all of the romances that I will be considering in this study, of what happens when the black knight is still black after he removes his helmet. At the same time, though, *The King of Tars* is a pre-Constantinople metrical romance and it circulated in manuscript. Standing in these respects outside the parameters of the central portion of this study, *The King of Tars* provides a useful beginning point since its solution to this dynamic between identity and difference is one that subsequent early modern romances will not be able to sustain for reasons that are historical, technological, and aesthetic.

In this romance, the King of Tars' daughter is beautiful and white, "non feirer woman miȝt ben, / As white as feþer of swan" (ll. 11–12), and the Sultan of Damascus falls in love with her and demands her hand in marriage. Initially, the King defies the Sultan and vows to spill his "hert blode" rather than give up his daughter to the pagan (ll. 41, 95). After a grim battle, in which more than thirty thousand Christian knights are killed, the King's daughter herself agrees to marry the Sultan in order to prevent further bloodshed and "to sauen Cristen kende" (l. 330). Right before their marriage, the Sultan himself becomes reluctant to marry a Christian and demands that she convert. The faithful daughter, who has been reassured in a dream that Jesus will not forsake her, promises that she will do so once she learns the truth of the Sultan's god.

After their marriage, the King's daughter gives birth to a mishapen lump of flesh, inanimate and unformed, "wiþouten blod & bon" (l. 582). The Sultan initially takes the monstrous birth as a sign of his wife's failure to truly embrace his religion. After his prayers to "miȝhtful Mahoun" go unanswered (l. 628), he allows his wife to have the monstrous child baptized and when she does the child is transformed. The "mark" of the initial birth that had obliterated all human identity and even life now disappears. The child produced by this Christian wife and her Muslim husband becomes an image of the genealogy of romance: beautiful and well-formed, "feirer child miȝt non be bore" (l. 781). The Sultan, who is now identified by the narrative as "blac" (l. 799), himself acknowledges

the power of the Christian God and converts. In doing so, he too is physically transformed, becoming as fair and white as his wife and child: "His
hide, þat blac & loþely was, / Al white bicom" (ll. 928–29) and indeed
"chaunged was his hewe" (l. 945). The conversion and transformation of
the Sultan become the means by which the romance's original military
battles are redeemed, as the Sultan now joins with the King of Tars to
defeat all of his former subjects who refuse to convert to Christianity with
him.

Recent criticism has been interested in *The King of Tars* because it has
provided a way to think about the meaning of "race" in a period that had
previously been seen as pre-racial.[6] Here, I am less interested in the issue
of race itself than in how *The King of Tars* literalizes the logic of romance
in the ways that Jameson suggests. In this romance, the commitments of
genre trump – or at least do not conflict with – the imperatives of racial,
ethnic, or religous identity, however those may be defined. *The King of
Tars* may be the most perfect literalization of the ethos of identity in
romance.

The King of Tars' daughter is perfectly, and always, white and beautiful in ways that mark her as a true child of Christianity. Her child is
at first not so much a mis-conception, an act of making that has been
perverted, as he is as yet unmade. The child is an unformed lump, and
the narrative thus three times reiterates the plea that they must "make it
fourmed after a man" (ll. 614, 668, 692). That is, the child should not be
understood as simply an image of a monstrosity produced by a perverted
mixing of Christian and Muslim, a kind of theologically-inflected version
of an Aristotelian accident.

Rather, the narrative premise here is that the child cannot be formed
because his father, the Sultan, does not yet have his own true identity. In
The King of Tars, the sight of the child retroactively creates the father's
identity: the child is not the genealogical proof of his birth and bloodline in the ways that romance traditionally insists; rather, birth achieves
the identity of the father. It is thus only after the child's transformation
and at the moment when the Sultan must recognize his now fair and
well-formed child that we first learn that the Sultan is black. It is at the
moment that he becomes white that the narrative describes how "blac &
loþely" the Sultan had been (l. 928).

In *The King of Tars*, Jameson's transition from identity to difference
is literal and precise: the black knight is black, until he is not. His identity is his appearance. Who and what he is always manifest within the
terms that the genre and its readers expect. From this perspective, it only

becomes necessary for the narrative to stress that the Sultan was black at the moment at which it momentarily seemed possible that his appearance might come to diverge from his essence. (This moment is clearly directed at the reader: it is not that the Sultan was not black before but rather that his identity was not one that the reader was asked to consider earlier.) Equally, conversion and conquest are both possible and true within the terms that Christianity expects. *The King of Tars* may anticipate and articulate the arguments that help make possible later attitudes toward the emergence of racial identity. This fourteenth-century romance may be a perfect instance of Jameson's "strong form" of romance. As we shall see, however, *The King of Tars* tells a story about the congruence of identity and appearance, as well as about conversion and conquest, that will no longer be possible in print romances after the Fall of Constantinople.

As I will suggest in this chapter, important transformations in the genre of romance and the kinds of stories it can tell begin as a result of historical changes, in Europe and in Spain, in particular, in church policies toward the possibilities of the two events that make *The King of Tars* possible: military conquest and religious conversion. These historical and social changes rewrite the generic possibilities for European romance: within the romances themselves identity and appearance repeatedly fracture against one another. Since the dynamic between identity and difference that appears within romances is largely a recognition narrative that is directed at the readers of romance, this also means that these historic shifts in genre happen in ways that, as later romances and commentaries on romance will make clear, ultimately impact readers' ability to see and recognize their own identities within these fictions.[7]

From a historical perspective, conversion is an important topic and one that leads to the development of theories of identity that contribute directly to the emergence of new models of racism from the mid-fifteenth century onward. There are three main components to any history of conversion in this period. First, within Christian Europe, there are the repeated waves of Jews and Moors who convert to Christianity. In Spain, for instance, large-scale conversions occur in 1109, 1366–69, 1391, and 1421. Second, there are the initiatives to convert Muslims living under Turkish rule to Christianity. These initiatives were a church policy that came out of the failures of the Crusades, which had initially embraced the idea of the military conquest as the primary vehicle for the spread of Christianity. In 1095, in his famous speech at the Council of Clermont, Pope Urban II, for instance, had instructed Crusaders to turn away from wars among Christians and instead go out to conquer in God's name: "Enter upon the road to the Holy Sepulchre; wrest that land from the wicked race, and subject it to yourselves."[8] From 1284 on, though, the Church became less certain that military power would allow them to achieve dominion over their religious enemies in the ways that they had hoped. As Robert S. Burns makes clear, Pope Innocent III and his successors increasingly advocated conversion as the way to defeat the Turks: Christianity needed to win victory through a battle for souls, rather than just lands.[9] Third, there were the large numbers of Christians living or working in lands controlled by the Ottoman or Marmeluk empires who converted to Islam.

Post-1453 romances tend to ignore or deny this third category of conversions, despite the fact that they probably comprised the largest numbers of actual conversions. Instead, they concentrate on the largely non-existent and thus essentially fictional possibility of converting Turkish Muslims or "infidels" living elsewhere outside of European Christendom. This plotline first gains prominence in the Catalan romance *Tirant lo Blanc* and dominates peninsular romances through the mid-sixteenth century. Studying the centrality of conversion to Iberian romance, Judith Whitlock notes, "nowhere is conversion more consistently in evidence than in the sixteenth-century Spanish romances of chivalry. It is a convention of the genre."[10]

From the perspective of cultural history, conversion becomes a part of romance as a response to the new military realities facing the Church. Just as earlier romances had promoted the policies and practices of the Crusades ("wrest that land from the wicked race, and subject it to yourselves") through their model of chivalric virtue, they now advanced and articulated the policies of conversion that the Church, in its foreign policy, envisioned as the new way to defeat the infidel threat.[11] Indeed, to the extent that chivalric romance had a long tradition of affiliation with the church policy of the Crusades, the comparative absence of actual real-life conversions of Turks and other Muslims to Christianity contributed directly to the strong compensatory presence of such stories in romances after the Fall of Constantinople.

In the face of crushing and ongoing defeats by the Turks in the fifteenth century and later, the narrative of triumphal conversion of the sort that we see at the heart of *The King of Tars*, and that defined medieval chivalric romance more generally, was in important ways lost to later romance writers. From a generic perspective, the historical shift to conversion as a church policy for victory implied a different narrative structure and created a different type of romance than crusading did. Romances such as Joanet Martorell's *Tirant lo Blanc* (1490), Montalvo's *The Labors of the*

Very Brave Knight Esplandián (1510; Book 5 of the *Amadis* cycle), Páez de Ribera's *Florisando* (also 1510; Book 6 of *Amadis*), and, as we shall see in Chapter 3, ultimately, Cervantes' *Don Quixote* (1605) offer a historically extended critique of what these romances understand as the mistaken and literally self-defeating violence of Christian against Christian that defined earlier romances, a violence that is not unlike what Urban had identified as the chief evil besetting his Christian knights, their aggression toward one another rather than against their true religious enemies. What in the first four books of *Amadis* had been paradigmatic victories of honor and virtue are reassessed in the fifth book, *Esplandián*, and critiqued as senseless and violent acts of self-aggression. As we shall see, Esplandián challenges both his father Amadis and the form of romance that he represents; importantly, he does so in language that closely follows Urban II's call to crusade: "frequently you perish by mutual wounds ... Let hatred depart from among you, let quarrels end, let wars cease .... Enter upon the road to the Sepulchre; wrest that land from the wicked race, and subject it to yourselves."[12]

Romances such as *Esplandián* follow calls to crusade and ultimately conversion by redefining the nature of combat: it is not just that fighting is carried out on a larger scale and that the enemies are now Turks, Moors, and other infidels. Rather, there is a key shift in the meaning attached to individual combat and collective war. The individual combat that dominates romances such as *Amadis* upholds virtue and honor through the articulation of shared values and commonalities of identity between individual combatants. *Tirant* and its successors, by contrast, posit radical and insurmountable differences of identity (religious belief, racial identity, and political values) and register those differences in part by replacing individual single-hand combat with large-scale, often multi-nation, aggregate warfare.

Within this larger structure, hand-to-hand combat continues to appear but, importantly, it does so precisely to affirm exceptional instances of common identity between those who would otherwise seem radically different from one another. In this sense, when the beautiful, dark-complexioned Queen Calafia and the black-armored Islamic Radiaro challenge the Christian knights Esplandián and Novadel in *Esplandián*, the terms of the combat (Muslim/Christian, white/black, male/female) go well beyond the boundaries of that "universal class" of the feudal nobility whose commonalities traditionally enabled the resolution of the basic contradiction that, for Jameson, is at the heart of romance: one's enemy is so precisely because he is a version of oneself.[13] Even without the "universal class," the shared membership in a landed Christian nobility that Jameson describes, these kinds of new combats still work to create identity between combatants. Ironically, even as the old model of chivalry is disparaged, those who meet traditional codes of chivalric honor, when defeated, become worthy of possible conversion that makes them versions of their opponents in precisely the way that traditional chivalry supposed.

Like the Church, though, writers of chivalric romance recognized that military conquest was not the ending to the story that the Turks presented to them. Romances such as *Esplandián* begin in a way that suggests that they are following the long familiar call to crusade but they do not stop there. These romances also introduce conversion as a central narrative premise. Conversions are not the concluding gesture to an already completed narrative, as they tend to be in the medieval sources; they instead constitute the driving force that makes military success and the narrative itself possible. The conversion of Queen Bramidonie in the medieval *Chanson de Roland*, for instance, appears at the end of the narrative as a confirmation of the truth of God and the virtuous identity of Charlemagne. That of Queen Calafia in *Esplandián*, the fifth book in the *Amadis* sequence, by contrast, stands as the beginning of a crucial new plotline. A fictional engagement with and enactment of established church policy, conversions are presented as a primary force that enables the narrative line itself. Thus, the military successes of Esplandián depend on the Turkish Frandalo; Tirant would not be able to save Constantinople without the Ethiopian Escariano and his nation of converted pagans. In some cases and in ways that will anticipate the structure of *Don Quixote*, the convert becomes a voice or conscience of the narrative. Romances thus provide an imaginative confirmation of the Church's theological arguments that conversion could enable the Church to defeat all enemies.

Yet, at the same time, introducing conversion into the heart of romance also destabilizes it. In its foreign policy and in its theological doctrine, the Church insisted that conversion was a powerful force – able to transform and defeat even the strongest or most recalcitrant of its enemies. On the domestic front, though, particularly in Spain, conversion was attacked and its efficacy repudiated. As we shall see, the Inquisition's adoption of race- (rather than faith-) based principles of identity challenged, and indeed were developed to challenge, the very possibility of conversion. When a single drop of stubborn Jewish blood could not be overcome by baptism and New Christians were still suspect after a hundred years of Christian worship, it was hard to know how conversion would conquer the swords of the Turk. Thus even as romances write out a key church policy, they also register the internal inconsistencies of the arguments that supported this policy by transposing the concerns about conversion that had arisen at home, out of domestic experiences with conversion, onto their imagining of foreign, distant, and exotic conversions. This overlaying of two different kinds of conversion stories (Spanish *conversos* and *moriscos* onto mythical Africans and almost Amazons) gives us more than just a commentary on the inconsistencies that riddled church statements and practices regarding conversion. More fundamentally, attacks on *conversos* became the basis for a new racially-based model of identity in Spain.

In the period that leads up to the imposition of the Spanish Inquisition, what begins as a model of genealogical racism also comes to be articulated in terms of increasing suspicion toward invisible or potentially hidden identities. The pure blood laws, in this context, are a specific instance of this tendency to the extent that they are concerned with qualities that are material and yet cannot be seen. When imported into romance, these two competing models of conversion – and the theories of identity and race that they imply – are expressed generically as a challenge to the commitment to visible identity that structured romance. What we see in the literary record recodes what we see in the historical register: when conversion is introduced to save romance narrative, race also enters in ways that threaten it and insist that identity is not subject to transformation. As was the case in Spain, racial identities develop within these romance narratives in conjunction with moments of conversion, but, crucially, and again following the historical trajectory, these newly racialized identities also challenge the very possibility of conversion that had been the new theological premise structuring the romance. What this means is that conversion narratives no longer confirm (heroic, Christian) identity, but instead often complicate that identity, and they do so in ways that get at the heart not just of romance's cultural assumptions but also of its generic ones. Ultimately, we will see the literary culmination of this fracturing of appearance and reality in Cervantes' *Don Quixote*. This fracturing breaks apart romance precisely on the grounds of how, in this new world after the Fall of Constantinople and the start of the Spanish Inquisition, we read the identities of others.

To understand how and why romances overlaid domestic attitudes toward conversion onto their nostalgic rewritings of the saving of Constantinople, it is necessary to recognize the complex relationship between race and conversion that developed, particularly in late fifteenth-century Spain, the primary point of origin for the chivalric romances that develop in response to both the Fall of Constantinople and the emergence of new understandings of genealogy. This is a historical claim that develops out of the monumental work of Benzion Netanyahu, and others, on the religious practices of the Spanish *conversos* from the twelfth through fifteenth centuries and on the political and theological arguments that various coalescing groups of "Old Christians" articulated against them.[14] Netanyahu argues that one of the most important, but critically overlooked, long-term consequences of the conversions in the first category (of Jews and Moors living within Spain) was the emergence of racism in the post-conversion periods. In contrast to earlier inquisitions and to established church policy, the Spanish Inquisition adopted a key principle of "race" to attack and discriminate against all those of "Jewish identity."[15] Introducing the idea of blood purity and the model of racial identity that that implied, Ivan Hannaford observes, "had the effect of turning the search for heresy within the faith into a search for the defilement of blood wherever it might be found."[16]

This concept of the Jews as belonging to a category of race rather than religion developed over a period of time and did so precisely as a consequence of the increasing assimilation of *conversos*, "New Christians," into the political, social, and economic culture of early modern Spain. The infamous *Sentencia-Estatuto*, the set of restrictive anti-*converso* decrees enacted in Toledo after the riots of 1449, thus designates all *conversos* as being of the "perverse lineage of the Jews."[17] Terms such as "natio" (nation) were applied to those of Jewish descent as a way of consolidating their identity as being separate and distinct, foreign, to the (true Christians) of Spain.[18] Recognizing that race-based definitions of identity posed potential problems for "Old Christians," many of whom had to be understood as the descendants of the original Jewish as well as gentile converts to Christianity during the time of the apostles and church patriarchs, anti-*marrano* polemists adopted an elaborate secondary category of race that confirmed that race was a matter of descent but one that did not go all the way back to the conversions that constituted the historic origins of Christianity. The anonymous author of *El libro del Alboraique* (c. 1480), for instance, thus separated Jews from the earliest Christians by arguing that those who had not converted at the time of the Pentecost had become a peculiarly degenerate and mixed race. According to this author, after the Destruction of the Second Temple (AD 70), the unconverted Jews intermarried with the women of Edom, Moab, Ammon, Egypt, and Babylon and, in doing so, became a "mixed race, bad and reprobate, quite unlike the race of the tribe of Judah."[19] This model of race emerged locally in the attacks and antagonisms against the *conversos* over the course of the late fourteenth and fifteenth centuries, intensified after 1449, and was ultimately consolidated and imposed across all of Spain when Isabella and Ferdinand instituted the Inquisition in 1480.

As Netanyahu demonstrates, the Spanish Inquisition followed these race-based attacks on *conversos* by defining being "Jewish" as a matter of descent rather than of belief. Adopted by the official body of the Inquisition in Spain (rather than simply by local magistrates and town councils, political agitators, or rioting masses), this policy went sharply against established church policy with respect to converts, the theological assumptions underlying baptism, and the church's historical understanding of itself as having been founded on acts of conversion.[20] It constituted an important and profound new theory of identity. Netanyahu stresses that this policy was adopted not because of any failures of conversion – his work overwhelmingly suggests that so-called New Christians, those Jews who had converted to Christianity and their descendants, were not secret "Judaizers" but rather were almost entirely assimilated members of the faithful.[21] That is, this new descent-based definition of who was a Jew and what that meant was a response to what ought to have been, from the Church's perspective, the success of their conversion policies. In essence, the "Jews" (of whom almost none were Jewish in their religious practices) become a "race" for the Inquisition precisely because their political opponents had no other way to distinguish them from other Christians, from themselves.

"Race" in these terms bridged what in other contexts functioned as two distinct identity models, genealogical theories of race as ancestry and new proto-racialist models of race as a feature of physical appearance. Genealogical models were not part of the attacks on Jews during the medieval period, if only because religious practice alone provided the basis for recurring encroachments against Jewish rights and privileges, while the Church tended to defend those who converted as part of a larger commitment to its theological positions on baptism and the sacraments. Thus, the introduction of genealogical models into this discussion in Spain is, relative to much of the rest of Europe, a somewhat belated one. Once attention and antagonism necessarily shifted from practicing Jews to assimilated *conversos*, what we see is an almost anachronistic, but in this context largely unprecedented, use of genealogical models. This genealogical model of identity drives claims about the Jews as a "degenerate" and "mixed" race, a foreign "nation" of people, the Jews as Jews in a blood that resists more powerfully than wine the miracles of grace-filled

transformation. Whereas elsewhere genealogical models of race are supplanted in the early modern period by proto-racialist ones, in Spain the
two phenomena go hand in hand.

When "Jews" were classified by their opponents as a race, that classification brought a concomitant fear that outer appearances might not
reveal true identities: First, could you see what someone believed? Could
you discern Judaizers from true Christians? And finally, could you see
who was "Jewish," who was a "New Christian," in an ancestral sense?
This sequence of fears prompted laws, policies, and identity texts such as
the infamous *Libre verde* which tried to make potentially hidden "racial
identities" visible and, I would argue, legible to all.[22] Within this historic
context, new meanings of "race" are not simply associated in some general
way with the subject of religious conversion. Rather, race emerged in this
context as a concept that was specifically designed to deny the theological
and social possibility of conversion: under this model, identity was either
pure or impure *and could not ever be changed*.

The concept that "race" constituted the basis for identity and that this
identity was incontrovertible and not susceptible to transformations of
grace obviously ran counter to central tenets of church doctrine. A denial
of the possibility of conversion was one to which the genre of romance was
inherently sympathetic. Romance had a strongly genealogical, kinship-
based model of identity; romance was also comfortable with the idea that
identity was fixed and immutable. What romance did have difficulties
with, though, was the secondary idea that essential features, qualities, of
identity might not be visible. The converted knight who appears so often
in the pages of romance is in part a hope for romance's imperial religious
success (mass conversion), but these knights are also potential threats
whose existence may challenge the premise that virtue is or can be made
visible and, with it, as we shall see, the basic structural model of romance
and its ability to convey such identities to its readers. If such knights
are virtuous but do not look as romance suggests that they will, then is
Christian virtue visible in the ways that romance seemed to promise?

Early printed romances such as *Tirant lo Blanc* and *The Labours of the
Very Brave Knight Esplandián* demonstrate how stories about conversion
threaten the model of identity that romance espoused and, with that, both
the terms of romance as a genre and the possibilities for self-recognition
that romance seemed to hold out to its readers. Within the historic context of the Inquisition, new meanings of "race" are not simply associated
in some general way with religious conversion. Rather, race emerged as
a concept that was used to deny the theological and social possibility of

conversion: under this model, identity was either pure or impure and could never be changed. As we shall see, this paradoxical sense that racial identity was a consequence of conversion, and yet also a challenge to its validity and even possibility, has profound implications for romance as a genre and for the acts of reading it could demand.

The Catalan romance *Tirant lo Blanc* begins as a traditional courtly romance and, indeed, stands as a kind of continuation of the Middle English *Guy of Warwick* and, through its extended citations of Ramon Llull's *Book of the Knightly Order*, a primer on the code of chivalry. *Tirant* was begun by a knight of the Valencian nobility, Joanot Martorell (writing in the 1460s), and, after Martorell's death in 1468, perhaps completed by Joan Roíç de Corelle.[23] It was published, in Catalan, under the title *Tirant lo Blanch* (Valencia, 1490), with one subsequent edition that decade and a substantially revised Spanish edition in 1511.[24] The structure of *Tirant* reflects the consequences of its dual authorship in ways that critics have suggested, but it also points to more general tendencies toward revision that are inherent in the genre of romance.[25] The romance's overall trajectory, like that of so many other romances from the late fifteenth century through the early seventeenth century, undertakes to rewrite the Fall of Constantinople. This desire expresses itself in revisions that take up two interrelated questions: First, can religious conversion save Constantinople? Second, can redefining romance save chivalry? As I will suggest, *Tirant* extends a larger romance impulse toward self-revision and modulates that impulse into a generic commentary that is also a theological and political assessment of religious practices. We will see a significant shift between the first sections of the romance (moving from London through Europe to Constantinople) and the last section of the romance (set in North Africa and moving back to Constantinople from there). As this romance is rewritten and changes narrative direction, conversion in *Tirant* becomes a narrative practice as much as a narrative subject.

The first sections of the romance, written by Martorell, tell the story of the chivalric adventures of the knight Tirant, "a gentleman of ancient Breton lineage,"[26] who first appears at a tournament being held to celebrate the marriage of the King of England to a French princess. After learning the tenets of the code of chivalry from an old hermit, himself once a knight and feudal lord, "knighted in Africa before a great battle with the Moors" (41),[27] Tirant achieves chivalric success in England and is subsequently made a Knight of the Garter. Widely acclaimed as an accomplished knight, Tirant then returns to his native land (133); when at the court of the King of France, he learns that Rhodes has been blockaded and is under siege and so sets out to assist the Master of Rhodes (138–55). He rescues the Rhodesians and then travels to the Holy Sepulchre and on to Egypt; returning to Sicily, he receives a desperate plea for assistance from the Emperor of Constantinople (160–85). In a love story that takes up familiar romance questions of political allegiance and personal identity within its amatory framework, Tirant fights the Turks on the Emperor's behalf and falls in love with his daughter, Carmesina.

In these first sections of the story, Tirant's identity is defined through origins that involve both familial and literary descent. Indeed, Martorell relies on a traditional genealogical model of identity, but tends to articulate that genealogical model as a form of literary and spiritual descent that ultimately becomes the basis for an argument against blood-based claims of virtue and nobility. Thus, at the outset, Tirant reveals his identity:

Since you wish to learn my name, I shall gladly tell you. I am called "Tirant" because my father was from the Tiranian March that borders England and "lo Blanc" because my mother Blanca was the Duke of Brittany's daughter. (40)[28]

By having Tirant reveal his familial identity so early in the romance, Martorell underlines his departure from the usual romance structure of identity recognition: despite whatever "ancient lineage" Tirant may have, here blood-based kinship will not be the primary determinant of Tirant's heroic and virtuous identity.[29]

Tirant instead becomes, in a more metaphoric sense, the "heir" to chivalry itself. Various father figures – both William of Warwick, who has separated himself from his son and heir, and later the Emperor of Constantinople, who welcomes Tirant after the death of his own son – adopt Tirant as a kind of surrogate son. Tirant is an heir to chivalry in a literary sense as well: he is modeled after the heroes of *Guy of Warwick* as well as after the strictures of Llull's *Book of the Knightly Order*. Martorell integrates this act of literary *imitatio* into the text itself in a manner that reflects the new power of the printed text to circulate and create the forms of social identity that *Tirant* envisions: given a copy of the *Tree of Battles*, Tirant patterns himself after its code of chivalry. In imagining Tirant in these terms, Martorell is advancing his larger argument that romances of chivalry become, for their readers, practices of chivalry. The romance repeatedly suggests to its readers that they, too, can claim kinship with Tirant and his virtue through acts of reading and enacting this fiction (50, 306).

Martorell's construction of a literary genealogy for Tirant as the heir to chivalry, a claim that we shall also see at the heart of Montalvo's *Esplandián*, fits into Martorell's larger arguments about the place that chivalry must have in the defense of Christendom. In the interval between leaving the court of London and arriving at that of Constantinople, Tirant's exploits provide a map of military action in fourteenth- and fifteenth-century Europe. Tirant liberates the knights of Rhodes, ransoms Christian slaves in Alexandria, and engages in piracy against Islamic strongholds along the coast of Andalusia. Taking the place of the traditional honor challenges that define identity in romances such as *Amadis*, these skirmishes reflect the historical realities of European action against the Ottoman and Marmeluk empires. These episodes establish Tirant as a virtuous and heroic knight; equally, they establish acts of individual chivalry as worthy and appropriate to the new military and religious contexts of the period.

At the same time, though, the de-emphasis of blood-based definitions of identity also involves a critique of the assumption that you can know who someone is – and what their virtue is – by knowing who their ancestors were. As we have seen, the re-introduction of *limpieza* statutes certainly made this question an explosive one throughout Spain by the end of the fifteenth century. In *Tirant*, the worst villains among the Christians inevitably turn out to be those with the highest rank, those who would presumably have the claims to the purest blood. Their consistent treachery stands in sharp contrast to the fidelity of Tirant, who is virtuous despite lacking "a drop of royal blood" (612). Challenges to Tirant's identity importantly reveal the basis of that identity, as Martorell understands it. Both in England and later in Constantinople, Tirant is repeatedly attacked as a foreigner and usurper: a "base foreigner of ill fame and unknown origin," "a vile foreigner" (238), and "a second Judas" (268).[30]

In this section of the book, Tirant's name is understood to refer not, as he had originally glossed it, to the identities of his parents and his Breton lineage. Rather, his opponents repeatedly assert that his name suggests that the only identity and privileges that he has are those that he has stolen from others to whom they more rightfully belong. Thus, the sailor Galançó unwittingly reveals to Tirant that

the Greeks are captained by some French devil who has won all his battles and whose name is Tirant. On my faith, he may have done everything they say, but his name is base and ugly, since "tyrant" means usurper of others' goods, or to put it more bluntly, a thief. (299)[31]

Given Martorell's own likely status as a member of the minor aristocracy of Valencia, it is probably too much to say that Tirant becomes a kind of structural Jew within the narrative, a Judas thief who has taken the court places and stolen identities legitimately belonging to others. Nonetheless, Martorell's construction of a primarily literary, rather than biological, genealogy for Tirant is part of a larger strategy of challenging blood-based models of identity in favor of the articulation of an aristocracy of merit. As the hermit William of Warwick makes clear at the outset, we should "not imagine that knights are of a higher lineage than others, since we all come from a mother and a father" (43).[32] This type of argument is familiar from other romances, but it is here deployed within a racialized context that ultimately works to break apart the identity structure of romance.

New proto-racialist models of identity were overlaid upon and indeed facilitated by pre-existing genealogical models of identity. What confers identity: belief and practice, or blood? As we have seen, this question demanded much attention from readers in the second half of the fifteenth century. In romance, of course, mortal combat often confers identity, as the victor acquires the honor, name, and symbolic identity of those he defeats. Martorell brings these usually separate questions together in two interlocking episodes that turn on questions about the "sign" of Tirant's identity. The first episode involves that central romance token of visual identity: the heraldic, armorial shield. The knight's shield embossed with the heraldic coat of arms is perhaps the most traditional marker of romance identity. The second episode, which follows up on the first, involves yellow tunics, one of the various "signs" of identity worn under penalty of law by religious minorities in Spain and across Europe, as well as in Morocco and other Islamic lands.

The first episode begins when four knights (who turn out to be the disguised kings of Friesland and Poland and the dukes of Bavaria and Austria) arrive at the court of the King of England to demand combat from worthy knights. The four knights, whose appearance and appurtenances are sumptuously described, claim equality among themselves ("all equals, brothers, and comrades in arms"; in their persons as in their belongings, "none was better than the others," 91, 92),[33] refuse to reveal their identities, but assure the English king that they are worthy opponents. They present to the king documents that testify that they have proven their birth and ancestry before the Roman Senate, the Cardinals of Pisa and Terranova, and even the Patriarch of Jerusalem. Their documents were witnessed by one Ambrosino di Mantova, a notary by imperial license, and serve

to declare publicly that they are knights of four quarters, for their fathers, mothers, grandfathers, and grandmothers were nobility, and therefore let no lord reproach their lineage. (94)[34]

Tirant quite literally puts his lineage onto the field against theirs: sending secretly to town, Tirant has four shields made up, painted with the arms of his father, his mother, his grandfather, and his grandmother (97). Tirant then enters the lists, under the somewhat paradoxical disguise of his own family identity, and, bringing a new shield to each successive encounter, defeats and kills each of the four knights in turn. Later, Tirant collects the shields of his dead opponents and has them sent back to Brittany to hang in his family chapel (110).

Tirant's defeat of the four challengers is, in part, simply a typical (and typically violent) chivalric battle to acquire identity. Yet, the curious insistence on the presence and testimony of notary evidence about these four knights "of the four quarters" makes it clear that this combat is not just about which knight is stronger or more agile: rather, these are legal trials connected to the demand that traditional genealogy now provide proofs of new kinds of identity. And, importantly, the strict patrilineal descent that dominates medieval romance is itself not enough here: for Tirant, as for the knights themselves, the line of the father must be confirmed by those of the mother and the grandparents, a requirement that evokes new standards for blood purity.

Martorell's envisioning of this encounter points to the widespread scrutiny put upon questions of proving identity. Indeed, this episode may also hint at the perhaps paradoxical historical irony that, as a result of the very high intermarriage rates between *converso* and aristocratic Christian families in the fourteenth and fifteenth centuries, to be an aristocrat was itself almost enough to be suspect in the eyes of the Inquisition. Thus, the relator, Fernán Díaz de Toledo, writing his *Instrucción* after the riots of 1449, warned that all of the noble lineages of Castile could trace their descent from *conversos*; in 1535, López Villabos extends this argument, suggesting that if *converso* blood is impure, then that impurity affects "the majority of the Spanish nobility."[35] Actual *limpieza* statutes are largely confined to conflicts in Castile and are in any case not introduced into Catalonia until later, but the questions that such statutes pose about identity are culturally dominant throughout the region.[36] In keeping with demands that suspected *conversos* be able to document pure blood "of four quarters," here the knights assert traditional aristocratic identity, but the terms in which they do so are ambiguous enough to remind us that the very bloodlines that made one noble might also make one a "member of that vile race."[37] These four knights who will not reveal their names and hide themselves behind "black velvet hoods with eyeholes" (93) and "Turkish-style hats" (96) display the contemporary dynamic by which racially-inflected demands to display and prove identity themselves created aesthetic and cultural practices dedicated to the concealment of identity.[38]

What identity does Tirant win by defeating these four knights and claiming the shields that protect, hide, and mark their identities? The answer that is probably most optimistic, at least for romance, is that by defeating opponents who so clearly hold higher ranks than he does, Tirant proves that he possesses a heroic identity that does not depend on genealogy, one that can overcome his lack of a single "drop of royal blood." The sequel to this episode in part confirms this reading, but it also suggests how questions about race increasingly trouble assertions of a universal Christian identity of the kind that Tirant and, by extension, romance itself needs to claim. That is, genealogical identity, itself often prejudicial with respect to merit, is being displaced, not necessarily in favor of some Christian equality of all believers, but rather by proto-racialist definitions of who can or cannot be accepted as part of that Christian community.

In the sequel episode, Tirant wins another great victory, but this time not by fighting. After leaving Jerusalem, Tirant and his companions travel to Alexandria where he encounters a Christian slave lamenting his fate. Posing as the man's relative, Tirant negotiates with his Saracen master to ransom him for fifty-five gold ducats. By selling all his silver, dishes, and jewels, Tirant is ultimately able to redeem four hundred and seventy-three Christian slaves. When they all arrive back in Rhodes, Tirant

bought many rolls of cloth and had capes, cloaks, doublets, stockings, shoes, and shirts made for the slaves. He collected their yellow shirts and sent them to his chapel in Brittany, where they were kept with the shields of the four knights he had slain. (161)[39]

Even more so than the first episode, Tirant's act of ransoming the enslaved Christians suggests that identity must be made up not through who you are born of but through what you do and how, in doing so, you claim spiritual kinship with Christianity. Here, chivalric battle is replaced by a Christ-like ransoming of souls. The ransoming is particularly evocative precisely because, unlike the usual ransoming of military prisoners and those captured into slavery, Tirant's involvement is not based on kinship. When Tirant fought the four kings and knights, he in a way disguised himself under his own family identity. Here, he initially pretends a family connection to arrange the first ransom, but the larger redemption is achieved as a "Good Samaritan" parable in which, as Marc Shell points out, being a true Christian differed from being a good Jew in supposing a universal brotherhood that demanded acts of "kindness" toward strangers, rather than toward kin and family.⁴⁰ In Tirant's family chapel, the four armorial shields are now supplemented, in a gesture of almost biblical proportions, that comes back one hundred fold, by four hundred and seventy-three of the yellow shirts that the enslaved Christians were forced to wear as the mark of their identity and status.

Martorell links these two episodes in a way that overlays two culturally dominant models for visible identity upon one another: as four becomes four hundred, the old identity of heraldry is supplanted by a new "sign" of Christianity. It is important to recognize, though, that such yellow tunics are a sign of Christian identity only in a pernicious sense. As most of Martorell's readers would have known, Christians living in Islamic lands often converted to Islam; the visual sign of their status as *renedagoes* was their "taking of the turban," a gesture of suspected false identity alluded to in the "Turkish-hats" of the kings and dukes that Tirant fights. Christian slaves and other religious minorities, by contrast, were marked by the yellow tunics that they were forced to wear in public.⁴¹

An imported, domesticated version of this practice, though, was in place through much of Christian Europe. Readers of *Tirant* would have more often directly encountered this "sign" of Christianity only in the inverse and exclusionary sense through their experiences with and cultural memories of the devices and signs that Jews and Moors living in Europe were required to wear to distinguish them from Christians. In 1215, the Fourth Lateran Council ruled that Jews had to wear a special sign.⁴² This edict was both enforced and waived, by turns, across Europe: in Catalonia, for instance, laws were put in place in 1411 requiring that "the Jews wear turbans with red signs and the Moslems hoods with a bright moon."⁴³ These larger cultural and religious conflicts over the imposition of the sign and its ability to mark identity in visible terms are registered here in *Tirant* in the narrative device of transposing onto an exotic foreign situation – Christians living in Morocco and other Islamic lands – what most readers would have experienced in its mirror version at home. If the yellow shirts are a sign of Christian triumph for universal brotherhood, rather than family name signaled by shields and devices, that triumph is for Tirant only achieved within the context of a racialization that perpetuates, rather than undoes, traditional blood-based identity.

Alternating between Tirant's military and amorous engagements, the first sections of this romance reach an impasse that seems to arise out of the increasing irrelevance of its traditional plotline. Tirant's love for the Emperor's daughter is requited, but their union is ultimately impeded because, whatever arguments have been made about his status as the heir to a Christian chivalry based on universal brotherhood, nothing that Tirant does can compensate for the fact that he does not possess a single drop of royal blood. He and the Greek Emperor's daughter Carmesina are married, yet the marriage remains secret and the narrative does not seem able to arrive at a solution that would transform what seems like it can only be the scandalous uncertainty of private marriage into the kind of legitimate, public union that can produce accepted heirs. This situation changes in the final portion of the romance. With the exception of a few chapters, this final section of *Tirant* reflects a substantial rethinking and critiquing of the assumptions of the first sections of the romance. At the heart of this revision, as I have suggested, is the recognition that military conquest, whether in the united armies of Christendom or in the heroic endeavors of mythical knights such as Tirant, is not enough to defeat the Turks. In keeping with this rewriting, the narrative here adopts conversion as both its central political commitment and narrative device.

This shift out of the old model of conquest to a new one of conversion is achieved within the narrative when Tirant, in a rage of mistaken sexual jealousy, beheads a Moorish slave. This episode may mark the beginning of the portion of the romance that was written by Joan Roíç de Corelle; it is certainly one whose seemingly unprovoked violence registers the radical disjuncture between the earlier and later sections of the romance. Here, Tirant fears that his beloved Carmesina might agree to marry the Grand Sultan of Babylon (317) and at the same time jealously and wrongly imagines that she has been unfaithful to him with "a black Moorish slave named Lauseta" (413).[44] At once denying this imagined possibility and yet enraged to the point of belief that she would "give her body to a black savage, making her beauty odious to all who love righteousness" (414),[45] Tirant ultimately beheads the man he believes has taken the place that is not yet even his. As he does so, he laments his loss: "Tell me pitiless damsel: did my appearance please you less than that black gardener's?" (431).[46]

This episode, which is not adequately accounted for within the terms of the narrative itself and which produces a deep fracturing of the romance, expresses the kind of racialist prejudice that becomes increasingly dominant in the early modern period. What is perhaps most interesting about this episode, though, is how a narrative frustration against the constraints of an older racial order (lack of kinship status) expresses itself in the form of a rage that attacks under the terms of new proto-racialist models of identity. When Tirant kills off this "black savage," he also kills off the traditional chivalric plotline with its fictions of transparent, blood-based identity that had until now dominated this romance.

This episode of racial violence radically alters the trajectory and assumptions of the narrative: Tirant and the center of the narrative now move to North Africa.[47] During this final section of the romance, Tirant leaves Constantinople in his furor over Carmesina's supposed infidelity and finds himself shipwrecked near Tlemcen in Northern Africa. Captured as a slave, he becomes a military hero fighting in the service of the King of Tlemcen, and, ultimately, converts these armies and those of their opponents to Christianity. With these armies of newly baptized African Christians, Tirant leads his forces north, defeats the encroaching Turks, and, in a nod to historical reality, temporarily saves Constantinople for European Christianity. As is the case in the larger historical context, claims about the power of conversion bring with them counter-arguments about the essential and unchanging truth of race that call into question the possibility of such conversions.

At the most literal narrative level, once conversion becomes a key subject of romance, visible forms of racial difference come with it. Whereas Tirant had previously been defined by his family connections and literary predecessors under the traditional understandings of race that dominate the first sections of the romance, he now becomes identified by his ethnic and religious identity. After his shipwreck he is saved because of his physical beauty. "Pale but handsome," "white, bright, and fair," he becomes known under the name "Blanc": "Should you wish to know who I am, I shall tell you the truth: my name is Blanc" (453, 454).[48] Tirant now creates a new etymology for his name: "my name is Blanc and the moon, which is white, bright, and fair, shines to show me the way. My hands stretch toward the moon, and thus with God's help I shall conquer Barbary" (454–55).[49] The new identity that Tirant acquires – and this new glossing of his name – reflects the larger historic shift that we have seen in models of race as a form of identity. More generally, what had been a somewhat belated romance in the medieval model now becomes a much more politically motivated, markedly post-1453 narrative about the conversion of souls as the only way to save Constantinople and Christianity from the onslaught of the Turks.[50]

With conversion comes race. At the heart of this second half of the romance is the dark-skinned Ethiopian, King Escariano, "a powerful black much taller than other men" (455).[51] The black Escariano is the African alter ego to the very white, northern Tirant. As white and black, as northerner and southerner, as a foreign knight with his "barbarian

Breton rabble" (208) at the court of Constantinople, on the one hand, and as the powerful opponent to the King of Tunis, on the other, Tirant and Escariano are mirror images of each other. They are both equally foreign from the perspective of the original readers of this romance. Escariano's desire, in the second half of the romance, to marry the daughter of the King of Tunisia gives us a version of Tirant's love for the daughter of the Emperor of Constantinople in the first half. The differences between these two marriage narratives suggest, though, how the conversion plot-line is part of a larger change in ethnic identity and in the possibilities for romance as a genre. In the first section of the romance, Tirant's love for Carmesina is part of a more traditional story about identity and vassalage. The impediments to Tirant's various successes arise out of political sus-picions about his identity as a "foreign knight." Tirant's courtly success, which ends in his secret marriage to the Emperor's daughter, should be a story about the achievement of a universal Christian aristocracy based on virtuous acts, one that overcomes various more limited forms of blood-based identity.

In the last section of *Tirant*, though, impediments to marriage involve racial and religious differences. Taken collectively, these marriage stories are a literary recognition of Netanyahu's claims that rises in the rates of intermarriage in the thirteenth and fourteenth centuries were a motiv-ating factor in the ensuing anti-Semitic racism that develops so strongly by the 1490s. For Martorell, in the first part of *Tirant*, "intermarriage" means something like the marriage between the King of England and the King of France's daughter. Difference is simply not a part of such alli-ances, a fact suggested in the physical appearance of the bride. As Tirant reports in his account of the betrothal dinner, "when the princess drank red wine, her whiteness was so extreme that one could watch it go down her throat" (40).[52] Like the princess herself, this marriage supposes a kind of complete transparency of and in identity. Once the narrative moves to the southern perimeters of Christendom, though, we begin to see mar-riages that cross boundaries of religion, ethnic identity, appearance, and geography.

Some possible marriages, proposed but not realized, are introduced to suggest that certain kinds of identity can be transcended, but not others. In one case, a poor Jew in Ethiopia refuses the king's command that he marry his daughter to a rich Jew's son on the grounds that he and his fam-ily are Jews of the race of David, but the rich Jew is of what he describes as the traitorous race of those Jews who persecuted Christ, the "lineage [of] those who took part in His crucifixion" (466).[53] The poor Jew refuses to "taint [his] blood with perpetual grief, since [his] children's lineage would be eternally corrupted" through such intermarriage (467).[54] This man is certain that nothing can change those who belong to this evil race of Jews and equally certain that his family's identity would be utterly and irremediably destroyed by contact with them.[55]

A second, related incident suggests that Islam is, in a different way, incapable of transforming identity. The Grand Sultan of Babylon proposes peace and marriage to the Emperor's daughter. He offers to allow his would-be bride to retain her own religion and to raise any daughters as Christians, but insists that sons would need to be raised as Muslims (317). Refusing, Carmesina reassures Tirant, "How can you think that I would marry an infidel?" (317).[56] In the first episode, the poor Jew speaks in the voice of anti-*converso* instigators; the second episode turns the well-known contemporary Islamic policies of toleration toward religious difference into a moral and biological failing. In either case, though, neither Judaism nor Islam has the power to transcend ancestry and identity in the way that, as we shall see, Christian conversion can. The domestic model of conversion that the Inquisition promoted – which regarded conversion as inefficacious when confronted with what it regarded as the essential, immutable, descent-based differences presented by Jews and Muslims – is here reattributed from individual peoples who might be converted (Jews and Muslims) and reconceived as a feature of their religions (Judaism and Islam).

In contrast to these cases, Escariano's desire for the King of Tunis' daughter, Emeraldine, offers readers a validation of the power of Christian conversion. A black Ethiopian living in the lands adjacent to Prester John's kingdoms, King Escariano is certainly a version of this mythic figure who seemed to hold out hope of a perhaps powerful Christian nation on the other side of the Turkish empire.[57] The power of the Prester John myth, as told by Mandeville and later Ariosto, lay precisely in the fact that Prester John was already Christian, providentially already a member of the faithful and ready to give aid against the Islamic threat. Escariano is instead initially a pagan. Escariano only becomes a kind of Prester John because he converts.

The reason that Escariano is not yet a Christian is because *Tirant* adopts the Church's robust model of conversion as a powerful force, rather than the Inquisition's account of it as weak. In *Tirant's* North Africa, conversion is not thwarted by differences among races or troubled by seeming incongruities between outer appearance and inner belief. The marriage of Escariano to Emeraldine crosses racial and geographic differences and provides a positive story about how conversion can transform religious identity. The courts of the white Tunisians and the black Ethiopians are brought together and all are brought into Christianity: the wedding festivities celebrate this union among peoples, "some of whom were black and some white, for the whites were Tunisians and the blacks Ethiopians" (549).[58]

Seemingly a more powerful successor to the universal aristocracy of virtue that Tirant had embodied in the first portion of the romance, conversion now provides an identity that promises to overcome not just racial difference but old forms of kinship and familial identity as well. Becoming through the act of baptism a "brother-in-arms" to Tirant, the converted Escariano thus kills his own brother (whose standing as a figure of both race- and family-bound identity is signaled by his armorial device, "the gold bejeweled monkey on his helmet") to prevent him from harming Tirant (486, 496–97). Conversion becomes for King Escariano the path to marriage (everyone in Ethiopia is first baptized and then they are all married [549]) and, at the same time, to military dominion over the Turks. Before the conversions, Escariano is powerful ("Except for the Great Khan, he was the mightiest lord on earth," 549), but afterwards even more so: "those baptized Christians are the bravest soldiers alive!" (490–91).[59] In Africa, conversion gives King Escariano precisely what Tirant lacks at home. A structure of desire, power, and possibility, conversion now drives the narrative. What the romance presents as happening at the level of plot – a series of cascading dominos that begins with Emeraldine's infatuation with the "blessed Christian" Tirant and then extends out to nations and peoples across Africa – is a literary fiction for what the church hoped would happen as a matter of policy: conversion would be a force that would overwhelm whole countries, subduing any military power, transforming identity, and bringing the salvation of Christianity.[60]

Ultimately, though, the end of the romance does not sustain this belief in the possibility of conversion. At the conclusion of *Tirant*, we must recognize that this romance about the power of Christian conversion is as nostalgic as, in its way, was the larger goal of rewriting the Fall of Constantinople. In the campaign on Constantinople, Tirant and King Escariano's armies separate from one another. When Tirant and his forces reach Constantinople, they capture the Sultan of Baralinda and the Grand Turk. With this victory, the Emperor appoints Tirant as his Caesar and Tirant accepts the succession and, with it, public betrothal to Carmesina (560–89). Committed to a full restoration of all the lands legendarily ruled by Justinian (588), Tirant almost immediately leaves Constantinople to unite forces with King Escariano. Following the path of Mandeville's *Travels*, the two knights and their troops travel across Andrianople, Strenes, Stagira, Trebizone, Olympia, into Hungary, Bosnia, Serbia, and through Arcadia, Persia, and Samarkand (591–99). Conversion continues to be important during this campaign: the narrative thus includes a key example of the conversion of the captain of the Turks at Stariga as a counterpart to the conversion of Escariano, the Ethiopian pagan (594). The romance stresses that this new campaign provides a fulfillment of the story of conversion that began in North Africa: Escariano stands as the godfather to the Turkish captain who, previously unnamed, now becomes in baptism a kind of second Escariano and is thus aptly "christened Sir John Escariano" (594). The power of conversion to create new identities also fittingly provides the chief military strength of Tirant's army.

David Quint has suggested that, after Virgil, epic commits itself to an ideology of empire that envisions the West triumphing over the East through a "principle of coherence" that in large part consists of an "ethnically homogeneous" identity in its peoples and troops.[61] Writing a story of romance conversion rather than imperial epic, *Tirant* instead imagines a unity of identity that crosses racial, ethnic, and geographic boundaries by making faith, not birth, the force that brings together God's armies. "From all nations," Tirant's four hundred thousand troops strike fear into all those who see them (595).[62] Diversity of birth becomes unity of faith and is all the more powerful because of that. The power of this army of four hundred thousand thus arises from a unity of identity that is founded on religious belief. Nonetheless, this final campaign, only briefly recounted, differs from Tirant's successes in North Africa. It involves not conquest, but reconquest of lost cities and populations ("whose Greek inhabitants rejoiced and whose renegade Christians returned to their faith," 591).[63] The narrative's cursory sweep back through the Greek empire finally suggests how, within imaginative literature, it may be easier to convert black pagans from the reaches of Ethiopia (a safely fictive possibility) than it is to convert Turkish Muslims or, for that matter, to win back renegade Christians (both intractable and often-encountered historical realities). The return to Christianity in the former Greek empire is less triumphal and less certain than are the distant conversions in Africa.

In the end, the racialist view of conversion seems to win out. The conversion narrative that Tirant initiates is not ultimately achievable or at least not sustainable. The narrative tends to agree with the poor Jew's suspicions that some tribes and races cannot ever change their identities.

At precisely the moment when all obstacles should be gone – the empire rescued and the wedding impending – Tirant suddenly and inexplicably dies, as he walks along the river with King Philip and King Escariano (601). His death is quickly followed by those of both the Emperor and his daughter. These deaths ignore the possibility that conversion held out and take the narrative back to the question of blood identity: on her own deathbed, Carmesina mourns Tirant as one "whose sole flaw was that he lacked a drop of royal blood" (612). With the loss of the Emperor, his named successor, and his only daughter, the imperial Greek dynasty dies out (615). (Carmesina's mother seems to be allowed to live at least in part because she is "too old to bear children" [619].) In this context, the romance at the end cannot imagine for its readers how Tirant can overcome his identity: what conversion did for Escariano it seems unable to do for Tirant.

The profound belief that conversion, however powerful it may be theologically, is not strong enough to create a happy ending can be seen in the treatment of Escariano at the conclusion of the romance. Escariano was Tirant's constant companion and alter ego in North Africa. Back in the Greek empire, though, the two are repeatedly separated from one another, and Escariano is notably kept out of Constantinople. Both at the initial victory and then in death (590, 608), Tirant enters Constantinople alone. Escariano seemed to be the military and theological force that made the salvation of Constantinople possible; yet, in the final chapters of the romance, the conversion of identity that he represented is not one that narrative is prepared to imagine as a possibility, at least not for or within European Christendom. Escariano may be converted and conversion may be powerful, but only as long as he, and his kind of conversion, remain safely in Africa (616, 620). In all, the romance of *Tirant* ends in bitter resignation; a fiction that seemed determined to retake Constantinople through the power of a conversion of identities abandons that cause.

Questions about race, conversion, and romance identity are also at the heart of the most influential of the Spanish romances, the *Amadis* romances. Garci Rodríguez de Montalvo adapted and revised a popular national myth that had been the basis of an original, now lost, "primitive" version of the Amadis story into the initial four books of what has become the *Amadis* cycle. Shifting from the Arthurian-style romances centered on Amadis of Gaul and his beloved Oriana that make up the first four books, Montalvo then undertook to conclude this sequence with what is now a much less well-known fifth book, *The Labors of the Very Brave Knight Esplandián*.[64] Dedicated to the adventures of Oriana

and Amadis' illegitimate son, Esplandián, Book 5 both revises and concludes Books 1–4 and, as is the case in the final section of *Tirant*, religious
conversion is at the heart of these critical revisions. Montalvo's largest
goal in making these revisions is to transform the individual honor combat of chivalry into a holy war against infidels. While asserting that no
one could equal his father in "boldness or fearless assault," Esplandián
explains Montalvo's narrative goals when he says that "the principal difference between Amadis and me will lie in the fact that God will give me
strength to fight against His enemies, the evil infidels, whereas Amadis
did not do this."[65] Following the dictates of church policy on conversion as a new form of crusade, Montalvo transforms chivalry into holy
war by introducing religious conversion into his romance. As we shall
see, however, Montalvo's narratives about religious conversion also bring
with them historically inseparable concepts of race that destabilize the
romance as a form.

The opening books of *Amadis* exemplify the values and commitments
of medieval chivalry; through the character of Amadis, they articulate
an ideal that was deeply nostalgic even when it was written. *Amadis*
begins by telling the story of how the unknown and lost knight, the
Child of the Sea, regains his rightful identity as the son of King Perion
of Gaul through acts of chivalric service to the princess Oriana, the
daughter of King Lisuarte of England. Throughout Books 1–4, chivalry
is a practice of identity. In this portion of the romance sequence, chivalric battles create identity in and between individual knights in much
the ways that Jameson indicates. Books 1–4 do not explicitly champion
the practices of the Crusades: the quintessential knight errant, Amadis
is not a liege knight to Lisuarte; he is a vassal only to love (and is thus
singularly the Queen's knight, not the King's); the action is confined to
Christian Europe, not the Holy Lands or the boundaries of the Greek
empire; Amadis never accepts lands or dominions and, as Queen Brisena
later recognizes, he is a knight "who had never acquired anything but
arms and a horse."[66] Yet, indirectly, these books do promote the ideals that drove the early Crusades. In part, *Amadis* is compatible with
the Crusades because the stated ideal of knight errancy, the righting of
wrongs suffered by those otherwise powerless, had a moral valence to
it that adapted to the perspective through which Crusaders understood
their participation in the Crusades. More importantly, *Amadis* also articulates a form of pan-European military nobility that transcended existing national, geographic, or political boundaries through its insistence
on an identity of virtue.

In much the same way that the last section of *Tirant* turns from geneal-ogy to racialism, the fifth book of the *Amadis* cycle, *Esplandián*, shifts from a medieval Crusade structure to a post-1453 conversion narrative. The Esplandián story is modeled on that of St. George. Like the St. George story (which promises rescue from the dragon only if the townspeople convert to Christianity), *Esplandián* is a conversion narrative that cent-ers on the lands of the Ottoman Empire (33). Montalvo directly invokes Isabella and Ferdinand and exhorts them to pursue their policies, the new more limited "crusades" of the late fifteenth century, those that centered on Granada and North Africa, as well perhaps as the domestic religious crusade implied by the Inquisition ("never to tire of or abandon that holy war they have begun against the infidels," 347).[67] Esplandián's identity – his fate as the bringer of religious truth – is appropriately first revealed in those portions of the text that Montalvo inserted in his revisions of Books 3 and 4 of the earlier narrative, at the moment when one of the two names inscribed from birth on his chest becomes legible as the hermit Nasciano starts to baptize the child.[68] It is baptism that Esplandián then brings, as a conversion of spirit to those who are already Christians such as Norandel, Amadis, and the hermit Nasciano, and as a transformation of identity to the Turkish Muslims and the African pagans.

Esplandián's goal is to rescue Constantinople from the threat posed by a multi-national army of Turks and other infidels and to marry the beautiful Leonorina, daughter of the Emperor of Greece. These goals are achieved primarily as a result not of particular valor on Esplandián's part but through his conversion of two pagans: Frandalo, a Turkish Muslim descended from a race of giants, and Queen Calafia, a black Amazon-like warrior from the mythical isle of California. These conversions make Esplandián's military successes possible, as did that of the Ethiopian Escarino in *Tirant*. At the same time and again in ways parallel to *Tirant*, what is converted is also the original model of chivalric practice and chiv-alric identity that had defined the first four books of the romance.

This act of transformation that *Esplandián* re-imposes back on the earl-ier sections of the *Amadis* narrative is thus expressed by Norandel, whose own search for adventure represents the old order of chivalry, as a form of religious conversion. Norandel's comments clearly express Montalvo's sense of the practice of narrative conversion in which he is engaged as an author:

I have gone through many adventures seeking the strange things around this world of ours ... [and] the thought I have had until now, which was to win honor and fame in exploits that had a past quality – most of which, by the way, have done very little good – has been *changed and converted* into seeking that by which, risking the death of my body, I can win glory and eternal life for my soul. (206, my emphasis)[69]

Much like Norandel, Montalvo's narrative has been changed and converted in ways that revalue honor and fame against faith.

The adoption of a conversion narrative as the heart of *Esplandián* involves a reassessment of more than just the kinds of battles that Christian knights must fight. (As Norandel notes, such exploits were concerned only with personal honor and fame and had done very little good.) It also requires a reassessment of the kind of identity that Christian chivalry had embraced. It is thus at this point that both conversion – a story about the transformation of identities – and race enter the narrative in ways that threaten its premises. This reassessment of identity is achieved first through a redefinition between Books 1–4 and Book 5, between *Amadis* and *Esplandián*, in the meaning of physical appearance, fairness, and beauty. This redefinition of the meaning of physical appearance parallels the larger historic shift in the concept of race during this period. In Books 1–4 beauty and physical appearance had been the primary trope that marked identity and demonstrated kinship among individuals. In Book 5, appearance instead is given by God rather than produced through blood and thus becomes a form of religious truth and key source of conversion.

At the same time, the traits of genealogical and racial identity that had defined many of the Christian characters in Books 1–4 are reattributed in *Esplandián* to the pagans and infidels. As a result, when characters such as Frandalo or Queen Calafia are converted what is at stake is not just the salvation of individual souls but also the transformation, the conversion in a larger sense, of traditional blood-based models of identity (now embodied by pagans and infidels) into claims for a universal Christian identity based on belief and the power of conversion. The shift from *Amadis* to *Esplandián* involves much the same rethinking of identity, conversion, and race that we saw in *Tirant*, but here that transformation occurs along an axis that is dominated by concerns about genealogy and appearance rather than primarily by interest in blood and religion as was the case in *Tirant*.

Martorell was a knight and member of the minor nobility in Valencia; Feliciano de Silva, the author of the sequel, *Amadis de Grecia*, which tacitly denies many of the theological arguments about conversion that Montalvo makes in *Esplandián*, was of a well-established noble family but married a woman of Jewish descent and concealed her *converso* identity by suggesting that she was the illegitimate daughter of his patron;[70] Cervantes was almost certainly, and known to be, of *converso* descent.[71] Montalvo was, by his own account, "regidor de Medina del Campo" and from what William Little characterizes as a "long pure bloodline."[72] These differences go some way to explaning how these authors approach the subject of religious conversion in their romances.

For Montalvo, physical appearance begins as a sign of kinship identity but ultimately in Book 5 becomes a sign of religious truth. Montalvo's shifting valuation of physical appearance (from genealogical blood identity to individual religious faith) anticipates and is congruent with the relationship between visible skin color and racial identity that racialism posits. For later readers, as we shall see in Chapters 2, 3, and 4, the meaning of physical appearance will have changed. Montalvo's attention to how visual qualities and visible differences define identity thus causes subsequent readers to react strongly to this feature of his text and to do so for reasons that arise out of their own, different, understandings of the relationship between identity and appearance.

In Books 1–4, beauty is the central trope of identity. It expresses the sense that virtue and other ineffable qualities are physically manifest in those who possess them. From a generic perspective, this understanding of identity makes it possible for both characters and readers to recognize virtue in others. Physical fairness is the single most important quality that distinguishes Amadis as a knight. He is brave and strong as a fighter and faithful as a lover, but before he is any of these things, he is handsome. Amadis, who was miraculously rescued from the sea and is known only under the name "Child of the Sea," first comes to the attention of King Languines and his wife as "the most beautiful child you have ever seen" (1: 46).[73] Others universally acknowledge Amadis' good looks: "He is very young and so handsome it is a marvel to see" (1: 84); "What knightly good looks" (1: 99); "They all marveled greatly at the extreme good looks of Amadis" (1: 164).[74]

This emphasis on Amadis' physical appearance should not be understood simply as a tendency, typical of romance, to idealize the qualities of its heroes or, by extension, of its aristocratic readership. Rather, Montalvo stresses Amadis' good looks as part of his commitment to the idea that identity is manifest and visible. Amadis is handsome because he is a good knight, and he is a good knight because he is handsome. This sense that Amadis' appearance is a component, an aspect in an almost physiological sense, of Amadis' military skill is captured in Queen Briolanja's response when she sees Amadis, coming from the battlefield, stained with rust from his armor. At this moment, Briolanja finds that Amadis is "the most handsome knight she had ever seen; and certainly such he was at that time, for he was not over twenty years of age and had his face stained with rust; but considering how becoming to him those blemishes were, and how with them he was rendering fame and honor so clean and bright, they enhanced greatly his bearing and good looks" (1: 376).[75] Just as rust from battle marks his face, Amadis' skill at arms expresses itself as a feature of his countenance.

In this narrative structure, physical fairness becomes not just an expression of traits or qualities but a version of identity itself, one that is ultimately grounded in a genealogical understanding of race as a form of connection among like peoples. To the extent that physical appearance is a mark or feature of identity, it also becomes a trope of recognition. Amadis' handsomeness becomes a chief means by which he is recognized by and reunited with his parents and brothers. Indeed, neither his father nor his mother recognizes their lost son; what they recognize is his handsomeness. Amadis encounters his father first and is knighted by him. Montalvo plays on the traditional sense that this ceremony involves a conferring of identity by stressing the fact that King Perion does not know the identity of the handsome youth that he knights. In the absence of name, Amadis' identity is limited to his countenance: Amadis' identity is his person, his face, the virtue of his physical being. King Perion thus begins the knighting ceremony with an exhortation about the meaning of this unknown knight's handsomeness: "In the name of God, and may he ordain that it be in you as well employed and as augmented in honor as he augmented your good looks" (1: 62).[76] When Amadis first arrives at King Perion's court, his mother's response mirrors his father's. In a recognition scene that would be familiar to readers of Heliodorus' *Aethiopika*, Queen Elisena "noticed how handsome he was; and recalling her sons whom she had lost, the tears came to her eyes. Thus she wept for him who stood before her and she did not recognize him" (1: 93).[77]

Physical appearance in *Amadis* is identity in the sense that it reveals individual qualities (virtue, bravery, fidelity), but it is also identity in the sense that it is a mark of family relationship. Thus, if characters can recognize Amadis in his handsomeness, readers are able to identify his brothers, Don Galaor and Don Florestan, through a handsomeness that demonstrates a kinship that is both moral and biological. In a repetition of his own knighting ceremony, Amadis knights his brother, without knowing who he is but seeing in him one "handsomer than any man he had ever seen" (1: 117).[78] When Don Galaor and Amadis are next to one another, they resemble each other so closely that they can almost not be told apart, "except that Don Galaor was a little more fair" (1: 296).[79] The same is also true of Don Florestan, their third and also lost brother: "they did not know Florestan, but he seemed to them very handsome, and before they reached him they were taking him for Amadis" (2: 501).[80]

Later sixteenth-century publishers of *Amadis* seem to have recognized both the congruence of these moments and the ways in which the question of appearance contributed an essential component to the reading of this romance. The Paris printer, Denis Janot, introduced a large number of woodblock prints in the Herberay editions of the *Amadis* cycle. As Mariann Rothstein makes clear, Janot reused the woodblock that had introduced readers to Amadis when he illustrated the scene of Amadis knighting his brother.[81] Janot's repetitions of woodblocks are not simply a cost-saving measure. Rather, this feature of the text involves a recognition that the narrative insists that this is the same beauty, the same physical appearance that defines the moral form of each of these characters. It is through their shared physical appearance that readers should know and recognize them. As these examples suggest, *Amadis* assumes that these two kinds of identity – character and family – are interchangeable with one another. This assumption will not be surprising, either as a cultural belief in the meaning and value of kinship or as a feature of romance. It is nonetheless this definition, which is at heart a definition of race in a genealogical sense, that will be most strongly challenged in Book 5 with Esplandián.

Like his father, Esplandián is very handsome. When the hermit rescues the unknown baby he "beheld him so handsome he was amazed" (2: 122).[82] When Esplandián appears at the court of King Lisuarte as a child, everyone again is "greatly amazed at how handsome the youth was" (2: 147).[83] In Esplandián's case, though, physical beauty is not a sign of who he is but of who God is. Esplandián's handsomeness manifests God's work: those who see him recognize the power of the Christian God and are transformed by that knowledge. The first indication that Montalvo has redefined the meaning of physical appearance comes at the beginning of Book 5. With this book, Montalvo shifts the narrative from Amadis to Esplandián and from Christian Europe to the lands of the Ottoman empire, "this land [where] all those who live here are his enemies" (83).[84] Sent off by the sorceress Urganda the Unknown in the magical Caravel of the Serpent, Esplandián arrives at the Forbidden Mountain, an unconquerable land on the boundary between the suzerain of Persia and the dominions of the Emperor of Constantinople. There, he meets the Christian hermit, Nasciano, who is overwhelmed by Esplandián's handsomeness: "I am quite amazed by you, and I would be even more amazed, if I believed you mortal, which I doubt, seeing how handsome you are" (83).[85]

While Nasciano takes Esplandián's appearance as confirmation of a religious truth that he already accepts, his appearance has a more powerful effect on those who are not yet Christians. The two major conversions of Book 5 are both achieved largely through the power of Esplandián's physical appearance rather than, as is the case in the conversions that are typical of medieval romance, as a consequence of God's might making itself known through combat on the battlefield. The first of these conversions is that of the valiant Frandalo, who is the nephew or possibly great-nephew of the powerful enchanter Arcaláus. Defeated by one of Esplandián's fellow novice knights from the Firm Island, Maneli the Prudent, Frandalo is captured and taken as a prisoner to Constantinople (168–80). Because of his lineage, physical stature, and past deeds, Frandalo is regarded by the people as an "evil, strong knight" (177) and identified by the Emperor as an "evil man … [who] has stolen enough of my realm alone to make and unmake two kings" (186).[86] Frandalo comes over to the side of the Christians after the Emperor, instead of having him imprisoned or put to death, offers to redeem him if he agrees to abandon "the evil and perverse sect" he has followed (192).[87] It is when Frandalo meets Esplandián on the eve of their first battle against Frandalo's former countrymen and kinsmen that he accepts baptism.

Frandalo's turn to Christianity is motivated by what he sees in Esplandián. When Esplandián exhorts him to convert

> Frandalo, *who was watching him and observing how handsome he was and how circumspect he was in his speech*, already knew the marvelous and very extraordinary feats of arms he had done, and he was truly convinced that such a person could not have been born of mortals, nor could he remain as he was without being protected by the law of truth. And even if he had never landed in such a strait where he had no choice but to promise the emperor what Esplandián was now requesting, *he now knew that merely seeing and hearing the knight were enough* to convert not only him but all pagans. (219, my emphasis)[88]

Montalvo underlines the importance of physical appearance as mark of religious truth by having Frandalo closely echo and repeat the words of the hermit Nasciano ("I would be even more amazed, if I believed you mortal, which I doubt, seeing how handsome you are" [83]; "he was truly convinced that such a person could not have been born of mortals," 219).

From a narrative perspective, the result of Frandalo's encounter with Esplandián is not unexpected: Frandalo converts, as do all his men, and many of his friends and relatives throughout the land (219). Esplandián's military successes and the movement of the narrative line are largely achieved through the figure of Frandalo, who contributes his considerable sea forces and uses his knowledge of his native country and its leaders on behalf of the Christians. Frandalo becomes Esplandián's chief comrade and the implied voice of the narrative.[89] Here, though, I would stress how Frandalo's conversion implies a reinterpretation in the meaning of physical appearance. Frandalo's appearance initially reveals his identity as a mixed-blood descendant of giants and pagan knights in much the same way that Amadis' appearance reveals his own lineage in Books 1–4. In that respect, Montalvo's depiction of Frandalo emerges out of the same genealogical model that characterized the older order of Amadisian chivalry. Esplandián's appearance, by contrast, reveals the truth of God. As this difference suggests, conversion narratives necessarily threaten kinship structures in the sense that they promise complete transformation: through conversion, you leave and change everything. Converts are thus no longer an expression of their family, kin, or past. This opposition plays out the two sides in contemporary debates about the efficacy of conversion: what Montalvo gives us in Frandalo is a fictional version of the argument that religious truth creates an identity that in conversion is more powerful than and thus supplants that of genealogical and racial identity.

The same emphasis on Esplandián's physical beauty also informs the second important conversion in *Esplandián*, that of Queen Calafia. The action of the fifth book leads somewhat inevitably and mythically to a great siege and battle for Constantinople. Enraged by Esplandián's victories over him and by what he takes to be the Emperor's violation of a peace treaty, King Armato appeals to "all soldans, caliphs, Tamerlanes, kings, and all other grandees of any sort who follow the pagan law in all regions on both the right hand and the left hand of the Orient" to join forces with him against the Christians and Esplandián (407).[90] Converging at the port of Ténedon, Armato's allies amass a huge force that reflects not just the racial, geographic, and political diversity of these pagan lands, but, in a fantasy that departed sharply from historic reality, their inherent dividedness. Answering the king's call, all the emperors and kings, "white as well as black" (410), gathered together a mass of peoples greater than any since the time of the giant Nimrod; coming together around Constantinople, "a horde of barbarian kings from white and black nations" joined in the battle (315).[91]

The most significant of the black nations who join the battle on the side of the infidels is that of Queen Calafia. Calafia is queen of a race of "black women" who are from the island of California, "which was very close to the region of the Earthly Paradise" (456–57), and who live with "no males among them at all, for their life style was similar to that of the Amazons" (457).[92] Queen Calafia brings her fierce gold-armored women warriors and their man-eating griffons to the battle, but she does not wage war against the Christians for religious or political reasons. Rather, in an inversion of the narrative assumption that she and her people constitute an ethnographical marvel for the reader, Calafia joins the pagan forces because she longs to "see the world and its various generations [races/nations]" (459).[93]

Calafia enters into this conflict with an aspiration to see the races and peoples of the world (459), but, importantly, what she ends up seeing is Esplandián, who represents not the races and generations of man, but rather the truth of God's creation. Like Frandalo, Calafia also converts and her conversion is, again, effected through the power of Esplandián's physical appearance. Calafia's interest in Esplandián is incited by a beautiful black damsel who serves as a messenger between the infidels and the Christians. Radíaro, the Sultan of Liquía, and Queen Calafia decide to challenge Amadis and Esplandián to an honor battle in advance of the main military engagement between the two armies. When the damsel returns with their answer, she also returns with a description of Esplandián for Calafia:

> They are all good-looking and well armed. But I tell you, oh queen, that the Serpentine Knight is among them. I believe a more stunningly handsome knight has never lived. One like him never existed in the past, does not exist in the present, and will never exist in the future. *No one has ever seen anyone like him, and they never will.* Oh queen! What can I tell you but that, if he belonged to our religion, we would certainly believe our gods had made him, and that they had used all of their creative power and knowledge to produce such a masterpiece from which they left nothing out. (477, my emphasis)[94]

Earlier in the narrative, the remarkable appearance of the black damsel had been described in terms that made this unnamed messenger between the two camps a figure of the new ethnographic difference that has been introduced into the world of *Esplandián* ("her face and hands were black, but her features were very pretty, and she seemed very beautiful," 439). In this passage, though, she now becomes the voice through which the narrative wonders at the appearance of Esplandián. In doing so, Montalvo transposes a narrative desire for identity founded on genealogy and ethnography into a commitment for identity based in faith.

After hearing the damsel's report, Calafia insists on seeing Esplandián in person before their challenge: she, too, is moved and emotionally defeated by his handsomeness. Having seen Esplandián and the religious truth he embodies (479), Calafia falls in love. When she is thwarted of her love by Esplandián's bond to Leonorina, she then converts. She and her sister marry Christians, who are Esplandián's kinsmen, and ultimately her whole island is imagined to be converted by the authority of patriarchal marriage and in turn becomes a site for Christian conquest of neighboring lands (502).

In aesthetic terms, the two women express the sense that Esplandián is incomparable and exceeds representation. In a theological sense, Montalvo supposes that seeing Esplandián is both an incitement to faith and an image of that faith. Montalvo's use of apocalyptic language modeled on the Gospel of John (encompassing past, present, future) makes it clear that, for those who see him, Esplandián is a version of the Word. As Esplandián in his person reveals the truth, so, tacitly, does *Esplandián* as a text: as the most forcefully religious of all the volumes in the *Amadis* cycle, this book ultimately seems to take Frandalo's words as its narrative premise: "he now knew that merely seeing and hearing the knight were enough to convert not only him but all pagans" (219). That is, Montalvo's emphasis on the religious truth that inheres physically in Esplandián makes it possible for him to suggest that the aesthetic pleasure of seeing and hearing his text *Esplandián* is for Montalvo's own readers a way of seeing and hearing a beauty and truth that must likewise come from God. This is a message that later readers clearly recognize and, for the most part, reject.

The emphasis on how Esplandián converts those who see him involves a change not just in the individual identities of those who convert but, more fundamentally, in the concept of identity itself. In *Tirant*, we saw how domestic antagonism and suspicion about the efficacy of conversion that emerged historically through the question of *conversos* and *moriscos* was displaced onto the foreign, missionary conversions in North Africa. In a similar manner, the older definition of race as a blood-based form of kinship, asserted so strongly in Books 1–4 of *Amadis*, is in Book 5 displaced onto the pagans and, in particular, onto Frandalo and Queen Calafia. Typologically, Frandalo, the mixed-blood Muslim giant, and Calafia, the black queen of the near Amazons, represent recurring fantasies of alterity against which early modern Europe tended to define itself. Montalvo, however, notably aligns these figures not so much with the emergent models of otherness as with the old forms of genealogy and tradition represented by Amadis himself. Whereas Esplandián seems to stand for the power of God as a maker and for the universal Christian identity that can be created anew by God and through baptism, Frandalo and Queen Calafia stand in for a model of aristocratic, blood-based identity that had previously, in Books 1–4, been associated with Amadis and the Christian knights.

Importantly, blood-based identity is displaced onto the converting infidels because that earlier model of chivalric identity is a key part of what is being transformed in these conversions. Throughout *Esplandián*, genealogical bloodlines are again stressed, but this time for the converting infidels and pagans rather than for the Christians. Both Frandalo and Calafia are characterized by the ideals and qualities that, in romance and the society implied by it, are marks of blood. Frandalo is universally regarded as a brave and fierce knight, and Calafia fights for glory and honor (459). Montalvo introduces them using terms usually reserved for the Christian aristocracy: she is the "very zealous Calafia" (460) and he, "the valiant Frandalo" (169).

Frandalo and Calafia's personal qualities are confirmed by their bloodlines. In the case of Frandalo, "on his mother's side, he came from the race of strong giants that are found throughout the seigniory of Persia. And, on his father's side, he was descended from brave and daring pagan knights" (171).[95] Montalvo returns to emphasize their bloodlines in the moments leading up to their conversions as a way of suggesting that religious conversion replaces racial and familial identity. Montalvo prefaces Frandalo's conversion by noting that he was "a pagan by birth as were those from whom he was descended" (213–14).[96] Calafia likewise emphasizes the quality and purity of her lineage, having a "royal bloodline so old that there is no record of its beginning" (502).[97] Conversion changes, transforms, blood identity. In much the same way that in *Tirant* old forms of kinship disappear and are replaced by spiritual brotherhood, here Esplandián initially does not speak to the pagan Calafia, but once she declares her intention to convert, he embraces her as a spiritual kin ("It is as if my father the king had begotten both of us," 503) and indeed offers to create new familial connections with her by marrying her to his cousin ("a knight whose virtue and lineage far exceed what you required," 503).[98] Conversion has transformed Frandalo and Calafia, but, perhaps as importantly, it has also transformed the model of identity that had defined the initial books of the *Amadis* cycle. This change is motivated by religious commitments and political needs of the post-Fall of Constantinople age, but this change necessarily also has generic consequences and ones that notably extend to the readers of this narrative.

Frandalo and Calafia are more than just exotic and foreign, not-yet-Christian versions of the knights of Firm Island. Importantly, Books 1–4 of *Amadis* draw on the concept of race only in its meaning as a term for understanding genealogical connections among like kinds of peoples. Book 5, by contrast, demonstrates its responsiveness to political and theological questions that were becoming urgent under the reign of Ferdinand and Isabella (the Inquisition and the military efforts against Granada, as well as the racial and religious dimensions of the Reconquest) and does so by introducing new, sometimes competing, definitions of race as a mark of visible difference. *Esplandián* critiques, through the figures of the converts Frandalo and Calafia, traditional models of racial identity. At the same time, though, race as an instance of physical difference is also a key component in how Montalvo represents the pagan warriors. This is true in a general way. The battle between the Christians and the pagans in some respects follows the traditional epic confrontation with otherness: like Boiardo and Ariosto and following Virgil, Montalvo contrasts the unity and homogeneity of the Christian knights ("all or most of you were born or raised in Great Britain … [and] despite great differences among various lands, the law was one and the same," 291)[99] with the diversity and multiplicity within and among the pagan forces ("a horde of barbarian kings from white and black nations," 315).

This diversity is especially true of Frandalo and Calafia, whose racial identities are physically visible to others. Frandalo is descended "from the race of strong giants," and it is this lineage that explains his great size and "husky" frame (171). Calafia is both black and beautiful and is closely associated with the damsel who serves as the go-between for Calafia (439). Throughout the romance, Frandalo and Calafia are consistently identified in racial terms because what conversion is imagined to overcome, within the historical context out of which this romance was written, is not so much religious difference as ethnic difference. Montalvo's concept of race encompasses both meanings of the term "generations": romance's traditional model of genealogical identity as well as his culture's emerging, religiously inflected, understanding of race as a form of visible racial difference. As we shall see in Chapter 3, it is the second of these definitions that engages the contemporary political situation most strongly, and it is thus this definition to which later readers in turn respond.

CHAPTER 2

The form and matter of race: Heliodorus' Aethiopika, hylomorphism, *and neo-Aristotelian readers*

What began in the 1490s as Montalvo's attempt to create a form of romance that would counter the new definitions of race that emerged out of the Inquisition and church policies on conversion ended in Paris in the 1540s with Nicolas de Herberay's reconception of these racial and religious arguments in his widely read French translations of the cycle. The next important romance that Renaissance readers turned to for questions about the nature of race and identity was Heliodorus' *Aethiopika*.[1] The *Aethiopika* was written c. AD 250; it appeared in both Greek and Latin editions (*editio princeps*, 1534), but most Renaissance readers first encountered the *Aethiopika* through Jacques Amyot's *L'Histoire Aethiopique de Heliodorus* (Paris, 1547).[2] Amyot's presentation of Heliodorus was enormously influential in the development of sixteenth-century romance and, perhaps more importantly, in the development of sixteenth-century genre theory. Amyot introduced his translation of Heliodorus as a morally and intellectually acceptable alternative to the *Amadis* romances that, as we shall see, were intensely popular at the French court through the middle of the sixteenth century.

The *Aethiopika* was, for Amyot, exemplary largely because in both its form and its subject this romance promoted a new kind of reading and, with that, a different kind of reader. Amyot's aesthetic assessment of Heliodorus emerged out of the way in which Renaissance understandings of Aristotelian poetic theory were inflected through the then more familiar terms of Aristotelian physics. Aristotelian physics concerns itself, as we shall see, with the relationship between matter and form in the creation of works of both art and nature. Heliodorus' romance self-consciously confounds distinctions that Aristotle had made between artificial and natural creations and does so in a way that challenges both category and identity (art/nature, romance/epic, white/black, Greek/Ethiopian).

Through Jacques Amyot's preface, the *Aethiopika* became an integral part of early modern critical debate over whether it was possible for romance to achieve the aesthetic and civic virtues of epic. What has not been recognized in this important moment of early modern critical controversy, though, is that when Renaissance readers accepted Amyot's identification of the *Aethiopika* as a mixed text that expressed romance material through an epic form they were not simply engaging in aesthetic categorization. Rather, these critical assessments also responded to questions of racial identity that were at the heart of Heliodorus' story as a whole. My larger interest in this chapter is to provide a way to think about how sixteenth-century debates about generic identity in romance, the categories of literary kind, influenced other cultural conversations about racial identity, the emergent categories of human kind.

Sixteenth-century literary theory was unusually vexed and contentious: it pulled in an enormous and even surprising amount of cultural energy.[3] This controversy was distinctive in the way that it centered on defining and defending the identity of literary genres. It was in the largest sense a debate about categories. As contemporary ethnographic texts make clear, the sixteenth century also saw new attention to creating and asserting definitions about types and categories of people. These debates about category – one seemingly literary and philosophical, the other more obviously ideological, human, and political – do not remain distinct from one another. Amyot's version of Heliodorus provides a powerful example of how early modern understandings of genre and literary category, what Rosalie L. Colie rightly referred to in an etymologically attentive way as "kind," were not separable from human narratives about genealogical descent and racial identity.[4]

The particularities of the intersection between Heliodorus and sixteenth-century debate over genre arise out of the distinctiveness of Aristotle's poetic theory. Before the sixteenth century, the *Poetics* was not central to poetic and rhetorical theory or to the Aristotelian philosophy of medieval scholasticism. In 1536, the revived Aldine press published Alessandro de'Pazzi's edition of the *Poetics*. Appearing in the trademark Aldine octavo format with both the Greek text and a Latin translation, this edition was almost immediately republished, in four subsequent versions (Basel, 1537 [2], Paris, 1538, 1542). This Aldine press edition was not the first or most philologically significant Renaissance edition of the *Poetics*, but it was important because its portable format and readable translation made it a vehicle for the dissemination of Aristotle's arguments about genre in the sixteenth century.[5] Ariosto's *Orlando Furioso* was published in 1516, but it was at the height of its popularity in the 1530s, at the moment when a whole new generation of readers and writers were being introduced to Aristotle's *Poetics*. The availability of Aristotle's *Poetics* helped stimulate a series of intense debates about literary form and genre. In some cases, this increased access to Aristotle's *Poetics* produced new critical responses. In other cases, writers who were engaged in the practical work of trying to find forms for the kinds of poems that they were already writing turned to Aristotle for arguments to explain and justify those activities.[6]

The impact of the *Poetics* was important in the highly polemical treatises, first circulated in the 1550s and continuing to appear through the 1580s, that take up the relative merits of epic and romance, and, ultimately, of Ariosto and Tasso. This debate turned on arguments about whether romance constituted a genre in its own right or was instead merely an imperfectly achieved form of epic. Aristotle provided an important source for arguments in the 1550s that sought to defend Ariosto and promote Italian chivalric romance as a distinct genre. G. B. Giraldi Cinthio's *Discorso intorno al comporre dei romanzi* (pub. 1554, but composed sometime in the 1540s), for instance, argued that romance was a distinct genre, separate from epic. His arguments, along with similar kinds of distinctions made in Giovanni Battista Pigna's *I romanzi* of 1554, were challenged in Antonio Sebastiano Minturno's *Arte poetica* (1564), which insisted that romance was not a separate genre and indeed should probably not be considered poetry at all.[7]

What began as a defense of Ariosto became a championing of Tasso, again through arguments founded in Aristotle, when this polemic became re-energized in the 1580s after the publication of Tasso's Counter-Reformation epic, *Gerusalemme liberata* (1580). Camillo Pellegrino's *Il Carrafa, o vero della epica poesia* (1584), Giason Denores' *Poetica* (1588), and Tasso's *Discorsi dell'arte poetica* (1587) and his revised and expanded *Discorsi del poema eroico* (1594) argue in various ways that romance is not a distinct genre, but rather a defective and degraded form of epic.[8]

Perhaps the most intellectually compelling response to Aristotle's *Poetics*, though, was associated with neither Tasso nor Ariosto. In 1547, Jacques Amyot published his translation of the *Aethiopika*. Amyot was a humanist educator, clergyman, and court figure, who initially secured preferment at the French court under François I, but who ultimately came to have considerable power as the Grand Aumônier de France, Conseiller d'État, and Bishop of Auxerre during the reigns of his former pupils, Charles IX and Henri III. Amyot is now probably best known for his lucid and powerful translations of Plutarch (*Les vies des hommes illustres*

[1559] and *Œuvres morales* [1572]).[9] It was Amyot's early scholarship on the first six books of Plutarch's *Vies* that brought him royal patronage, but Amyot may have intended his work on Heliodorus to be his introduction to the royal court.[10]

Amyot began his translation with a powerful preface that attacked Amadisian romance in much the same terms that later writers would use to challenge *Orlando Furioso*, and he presented Heliodorus' *Aethiopika* as an alternative form of romance. A preliminary to his later introduction to Plutarch, this preface was addressed to François I and attacked what Amyot saw as the dangerous popularity of the Herberay translations of the books of *Amadis*.[11] This critique was indebted to Amyot's understanding of Aristotle and probably emerges out of what Martin Lowry has identified as the transmission of debates about poetic theory that flourished from the Italian academies of the 1530s to Paris in the early 1540s.[12] Amyot's invocation of Heliodorus as an alternative to *Amadis* is, however, more than just a precursor to the Tasso/Ariosto debate. This episode highlights the intellectual and philosophical assumptions that drove Aristotle's poetic categories, assumptions that began in physics and ended with genealogy.

For Aristotle, poetic theory meant genre theory. Aristotle was unusual in insisting that poems had inherent or internal forms. As Daniel Javitch points out, "most ancient critics (Horace, among them) measured the effectiveness and value of a poetic work in terms of external standards of truthfulness and of morality, and not by the degree to which it contributed to realizing what Aristotle took to be its particular form and function," but Aristotle instead understood poetry "in terms of the inherent or internal requirements of their forms." It is in this context that Daniel L. Selden thus characterizes Aristotle's poetic theory as "a remarkable effort to displace discussion to the realm of natural forms."[13] For Aristotle, questions of aesthetics are hard to separate from questions about physics. Aristotle is not primarily concerned with questions of mimesis (with what is represented) or with those of rhetoric (with what effect an author or rhetor might have on an audience). Instead, he is interested in the qualities that are distinctive to, and more properly inherent in, a particular work or kind of work of art.

Aristotle thus begins the *Poetics* by emphasizing that he is undertaking an explanation "not only of poetry in general but also of its species and their respective capacities" (1447a10–11). Aristotle insisted variously that tragedy must produce "pity and fear" as its own "proper pleasure" (1453b12–13, 11), "there are six parts consequently of every tragedy, that make it the sort of tragedy it is" (1450a8–10), tragedy requires both "reversal and discovery" (1452b10), but the epic is the genre that best encompasses the marvelous (1460a14). For many readers, Aristotle seemed to be offering a formula for literature: early modern readers thus often responded to the *Poetics* as an exercise in literary taxonomy, applying, accepting, or revising a seeming checklist that they were able to draw out of his text. Aristotle, however, emphasizes the features that were "proper" to a given genre and to the "species" of poetry (the qualities that make a work of art the kind of work that it is) because he understands poetry as a made object whose properties express the teleological causes that inform it.

Aristotle's conception of poetry as the realization of form is fundamentally consistent with and may be best understood as a somewhat paradoxical extension of his more general theories of physics. Renaissance readers recognized, in ways that modern critics have not, that Aristotle's doctrine of form applied to his account of poetry as well as to his model of physics. As Aristotle makes clear in the *Physics*, the forms that works of art can take are allied to the forms in and through which matter is realized. That is, the relationship between the essence of a poem and the form in which it is realized is basically a sort of physics that is determined by Aristotle's understanding of physical matter. For instance, Aristotle's arguments about poetic works having a beginning, middle, and end derive from the organic teleology that informs his model of physical change and identity. In an assessment of the importance of the doctrine of immanent form in Aristotle's thought as a whole, Norma E. Emerton notes that Aristotle's "conception of form was a rich and varied one, operating at different explanatory levels and bringing together many aspects of his thought."[14] Emerton is right to emphasize both the centrality of the doctrine of form to Aristotle's own philosophy and its dominance in the European philosophical tradition (she characterizes Aristotelian *hylomorphism* as "normative for European philosophy").[15] Colie's account of genre theory in the Renaissance provides the larger outlines within which this affiliation must be understood: genre was for Renaissance authors a "mode of thought" as well as form of poetry, and understanding genre theory meant understanding not just categorical difference but rather "how literary works *were thought to come into being*" (my emphasis).[16]

Aristotle emphasizes the importance of form in physics and of genre in poetry, and does so for similar reasons and out of a consistent philosophical perspective, but the two processes are not the same. It is worth thinking further here about the nature, extent, and limits of these affinities.

Aristotle's model of physics is structured around a central concept of *hylomorphism* (wood [matter]; shape). Developed most fully in the *Physics* and *Metaphysics*, this concept provided a way to understand the relationship between form and matter, and in particular, for articulating how matter was realized in and through form. Aristotle's version of *hylomorphism* was intended as the cornerstone of his commitment to dualism. This model of physics was a modification of Plato's theory of "Forms." (Plato's forms were transcendent; they gave shape to physical bodies, but themselves pre-existed and transcended such bodies; Aristotle's forms were instead immanent and could only be separated from primary matter hypothetically and speculatively, rather than actually.) On the other hand, *hylomorphism* was also Aristotle's corrective to natural philosophies, such as those of Empedocles and Democritus, which focused almost entirely on matter and seemed to ignore form and essence.[17]

In differentiating himself from both Plato and the pre-Socratics, Aristotle is interested in trying to understand in what sense primary matter (which is distinct from substance, though never in fact achieved without it, but which can only be defined as "that which becomes," *Physics* 190a33–34) does and does not change in that process of becoming substance. Matter is that which survives change, and, through form, matter both "comes to be and ceases to be in one sense, while in another it does not" (*Physics* 192a25–26). From the kind of perspective that Empedocles took, nature is all about matter: "nature is the underlying matter of things which have in themselves a principle of motion or change" (*Physics* 193a28–29).[18] Aristotle, by contrast, insisted that form was the defining feature of substance: "nature is the shape or form which is specified in the definition of the thing" (193a30–31).

Aristotle differentiates matter from form but does so by way of a secondary distinction that he makes between art and nature. On the one hand, art differs from nature because it does not have an "innate impulse to change" (*Physics* 192b17–18). A wooden statue may decay, but that is a change to the wood, as a thing of nature, rather than to the statue itself, as a thing of art. Works of art thus do not participate in the process of becoming, the transformation of matter into substance through form, in quite the same way that nature does. In keeping with this, artificial things will have causes that are external, whereas living things have causes that are internal. On the other hand, art provides what turns out to be the best examples of how matter becomes substance. Primary matter is hard to grasp: it cannot be apprehended in its own right and, while it underlies form, it is never truly distinct or separable from it. Teleology ("for the sake of what") is also more evident in art than it is in nature. Aristotle thus uses examples drawn from art as a way to illustrate his claims about nature, although it is also arguable that he understands nature in the way that he does because of how he experiences art. "If a house, e.g., had been a thing made by nature, it would have been made in the same way as it is now by art; and if things made by nature were made not only by nature but also by art, they would come to be in the same way as by nature" (*Physics* 199a12–15). Or, again, "If the ship-building art were in the wood, it would produce the same results by nature" (*Physics* 199b28–30). Aristotle's genre theory emerges out of his physics, but his physics in certain respects also depends on his understanding of art.

In the sixteenth century, most readers were more familiar with Aristotle's *Physics* and *Metaphysics* than with his *Poetics*. Charles Schmitt reports, for instance, on statutes governing the university curriculums during the sixteenth century: natural philosophy "in all of the universities" was limited to Aristotle's texts on physics, and in the field of metaphysics Aristotle "seems to have been universally used."[19] Such readers brought this philosophical context to their understanding of the newly available *Poetics* and to the fictions that they read through the *Poetics*. The way in which Aristotelian physics and the teleology it implied created a general structure of thought and a philosophical basis for understanding poetry can be seen in the many sixteenth-century poetic treatises that are largely Horatian in their details and rhetorical in their strategies, but nonetheless use Aristotle's "four causes" to introduce and structure their arguments.[20] Other writers integrate arguments and examples from works like the *Generation of Animals*, the *History of Animals*, the *Topics*, and the *Physics* into their literary critical treatises: Francesco Filipe Pedemonte, for instance, moves from natural history to poetry, citing Aristotle on the beautiful animal to gloss his definition of the proper magnitude of a poem.[21]

Torquato Tasso explicitly recognizes and elaborates on the affiliations between Aristotelian poetics and physics. Tasso begins with a traditional rhetorical structure, suggesting that writing poetry involves choosing the right subject, putting it into a proper form, and then adorning it with ornaments that are appropriate to its nature (inventio, dispositio, elecutio).[22] In elaborating his version of a rhetorical structure that was usually associated with Horace, Tasso notably follows Aristotle and, most particularly, the *Physics*. His attention to the differentiation of works into kinds is not simply classificatory, but emerges out of and cannot be separated from his understanding of how and out of what aesthetic works are created. Tasso thus compares the "raw material" with which the poet works, and which the poet must know and understand, to the iron and wood used by the craftsman: "Just as the shipwright is obliged not only to know what the form of ships should be, but also to recognize what sort of wood is most suited to itself to take on this form, it likewise behooves the poet not only to possess the skill to give form to his subject but also the judgment to recognize it" (Tasso, 1587, 99). Tasso's example is not taken from Aristotle's *Poetics*, but rather is an inversion and application to poetic practice of the "craftsman" examples that Aristotle had used in the *Physics* to explain the different material and efficient causes of the transformation of matter (e.g., *Physics* 194b5–8).

Where Aristotle had used art to explain the transformation of nature (saying, for instance, that "the underlying nature [of primary matter] can be known by analogy," 191a9), Renaissance readers of Aristotle's *Poetics* use nature to explain art. What Tasso says quite explicitly, other readers may have registered more indirectly: "In the beginning of this discourse, we compared what we have come to call the raw material [that which becomes poetry] with what natural philosophers call primary matter" (Tasso, 1587, 110).[23] As Maggie Günsberg notes, "*materia* denotes not only the subject-matter to be used by the poet or orator, but also matter in general." As such, I would suggest that early modern arguments about poetic matter and form necessarily also involve making "philosophical categorizations."[24] Like Tasso, Amyot understands poetic matter and form within the context of his understanding of natural philosophy. Indeed, it is precisely his sense that such distinctions involve "philosophical categorizations" that will explain what would otherwise seem to be his slightly odd insistence that the *Aethiopika* is a good romance because it contains within it examples of natural philosophy ("il y a en quelques lieux de beaux discours tirez de la Philosophie Naturelle," *iiii[r–v]).

Aristotelian dualism provided a theory of matter that was in the largest sense also an account of creation and identity, at once natural, artificial, and human. It may be possible to get a better sense of the impact that this larger framework had on how Aristotle's *Poetics* were understood in the Renaissance if we imagine that the *Poetics* had not become widely available until the middle of the seventeenth century. Monism, the revival of Lucretian atomism, Cartesian dualism, mechanism, and Paracelsianism: the philosophical movements that dominated seventeenth-century intellectual culture all involve assumptions about matter that differ radically from Aristotle's comfortable dualism, and those assumptions in turn changed how many seventeenth-century poets understood the acts of poetic creation in which they were involved.

In the case of *Paradise Lost*, Milton's depiction of Chaos, the Battle in Heaven, the Fall, and the very concept of free will thus all emerge out of his commitment to a monistic understanding of matter. "Contemporary debate over substance," as Steven Fallon makes clear, informs how Milton understands the creation of the physical world;[25] equally importantly, those debates also inform how Milton understands the creation of poetry and, as "Areopagitica" makes clear, how he understands the practice of reading.[26] This debate does not yet exist in the sixteenth century. Milton undertook his own project of redefining epic and romance, but he does so under quite different theoretical terms than did Tasso and other late sixteenth-century writers. Almost certainly, the *Poetics* would have had a much less influential role in the development of Renaissance poetic theory and practice had its arguments not been supported and reinforced by the larger intellectual and cultural commitments of sixteenth-century neo-Aristotelian dualism.

The philosophical context of *hylomorphism* provides an important but overlooked frame for early modern responses to Heliodorus' *Aethiopika*. The *Aethiopika* is a story about the adventures and identity of Charikleia, the daughter of the king and queen of Ethiopia, who was born with fair skin because her mother looked at a painting of Andromeda at the moment of her conception. In both his preface and his translation, Amyot presents Heliodorus' work as a model for a modern kind of epic. Read through the perspective of the *Poetics*, the *Aethiopika* does conform to some key features of Aristotelian genre theory. Read through the perspective of the *Physics* and the *Metaphysics*, as early modern readers such as Amyot were inclined to do, though, the *Aethiopika* utterly vexes Aristotelian assumptions about the relationships between both matter and form, on the one hand, and between nature and art, on the other.

Heliodorus gives us a story in which nature (the girl, Charikleia) is created from art (the painting, Andromeda). In her very person, Charikleia violates Aristotle's two fundamental distinctions between art and nature. For Aristotle, art is a lesser form of creation; it is created out of nature, but it never creates nature. As a corollary, living beings have their causes within them, whereas artificial things have their causes without (192b12–23, 199b16–19).[27] In imagining that Charikleia's physical appearance (her substantial form) is produced, even in part, by the image of Andromeda (as either material or efficient cause, however poetically rendered), Heliodorus' narrative premise reverses both the art/nature distinction and the matter/form process. The medieval Christianization of Aristotle meant that "substantial form" was generally glossed by medieval and early modern scholastics as "soul," rather than as physical appearance or shape, but Aristotle himself notably uses skin color [the whitening of a man] as a key instance, almost a trope, for distinguishing matter from form with respect to that which does not survive change. In ways that resonate for both Heliodorus and early modern readers, Aristotle's examples invoke skin color as a paradigm instance of an accidental quality rather than as its essence or definition [e.g., *Physics* 185b29–30].[28]

Heliodorus' interest in the fabulous birth of Charikleia is more than just a slightly gimmicky plot device or a fictional rendering of philosophical theories about the maternal imagination. As we shall see, Heliodorus makes her birth integral to the story by tying it to the narrative's insistence that Charikleia's identity be recognized both by other characters within the story and by his readers in ways that emerge out of the same kinds of acts of aesthetic response that initially created her distinctive appearance and identity.

Amyot's preface, which is about ten pages long and is included, with some important variations, in subsequent editions and translations of the book, takes up the implications of Heliodorus' sly poetic challenge to Aristotelian physics. Amyot most directly aligns himself with contemporary interest in Aristotelian genre theory in the way that he positions *L'Histoire Aethiopique* as different in kind from other romances. Amyot does not mention *Amadis* directly, but he has both Aristotle and Amadisian romance in mind when he describes how a good fiction can include marvels ("choses estranges, & pleines de merveilles," iiiᵛ), but must integrate them into a larger narrative that has the appearance and probability of truth.[29] Most romances fail to meet this criterion: Amyot particularly condemns "la plus grande partie des livres de ceste sort, qui sont anciennement esté escritz en nostre langue" (*iiiᵛ). For Amyot, traditional romances are untrue ("escritz mensongers," *iiʳ) and his preface undertakes a sustained attack on romance through the articulation of a quasi-Aristotelian set of criteria (beginning *in medias res*, mingling fact and fiction into a single whole, arriving at an end that is ordered by and expressed from the beginning, providing a structure and content that both produce knowledge for the reader).

Contemporary readers responded strongly to this attack. Assessing the impact of the twenty-six contemporary editions of Amyot's Heliodorus, Marc Fumaroli characterizes Amyot's preface to Heliodorus as "a determining event" in the history of the European novel.· After 1547, translations and adaptations of traditional romances – which had before the Amyot preface seemed curiously immune to the attacks of Juan Luis Vives and other humanists – began to include their own prefaces to counter Amyot's polemic. By 1660, this increased scrutiny was accompanied by a decline in the publication and translation of new romances.[31] If Amyot's preface marked the end to the dominance of the Amadisian romance, it also incited experimentation with new kinds of epic forms.

Writers accepted Amyot's assertions about the essentially epic qualities of Heliodorus' work. Yet, they do so less as a movement away from traditional Amadisian romance, than as part of a larger critical movement to redefine and adapt classical epic within early modern literary culture. Julius Caesar Scaliger, for instance, praised Heliodorus' work as one "that should be most carefully conned by the epic poet as furnishing the best model for heroic poetry."[32] Tasso, who models his Clorinda on Heliodorus' Charikleia, identifies the *Aethiopika* as a romance but only in the context of arguing that romance is not generically distinct from epic.[33] Abraham Fraunce's decision to compose "Heliodorus his Æthiopical History" (1591) in quantitative hexameter was part of an attempt to use familiar epic matter to establish new metrical forms for English poetry.[34] Pierre Vallet captures the generic multiplicity that readers found in Heliodorus in the composition of his 1613 edition: he integrates the narrative digest that was often used to condense long romances with an emblem book format that was more in keeping with the moral and civic lessons of epic.[35] Philip Sidney not only identifies Theagenes as the truest of lovers in *The Defence of Poesy*, but also uses Heliodorus' narrative as a model for transforming what began as a "heroic" poem into a new kind of epic when he revises the *Arcadia*.[36]

Renaissance writers accepted Amyot's assertions about the essentially epic qualities to Heliodorus' work, then, but they did so as part of a larger critical movement to redefine the notion of generic purity that had been particularly associated with epic. The examples of Scaliger, Tasso, Fraunce, and Sidney suggest how Heliodorus becomes associated with the new epic and with the forms of generic multiplicity that were thought to characterize it. If these claims seem to us surprising in some respects, we should not conclude that this assessment arises out of bad reading or bad theory on the part of Renaissance readers of Heliodorus. The critical controversy that surrounded the *Aethiopika* is not primarily a product of debate over the relative merits of Amadis and Achilles, or of the differing cultural values attached to epic over romance. Claims that the *Aethiopika* represents a "heroic romance" or "romantic epic" express, as I see it, a displaced critical response to the question of hybrid identity that is the central thematic concern of the work. Understanding the identity of the work within new critical paradigms became a way for Renaissance readers to respond to the apparent hybridity, the mixing of race, identity, and category, that is the key thematic and intellectual concern of the narrative as a whole. Grouping literary works into genres is not the same as classifying people into identity groups. What is being classified and the stakes of those classifications are very different things. I would suggest, though, that the intense cultural energies that, in seemingly quite different spheres, went into creating and defending new understandings of both literary and racial "kind" in the sixteenth century were not historic coincidences.

The impact of Aristotle's *Poetics* was strengthened by its affiliations with a theory of "form" that was primarily understood to apply to living things. Certainly, on the literary side, cross-over of the sort that I am describing between discussions about literary genre and racial identity is intensified by the degree to which the Aristotelian model was recognized to be an explanation of creation, category, and identity in living beings. Both Renaissance understandings of "kind" carry the sense of a category identity that includes an assertion of three key components: creation, descent, and meaning. To put it another way, Renaissance interest in Heliodorus was dominated by questions of genre, but, from at least the nineteenth century, readers of Heliodorus have focused primarily on questions of race. This apparent disparity does not just arise out of changing cultural and aesthetic contexts. Rather, genre and race are two sides to the coin of "kind": they are both at the heart of Heliodorus' narrative and, equally importantly, both part of how Amyot's preface framed this text for Renaissance readers, philosophers, and artists.

To fully understand the implications of sixteenth-century connections between literary kind and racial type, we need to see how Amyot's Aristotelianism goes beyond his influential claims about generic categories. In addition to focusing on romance as a genre, Amyot also makes reading central to his arguments about *L'Histoire Aethiopique*. The fundamentally hylomorphic inflections that governed Aristotle's thinking about poetics involved attention to poetry as a made object whose properties reflect the teleologies inherent in its making. This philosophical assumption tends to imply three theoretical consequences, all of which appear in Amyot's preface. First, as we have seen, this involves an attention to genre as an expression of the formal qualities that make a work the kind of work that it is. Second, it leads to an assumption that the subject matter is also a part of the formal definition of a work: the content of the work must be an expression of its identity and appropriate to its form. Speaking about the philosophical context, Emerton notes that, for Aristotle, "the matter in a body is always infused by a form, even though in the process of change one form may replace another, and *the form infuses and acts upon only that kind of matter which is suitable to it*, so that matter and form are always fitted to each other" (my emphasis).[37]

In keeping with this assumption, Amyot thus stresses the necessary integrity between the intellectual content of the *Aethiopika* and its formal structure. He attacks Amadisian romances because they lack intellectual content (in these, "il n'y a nulle erudition, nulle cognoissance de l'antiquité," *iii^v) and praises the *Aethiopika* because, among its other virtues, the text contains moral and natural philosophy ("il y a en quelques lieux de beaux discours tirez de la Philosophie Naturelle & Morale," *iiii$^{r–v}$). Throughout, the understanding that form must be appropriate to content underlies Amyot's comments about how the *Aethiopika* appropriately mixes fact and fiction, the marvelous and the verisimilar, within a narrative structure that Amyot characterizes as concerned with knowledge and judgment. Third, this emphasis also implies an interest in the poet as a craftsman, as the maker of the text, able to take the verbal primary matter (what Tasso describes as "that which has not yet received any touch of the orator's or the poet's artistry and is called the raw material," 99) and hammer it into the substantial form of the poem.

Going beyond these basic theoretical assumptions, though, Amyot also applies a tacitly Aristotelian framework to his treatment of reading by extending this final category (*materia/forma*) to the relationship between texts and readers. Early modern poetic theory tended to take up questions involving audience (usually this meant theatrical or oratorical audiences, but, after the advent of print culture, this could also be extended to readers) through the perspective of rhetoric. Horace provides what is perhaps the dominant model here: the *Art of Poetry* thus emphasized the "pliant mind" of the audience that may be "soothed with pleasure" or "provoked with rage"; effective poetry "smites the listening ear"; the would-be poet should instruct and delight by using short precepts with "impression strong" so that "minds may catch their quick." Amyot cites Horace and specifies that he is following his precepts ("suyent les precepts du Poete Horace," *iii^r).

When he turns his attention to reading, though, Amyot does not give us an account of a reader who is moved, persuaded, or controlled by the words of the poet. Horatian attention to the poet as a kind of rhetor disappears in Amyot. Rather than being moved by the author, Amyot's reader is instead transformed by the text, and Amyot presents the act of reading as essentially somatic. He transforms Horace's rhetorical version of poetry into an Aristotelian account of the transformation of matter into substance, a transformation in which the reader is the clay that is being shaped by the texts he reads. For Amyot, the *materia/forma* transformation applies not just to the words that are shaped into texts but extends also to the reader who is shaped by the text he reads.

This argument emerges in the context of Amyot's description of the *Aethiopika* as a text whose teleology expresses itself in and through its form. Beginning *in media res* in the manner of epic poetry (iiii^v), the *Aethiopika* is ordered so that the end is an expression of its beginning; the narrative is in some way square to itself. The form of the book in turn implies the form of the reader. In the same way that the fiction comes into being through the form, so, from this implied theoretical perspective, does the reader become actualized by the act of reading. This distinctive feature of the *Aethiopika* can be best seen through the counter-examples provided by Amadisian romance, which, for Amyot, work on the passions and bodies of their readers. Invoking Petrarch, Amyot suggests that traditional romances are like the nightmares that arise out of a fevered brain ("il semble que ce soient plus tost songes de quelque malade resuant en fievre chaude," *iiiii^r). Those who indiscriminately read the wrong kind of romances are like children whose nurses have told them too many fairy-tales; bad romances are like contaminated breast milk, and what readers imbibe (abreuver) may corrupt and degrade them, leaving a vicious imprint on them (vitieuse impression, *ii^r). Transforming only the body, these books in some sense confine themselves to a flat Empedoclean universe, stuck in a monistic world of physical materiality.

The *Aethiopika*, as Amyot reads it, is by contrast the product of an Aristotelian world in which matter only exists within the frame of form. The *Aethiopika* is distinctive because it works not just on the body, but on the mind of the reader and does so in large part because of its infusion of matter and form:

The ordering of the narrative is, however, distinctive because he begins in the middle of his story in the manner of the epic poets. On the one hand, this produces a great amazement in readers and incites in them a passionate desire to understand the beginning and, yet, leads them so successfully into the skillful sequence of his story so that the resolution to what you find right at the start of the first book does not come until you have read the end of the fifth ... In this manner, your understanding always remains suspended until you come to the conclusion, which leaves the reader satisfied in the same way as are those who at last achieve an ardently desired and long-awaited pleasure.[38]

The reader's lack of knowledge produces desire and that passion structures the act of reading, but the act is directed toward the rational end of knowing, and the end of the book produces knowledge and, with it, satisfaction.

This theory of reading that Amyot articulates is consistent with Aristotle's assumptions about matter and form in genre. Amyot upholds Aristotle, but he also responds to the ways in which Heliodorus involves his readers in the construction of Charikleia's identity. Heliodorus' story centers on the love of Theagenes, an Ainiane who claims descent from Achilles, and Charikleia, who initially seems to be the daughter of a Delphic priest but who turns out to be the daughter of the king and queen of Ethiopia. Theagenes and Charikleia fall in love at first sight, and the oracle at Delphi predicts that "To the black land of the Sun will they travel / Where they will reap the reward of those whose lives are passed in virtue: / A crown of white on brows of black."[39] The narrative is an unfolding of this prophecy: with the help of the Egyptian sage Kalasiris, Theagenes and Charikleia leave Delphi to claim Charikleia's birthright in Ethiopia.

The narrative opens in Egypt, at the midpoint of the adventures that take Theagenes and Charikleia from Delphi to Meroe. In the opening book, we are introduced to Theagenes and Charikleia through the perspective of Egyptian bandits who discover the lovers, alive but wounded, alongside a pirate ship full of plunder and a beach covered with dead bodies. Theagenes and Charikleia are captured by the Egyptian bandit Thyamis, who in turn is almost immediately attacked by rival bandits and the forces of the Persian army. In the conflict, Theagenes, Charikleia, and Knemon, an Athenian exile, all escape from their captors (Book 2). Through stories told by Kalasiris in Book 4, we learn how the lovers found themselves in this situation. We also learn that Charikleia was born with "skin of gleaming white" because her mother Persinna had been looking at a painting of Andromeda at the moment of the child's conception (433), and it was for this reason that her mother abandoned her at birth. In the meantime, Theagenes is recaptured and taken away to be given to the satrap of Persia, but in Book 5 Charikleia is reunited with Kalasiris at the home of an Egyptian merchant, Nausikles.

Attempts to rescue Theagenes lead the characters to Memphis. Theagenes and Charikleia are temporarily reunited, but they become involved with Arsake, the wife of the Persian overlord, Oroondates.

Theagenes is imprisoned by Arsake, and Charikleia is put on trial for the murder of one of Arsake's maidservants. The two lovers are then brought to Oroondates, who is engaged in a war with the Ethiopian king, Hydaspes (Book 8). In the fighting, Theagenes and Charikleia are captured by the Ethiopian forces, and in Book 9 they are taken to Ethiopia to be offered up as sacrifices to the sun gods. In the final book, Charikleia and Theagenes prove their chastity and valor in front of the people of Meroe, who are much moved by their appearance and pity their situation. After Charikleia claims her identity as the heir to the throne, in an extended Aristotelian recognition scene, and also reveals that she is married to Theagenes, the Ethiopians renounce the practice of human sacrifice, and the two lovers fulfill the final part of the prophecy by taking the miters of priesthood in the royal family of Ethiopia.

The central question of the story is who is Charikleia? Or, more properly, what is the nature and source of her identity? In a recent essay on generic categorization, Thomas Pavel identifies the *Aethiopika* as an example of idealist fiction. The *Aethiopika* and other idealist fictions, he notes, "emphasize the axiological abstraction of the characters, the eminent visibility of their moral beauty," which appears certain and fixed within an otherwise "wildly contingent world."[40] From this perspective, Charikleia is who she is, visibly and without change, from the start of the narrative and from the moment of her birth. (We can see this understanding of her identity in both the narrative's insistence on her virginity and her submission to the forces of fate.) Taking a different perspective, though, Sujata Iyengar persuasively argues that Heliodorus relies on (pre-modern) conceptions of race, which include both descent and social category. Because this is "a race that can only come into existence once it is recognized," Charikleia's identity is thus only "materialized through her actions." Put bluntly, "Charikleia's translation to Africa makes her black; falling in love makes her female and heterosexual."[41] (It is for this reason, then, that we know of the other recognition tokens earlier in the narrative but, in ways that might otherwise seem surprising, do not learn of Charikleia's birthmark, the black band that encircles her arm, until the last book.) Is Charikleia's identity fixed and constant? Or, is it materialized through her actions? Must it be recognized to exist? Pavel and Iyengar are relying on different models of identity, and, in important ways, both are right. In part, their differing assessments turn on a kind of critical perspectivalism: thinking about identity through the perspective of genre produces one kind of answer, while thinking about it through that of race produces another one.

I would suggest that Charikleia's identity and the degree to which one understands it as fixed and manifest, on the one hand, or fluid and latent, on the other, depends on how we understand her form. The *Aethiopika* is a deliberate and highly self-conscious fiction, which responds at an aesthetic and ideological level to Homer's model for epic and at a philosophical level to Aristotle's physics. In this context, Charikleia is an Aristotelian character. From this perspective, her identity – both her substantial form, shaped to the likeness of the painting of Andromeda (433), and her qualities – must be fixed precisely because they are expressions of the kind of teleological identity that makes Charikleia who she is. Heliodorus insists, through Persinna's letter, that the infant Charikleia was an "exact likeness" to the image of Andromeda (433). The likeness – which seems to go beyond skin color – is again invoked in the final book with the now much older Charikleia when Persinna enjoins her husband to "take a close look at Andromeda, and you will find that she is reproduced in this girl exactly as she appears in the painting ... the exactitude of the likeness struck them with delighted astonishment" (569).

In suggesting that Charikleia, both as an infant and as a grown woman, is and remains the "exact likeness" of the painting, Heliodorus seems to be toying with Aristotle's description of artificial creations as coming from an external source and thus having no principle of change within them. More substantially, Heliodorus suggests that Charikleia's unchanging nature includes both her character and her appearance because, as Aristotle puts it, "nature is the shape or form which is specified in the definition of the thing" (*Physics* 193a30–31). As we shall see, though, Charikleia's identity is also fluid to the extent that Heliodorus demands that his readers participate in an aesthetic act that tacitly re-enacts that shaping of her identity in their own recognition of her identity.

Throughout the text, Charikleia expresses a teleology through her form in ways that adhere to Aristotelian assumptions. The priest Charikles describes to Kalasiris how it was that he came to rescue the exposed child: "I chanced upon her and took her up, for once a soul had taken human form it would have been a sin for me to pass it by in its hour of peril – this is the sole precept of the naked sages of my country" (404). Charikles' comments in part foreshadow the narrative's condemnation of human sacrifice in the final book. It is worth noting, though, that Charikles feels obligated to save not the infant herself, as a living creature, but her soul, the idea that informs her being. Charikleia was abandoned by her mother precisely because an idea (the image of the painting) that may not have been hers gave shape to her child. As Persinna explains in a letter that she leaves with her abandoned child: "the painting had presented me with the image of Andromeda ... and [the painting, the image] had unfortunately shaped the embryo to her exact likeness" (433). It is for the same reason, though, that Charikles must save her. Charikleia must be rescued because she is a made thing, one which expresses an idea through the form of its body.

Heliodorus gives his readers a highly self-conscious, literary rendering of the realization of the philosophy of matter and form. Yet, the narrative as a whole playfully confounds the distinctions and analogies between natural and artificial that Aristotle used to explain his physics. In the *Aethiopika*, art creates character (and characters); it is the source of identity. Charikleia is associated with works of art that seem, in the phrase of the English translator Thomas Underdowne, to "break nature."[42] At the temple in Delphi, Charikleia wears a band of gold in the shape of two intertwined serpents around her breast. Kalasiris describes the craftsmanship in this masterpiece in which the goldsmith "had locked all his art" (412): "You would have said not that the serpents seemed to be moving but that they were actually in motion" (412). Charikleia herself is repeatedly seen by the other characters as a work of art. The bandits through whose eyes we are first introduced to Charikleia gaze in wonder at her: "was this girl the statue of a goddess, a living statue?" (357). Kalasiris likewise describes her effect on those who see her: "in physical beauty she is so superior to all other women that all eyes, Greek and foreign alike, turn toward her, and wherever she appears in the temples, colonnades, and squares, she is like a statue of ideal beauty that draws all eyes and hearts to itself" (406).

As these examples make clear, Charikleia is more than a kind of painting come to life. By depicting her as a statue, Heliodorus figures Charikleia as an instance of *ekphrasis*. She is, that is, a three-dimensional sculpture that re-presents the two-dimensional form of the painting. *Ekphrasis* was understood, philosophically, as an aesthetic practice that involved the transfer of "ideas" from one art form to another; it was an example, at a further remove than simple mimesis, of the relationship between matter and form. In suggesting that Charikleia is an ekphratic rendering of the Andromeda painting, Heliodorus is thus again associating Charikleia with questions about the nature of identity that are raised by Aristotelian *hylomorphism*.

It is not just Charikleia, though, that we see as a work of art. In his account of the arrival of the Ainianian delegation at Delphi, Kalasiris provides a detailed description of the first appearance of Theagenes:

In came the young man, who really did have something redolent of Achilles about him in his expression and dignity. He carried his head erect, and had a mane of hair swept back from his forehead; his nose proclaimed his courage by the defiant flaring of his nostrils; his eyes were not quite slate blue but more black tinged with blue, with a gaze that was awesome and yet not unattractive, rather like the sea when its swelling billows subside, and a smooth calm begins to spread across the surface. (408)

As B. P. Reardon notes, Philostratus in his *Heroikos* depicts Achilles in remarkably similar terms, and both works are themselves descriptions of what was probably a well-known contemporary statue or painting of Achilles (408 n. 75).[43] Theagenes would thus have been understood by astute readers as a copy of an "original" artwork. That is, Theagenes, at one diegetic level, is a copy of Achilles, just as Charikleia is of Andromeda at the next one. In both cases, though, Heliodorus' lovers are copies not of the human originals but of the mimetic representations of them. In this scene, Theagenes is asserting the purity of his race and the legitimacy of his descent from Achilles. As Kalasiris proclaims, "there are none of more noble ancestry than they. They are Hellenes in the truest sense of the word, for they trace their descent from Hellen, the son of Deukalion" (407). Heliodorus' *ekphrasis* has the effect of making Theagenes into an aesthetic, as well as biological, descendent of Achilles. With this gesture, Heliodorus thus creates a version of the aesthetic genealogy that Charikleia herself has within the fiction.

As the example of Theagenes suggests, *ekphrasis* is for Heliodorus about the relationship between art and identity. Heliodorus' depiction of Theagenes is part of a critical impulse, prominent among the Greek novels of the second and third centuries, to rewrite Homeric epic from the periphery of the empire. Seen in the context of the literary achievements and political movements of the third century, the *Aethiopika* is one of the imperial Greek novels whose experimentation with narrative form arises out of a questioning not just of established genres but also of the cultural narratives that they supported.[44] In the case of the *Aethiopika*, Tim Whitmarsh thus argues that filiation becomes Heliodorus' way of rewriting the *Odyssey* to comment on how Homeric epic insists on an explicitly imperial lineage and teleology.[45] As Whitmarsh points out, patrimony and descent (real and surrogate fathers, blood lines, race and clan) often trope for literary descent in the *Aethiopika*. Heliodorus experiments with generic identity as a way to comment on the nature of epic and its claims to create cultural identity. Heliodorus initially insists on the purity of Theagenes' Greek identity, but then the narrative overwrites that identity with Charikleia's Ethiopian one.[46] Insofar as that Greek identity is aesthetic and specifically generic, the narrative's movement from Delphi to Meroe necessarily also involves the overwriting of Greek epic and the cultural values it implied.

Heliodorus does not use *ekphrasis* at the one moment that his readers might most surely expect it. In keeping with this rewriting of Homeric descent narratives, Heliodorus adapts and reverses the story of Andromeda within his narrative to achieve a critique that is at once racial and aesthetic. The story of how Persinna gazed upon a picture of Andromeda as an explanation for her daughter's light coloring provides a narrative of the cultural assimilation of other races into the Greek empire. Heliodorus' suggestion that a picture of Andromeda might produce a fair-skinned child calls attention to the otherwise anomalous fact that although Andromeda was herself the daughter of Cepheus and Cassiopeia, the king and queen of Ethiopia, most Greek writers and artists nonetheless represented her as fair-skinned. Achilles Tatius, for instance, alludes to this artistic tradition when he incorporates into *Leucippe and Clitophon* a vivid and extended *ekphrasis* of a wall painting of Andromeda: "her cheeks are not quite perfectly pale, but brushed with a light red wash" while "the color of her arms shaded from a pure white to livid."[47] Andromeda is "brushed" and "shaded" white not so much because she is beautiful but rather because her beauty makes her a figure of art for Greek culture.

In responding to *Leucippe and Clitophon*, Heliodorus' larger point is that not only should Charikleia be dark skinned, but so should Andromeda, and for precisely the same reasons. As Heliodorus makes clear, the Andromeda painting decorates the royal bedchamber because Perseus and Andromeda, along with Eos' child Memnon, are the mythic "founders" of the Ethiopian royal family (432). The Andromeda story at the center of the *Aethiopikia* functions within Heliodorus' text as an image of an assimilation of the peripheries of the empire into Greek art and culture that anticipates the narrative transformations undergone by Charikleia and the authorial one enacted by Heliodorus.[48]

Yet, even as Heliodorus invokes *Leucippe and Clitophon* in his narrative of the birth of Charikleia, his version is not a citation or an *ekphrasis*. Achilles gives his readers an extended description of the painting of Andromeda and Prometheus. Heliodorus makes this moment in *Leucippe and Clitophon* the starting point for his own narrative. He does not, however, include any comparable detail in the two key moments when the painting is discussed in his text, and this omission is notable. In Book 4, Persinna's letter provides only one descriptive detail: Andromeda, she writes, "was depicted stark naked, for Perseus was in the very act of releasing her from the rocks" (433). The final scene does not include any description of the painting, beyond Persinna's comment that Andromeda "is reproduced in this girl exactly as she appears in the painting" (569). Heliodorus omits any real detail to his accounts of the one work of art whose frame is, as it were, set inside the frame of the narrative. Heliodorus' readers must, in ways that will become important in Renaissance responses to the *Aethiopika*, imagine for themselves what Achilles Tatius so fully describes for his readers. Heliodorus may imply that his readers have brought a visual picture of Achilles Tatius' Andromeda with them to his fiction, but this omission ultimately means that he refuses to engage in the kind of assimilatory poetics that is at stake in Achilles Tatius' white Andromeda.

The question of the relationship between art and identity becomes most prominent in Heliodorus' rewriting of the classic Aristotelian recognition scene. Once again, this rewriting puts demands on Heliodorus' readers that are at odds with the assumptions of Homeric epic. The *Aethiopika* is not so much a search for identity as it is a quest for recognition. Charikleia in some respects always has her identity, which never changes, and it is just a question of others realizing that identity. Among those who must recognize Charikleia are Heliodorus' readers.

In the final book of the romance, Heliodorus gives us the basic Aristotelian forms of recognition, along with one notable addition. The proving of Charikleia's identity in Book 10 is framed by the test of chastity on the sacrificial gridiron which provides "visible proof" that "the greatest ornament to her beauty was chastity" (564) and Sisimithres' assertion that "a person's character [is] important as the color of his face in reaching a judgment" (566). Within the context of this need to provide a visible proof of her own invisible identity, Charikleia produces the following evidence: a band of cloth into which Persinna wove the story of her birth, her mother's necklaces and her father's ring as further "tokens of recognition" (572), and her birthmark, a "ring of ebony staining the ivory of her arm" (569). None of these proofs, however, convinces Persinna of Charikleia's true identity. Rather, Persinna sees in Charikleia a version of the daughter she lost; thus, from the first time Persinna sees Charikleia, she sees her – and can only see her – from the perspective of a mother. Indeed, Persinna looks at Charikleia and is touched in the same way she was earlier when she first looked at the picture of Andromeda. Charikleia triggers this reaction by looking to Persinna for validation of her identity. Charikleia "stared so long and so hard" at Persinna that the queen is moved until she is "seized with a fit of palpitations [and] perspiration streamed from every pore" (562, 567).

Re-enacting in important ways the unusual circumstances of her birth, Charikleia ultimately relies on what she identifies as the "one incontrovertible token of recognition": that is, the "maternal instinct, which, by the workings of an unspoken affinity, disposes the parent to feel affection for the child the instant she sets eyes on it ... the one thing that would make all other tokens convincing" (555–56). King Hydaspes and the Egyptian spectators are convinced of the truth of Charikleia's story when they compare Charikleia to her "original," the painting of Andromeda which is "reproduced in this girl exactly as she appears in the painting" (569). Charikleia's mother, by contrast, realizes the truth about her daughter by an "affect" that she feels when she sees her, one that replicates the emotion that created her daughter in the first place.

In this final scene, the mother's recreation differs from the father's recognition. Charikleia's identity is created both at the beginning and the end through the eyes of her mother, through an act of maternal imagination and recognition. It is this maternal gaze that most fundamentally challenges both Greek epic and identity; it is this alternative that is at the heart of Amyot's theory of reading and that will trouble Renaissance responses to the *Aethiopika*.

These narrative features of the *Aethiopika* are intensified by the particular moment at which they are translated back into European literary history and culture. Many critics have agreed that skin color changes its meaning during the early modern period, becoming a determining marker of racial identity. Shifting away from traditional definitions of race that followed genealogical terms, early modern European culture increasingly accepted skin color as what Michael Neill has identified as "the most important criterion for defining otherness."[49] Recent work in early modern race studies has emphasized the multiple and often contradictory models that came together to create and contest what became, by the late seventeenth century, increasingly familiar and stable categories of racial difference. These models include, among others, emergent discourses of racialism, geo-humoral models of complexion, and the transformation through scienticism of bloodline genealogy into blood laws, as well as the claims of nationalism as a form of identity.[50] Within these parameters, though, it is worth remembering that new racial definitions – and the models for identity that they imply – are in part realized through the literary and narrative forms in which they are enacted. Understanding race in terms of visible appearance necessarily raises questions of representation since physical appearance was becoming a sign of who or what one is. With its emphasis on true genealogy as something that exceeds simple physical appearance (Charikleia's skin color) and yet is nonetheless in some way produced through art by a physical appearance (Andromeda's skin color), the *Aethiopika* resonates with contemporary concerns about the nature and origin not so much of skin color but of identity itself.

In the final section of this chapter, I would like to direct attention to the recognition scene as a particularly charged moment in early modern responses to the *Aethiopika*. Historic responses to the recognition scene provide evidence of the consequences to how Heliodorus constructs the recognition scene so as to require the reader to participate in an act of literary genealogy that runs counter to the more explicit goals of the narrative. The narrative tension within the recognition scene – and the serious demands it makes of readers or viewers – is intensified by the construction of racial identity within the visual culture of early modern Europe. Consider two early modern treatments of this central recognition scene: those in Tasso's adaptation of Heliodorus in the *Gerusalemme Liberata* (c. 1565) and Pierre Vallet's condensed, illustrated epitome of *Les Adventures amoureuse* [sic] *de Theagenes et Cariclee* (1613). These works follow Heliodorus in mixing biological and aesthetic genealogy, but they depart from his model by strongly discouraging their readers from modeling themselves as readers on Heliodorus' Persinna. Neither Tasso nor Vallet imagined their readers in terms that would allow them to be a new Persinna.

Tasso's *Discourses on the Art of Poetry*, which were published in 1587 but composed in the early 1560s, return to the questions raised by Ariosto through a perspective provided by Amyot and Heliodorus. Taking the neo-Aristotelian position that romance and epic are not distinct genres, Tasso argues that the heroic poem must be epic in both its subject matter and its form (Tasso, 1587, 120–30). In adopting this position, Tasso exemplifies the early modern sense that form is essential to the expression of epic. For instance, Tasso's great complaint about Ariosto concerned the size and multiplicity of *Orlando Furioso*. For Tasso, the "matter" that constitutes a literary work is much like "what natural philosophers call primary matter": in both cases, size is "its constant and external attribute, evident before the birth of form and remaining after form decays" (Tasso, 1587, 110).

As Tasso saw it, Ariosto did not so much write a romantic epic as fail to recognize or realize the underlying unity that belonged to his work. Calling attention to the "organic" metaphors that recur in Tasso's critical writings, Andrew Fichter thus demonstrates how for Tasso true poetry must reflect "the unity of creation in the medium of poetic form."[51] Yet, as with Amyot, what begins as a physical quality also becomes a physiological one – the innate characteristics of the story cannot be separated from the physical and intellectual qualities of its readers. For Amyot romance created desire in the body, but the *Aethiopika* was epic insofar as it stimulated intellectual rather than physical desire. Following this argument, Tasso defines epic through the structure and demands of the mind. The epic story should thus be no longer or larger than the ordinary human memory. Tasso explains, "just as the eye is the right judge of comely stature in the body – for that body has suitable size whose sight does not confound the eye and whose proportions the eye can appraise, taking in all its members at a glance – so is the ordinary human memory the right index of the appropriate length of the epic" (Tasso, 1587, 117). Adapting claims about proportion as an essential component of beauty that are standards of the visual arts, Tasso critically constructs the act of reading as a form of looking. In doing so, he describes the interconnection among reading, seeing, and making that informs his own critical commentaries and fictional rewriting of Heliodorus.

While Tasso mentions the loves of Theagenes and Charikleia and also demonstrates familiarity with Amyot's preface in the *Discourses*, his more significant response to Heliodorus' poetic practices appears in the *Gerusalemme liberata* when he transforms Heliodorus' Charikleia into Clorinda.[52] Tasso's arguments in the *Discourses* are consonant with his rewriting of Heliodorus' Charikleia as Clorinda. Like her original, Clorinda is a fair-skinned Ethiopian who is born of black parents as a result of her mother's act of having looked at images of a fair maiden being attacked by a monster. As the eunuch Arsetes recounts, her father, the Ethiopian king Senapus, become jealous of his wife's fidelity and locks her away in a room "painted with a tale of piety and with figures of devotion" (12.23). Rather than Perseus rescuing Andromeda, Tasso imagines St. George protecting a virgin: "A virgin – her lovely face white and her cheeks crimson – is bound there, close by a dragon" (12.23). As a result of her daily devotions before this image, Clorinda's mother gives birth to a "fair-complexioned" daughter whose very whiteness, like Charikleia's, seems to mark a moral "blackness" within her mother (12.23, 12.21). Tasso follows Heliodorus in taking as a moment of origin a daughter who is the image of her mother's mind rather than her father's body.

Beyond this point, though, Tasso radically rewrites Heliodorus' narrative. While Tasso begins in the same place as Heliodorus, he concludes quite differently. In Heliodorus, Charikleia is the heroine of the book. The "great ends" of the narrative center on the recognition of Charikleia: Book 10 offers readers an extended series of recognitions experienced by the judge Sisimithres, who took her from Ethiopia as a child; by Charicles, the surrogate father and namesake who raised her in Greece; by her parents, King Hydaspes and Queen Persinna; and even by the crowd of Ethiopians who watch but cannot understand the events that they see (555, 586). The discovery process in Book 10 is protracted: it is not simply enough, as Theagenes imagines, for Charikleia to "tell the king the truth" about who she is (555). We hear the full story of her origins – told not sequentially but through the contributions of everyone who was involved in Charikleia's birth and life. Heliodorus' version of the recognition scene in turn extends the many recognitions and mistakings that make up the narrative as a whole. For instance, Theagenes (along with most of the other male characters in the novel) falls in "love-at-first-sight" with Charikleia in a way that anticipates the responses of her parents in Book 10 (414). All the way through the process, the reader is both prepared for and made a participant in the act of recognizing Charikleia. In Heliodorus the reader is made to participate in and become complicit with that maternal instinct through which Persinna first creates and then recognizes her daughter.

Tasso, by contrast, rewrites the Charikleia story in order to eliminate the reader's involvement in this moment of recognition and the kinds of narratives such participation may imply. When the story of Clorinda's origins is initially recounted it is explicitly not a recognition scene. Arsetes tells the story to Clorinda when he sees that she has changed her signature white armor for rusty black armor that will prevent her from being seen by others (12.18). Trying to hide herself, she goes, as it were, from white to black. Arsetes tells her the story of her origins less to discover her than to protect her from the dangers of her disguise. His hope is that telling her of who she truly is – that is to say, black if Christian – will prevent her from putting on this black disguise. Ignoring his story, she ventures off and is killed precisely because Tancred fails to recognize her in her black armor. Because Arsetes' story provided only an unheeded warning and not the recognition Charikleia needed to claim her true identity, the one who loves her becomes the one who mistakenly kills her (12.67). Tasso underlines his rewriting of the Heliodoran recognition scene when lover-killer and victim recognize each other as she dies. As the narrator bemoans, "Alas, the sight! alas the recognition!" (12.67). This arrested recognition extends to the reader in the sense that the narrative tries to prevent Clorinda from recognizing her black origin by killing her at the moment she puts on black armor. Tasso thus insures that his heroine remains a "pale" dead character, her whiteness, but not her life, inviolable (12.81).

In commenting on Tasso's treatment of this scene, Valeria Finucci emphasizes how Clorinda is constructed as a "monster" and concludes that "a happy ending for a white Ethiopian princess is … out of the question, because it could breed fears of miscegenation, since Tasso's outward purpose in the *Liberata* is to create a heroic genealogy for his patron, of the Este family of Ferrara."[53] For Finucci, Clorinda remains monstrously outside the main line of Tasso's narrative because assimilating her more fully into the text would raise questions about mixing of bloods, races, and religions in ways that would taint the heraldic impulses of Tasso's fiction. Yet, Clorinda is "monstrous" not just as a certain kind of unthinkable creature but as a figure for a certain kind of a story. Clorinda offers us a way, that is, to see how Tasso rewrites not just Heliodorus' story but also his narrative aesthetics. Tasso's need to kill Ariosto – and the formal innovations to epic that he represents – is achieved in part by killing Clorinda.

Tasso's story requires race as part of the narrative, yet his treatment of Clorinda makes her race in important ways invisible to the reader. His narrative works to write race out of the story, and he does so in order to take away from the reader the ability to connect race with genealogy. If you never see Clorinda visually then you can never have Clorinda's mother's power. Tasso in the *Discourses on Poetry* had followed Amyot in his argument that epic matter had to fit the mind of its readers. Here, though, Tasso eliminates at least one model that was present in Heliodorus for the reader to make the narrative. Tasso begins his story as genealogical investigation. Yet, when the narrative kills Clorinda it kills any possibility of descent from within that narrative.

Renaissance readers of Heliodorus, even when not as directly theoretical as Tasso, follow his example in de-emphasizing the recognition scene as a way of eliminating the possibility of replicating through readers his racial narrative. In the letter that she sends with her abandoned daughter, Persinna describes the ancestral painting that created this new descent line for her child:

Our line descends from the Sun and Dionysos among gods and from Perseus and Andromeda and from Memnon too among heroes. Those who in the course of time came to build the royal palace decorated it with scenes from the stories of these figures: they painted the likenesses and exploits of the others in the men's quarters and the colonnade, but made use of the romance of Perseus and Andromeda to adorn the bedchambers. (432)

In much the same way that the romance of Perseus and Andromeda adorned the royal bedchamber of Heliodorus' Persinna, the story of Theagenes and Charikleia adorned the bedchambers of early modern Europe. One consequence of Amyot's translation of *L'Histoire Aethiopique* was a vogue of courtly painting cycles that depict scenes from Heliodorus' romance.

The first and probably most well known of these was a fifteen-painting cycle (c. 1600–1606) done by Ambroise Dubois [Ambrosius Bosschaert] for what is now the Louis XIII salon at Fontainebleau. It was in this bed-chamber that Marie de Medici gave birth to the future Louis XIII on September 27, 1601, and Dubois, who was appointed "peintre de la reine" in 1606, undertook the cycle in conjunction with celebration and com-memorations for the baptism of the dauphin in 1606.[54] Under the patron-age of Marie de Medici, the *Aethiopika* became a subject of a series of related court painting cycles, done for court bedchambers and often and perhaps rather remarkably commissioned as wedding commemora-tions, in the first half of the seventeenth century.[55] Wolfgang Stechow has tracked the interlacing of kinship and patronage structures that informed the transmission of this visual epithalamia across these courts.

Here, I would like to focus attention on Dubois' painting cycle, done for Marie de Medici, along with a second work, Pierre Vallet's *Les Adventures amoureuse de Theagenes et Cariclee* (Paris, 1613), a published epit-ome of images from the novel, dedicated to her son, Louis XIII. Neither of these works is particularly original artistically. Considered from aes-thetic standards, for instance, the works of both Abraham Bloemaert and Karel van Mander III are considerably more distinguished.[56] The Dubois cycle is notable, though, when we consider it as a contemporary reading of Heliodorus and one which is done in a medium, painting, that is at the heart of the fictional premise of the book. Dubois read the Amyot Heliodorus and was, indeed, working at Fontainebleau with Amyot's library.[57] His cycle offers what I would suggest is a theory of the relation-ship between art and identity that runs counter to Amyot's and does so by rejecting his model of reading. Dubois may not be particularly interesting in these works as a painter, but he is compelling as a kind of first reader of Amyot's text. As Stechow points out, the Dubois paintings represent "the first cycle from the *Aethiopika* and, as far as we know, the artist had no pictorial tradition whatever at his disposal, not even in prints."[58] Dubois' depictions of the narrative are thus entirely text-based.

Dubois begins as a reader, but the premise of the *Aethiopika* also tacitly imagines that an artist was (and, in ways that Renaissance illustrators of Heliodorus seemed to recognize, could perhaps again be) the figure who stood at the very beginning of this story. During this period when Dubois was painting the *Aethiopika* cycle, he was also at work on a cycle of scenes from *Gerusalemme liberata*, also for Fontainebleau. It is perhaps not surprising, then, that Dubois' paintings follow a trajectory that is much like Tasso's rewriting of the recognition of Charikleia as the fatal mistaking of Clorinda. Dubois painted this cycle for Marie de Medici, but, like Tasso's romance, the cycle is designed to avoid putting her, or other would-be viewers, in a position that might allow them to see in his paintings what Persinna had seen in the original painting of Andromeda.

As a visual representation of the narrative, Dubois' cycle is conspicuously partial. The fifteen paintings in this cycle deal only with events from the first five books of Heliodorus' romance: these events take us from the initial meeting between the two lovers at the temple of Delphi, to their capture by brigands, brief separation, and happy reunion in the caves along the Nile. The scenes that Dubois selected (which combine events narrated by Kalasiris with those that we learn directly in the opening books) are designed to present the romance as a straightforward love story. Dubois eliminates the teleological narrative structure of readerly suspense that Amyot praised, and he also eliminates the diasporic narrative movement that takes Heliodorus' reader out of Greece, into Egypt and Ethiopia. In short, Dubois gives his audience a courtly love story suited to a pan-European aristocracy. Throughout the sequence, Charikleia is consistently, luminously "whitened." Charikleia's whiteness functions to aestheticize her: with coloration that looks more like marble than like flesh, Dubois' Charikleia has a sculptural quality that tacitly reminds us of her origin in a painting and of Heliodorus' figurative ekphrasis of her within the romance.[59] The blue/white tones of her skin also make Charikleia a kind of visual/chromatic double to the Clorinda (whose white skin is set off by her blue clothing) in his *Gerusalemme liberata* cycle. Charikleia's whiteness cannot be read as a mark of race or origin and must instead, in ways that are nonetheless not racially innocent, be understood as a sign of class and gender.

The whitening of Charikleia clearly accords with Dubois' interest in rereading the *Aethiopika* in terms of a pan-European Christian aristocracy. Much of Heliodorus' narrative must be eliminated to conform to such a narrative: in order to transpose the events of the romance into a visual medium, Dubois reorders his images so that they conform to the chronological order of the events as they happened, rather than as they are narrated. This reordering has the effect of highlighting Dubois' decision to omit representations of both the conception scene with which the story began and the recognition scene with which it ends. Indeed, Dubois eliminates all the scenes that take place in Ethiopia. As the near contemporary work of Karel van Mander III makes clear, these are indeed the most dramatic and visually legible elements of the text, so Dubois' decision to exclude them is noteworthy.[60]

Dubois' images enact the story but do not represent it. Dubois produced a series of paintings that would in some way paint over the events that follow directly from what Persinna describes in her letter. She concludes her vivid description of the royal palace and bedchamber: "It was there one day that your father and I happened to be taking a siesta in the drowsy heat of the summer ... That day your father made love to me, swearing that he was commanded to do so by a dream, and I knew instantly that the act of love left me pregnant" (433). One might imagine that, as the queen's painter, Dubois might well have intended to read Heliodorus' text as narrative that affirmed a woman's power over creation and conception in ways that would celebrate his patron, Marie de Medici, and the birth of her son. Yet, Dubois does not do so because he does not structure his paintings to give his queen the same aesthetic power that Persinna has in Heliodorus. Much like Tasso, Dubois eliminates any possibility of creating a new Persinna who might inadvertently replicate the events of Heliodorus' story.

This tendency to eliminate Heliodorus' emphasis on color and art also typifies Pierre Vallet's *Adventures amoureuse*. Like Dubois, Vallet was closely associated with Marie de Medici, and he held appointment as the first royal botanical painter under Henri IV and Marie de Medici. Vallet was probably best known for his botanical illustrations: he published *Le Jardin du roy très Chrestien Henry IV* (Paris, 1608) and later expanded this volume as *Le Jardin du roy très Chrestien, Louis XIII, roy de France et de Navarre* (Paris, 1623). In his preface to the Heliodorus epitome, Vallet begins by invoking what seems like a Heliodoran language of vision, but he does so in order to situate such power not with the mother but with her son, the boy king Louis XIII, to whom he dedicates his volume. Addressing the king, Vallet thus contrasts the delights of the body with those "chaste douçeurs des Muses" and promises to "faire revivre en ces peintures" the pure love of Theagenes and Charikleia.[61] In an elaborate royal compliment, Vallet suggests that if the twelve-year-old Louis derives delight from such representations of virtue, he himself in a way produced those representations for, according to Vallet, it was seeing his virtue that prompted Vallet to undertake this translation.[62]

Within the text itself, though, Vallet's otherwise highly visual text works to draw attention away from both art and race. As an illustrator, Vallet was elsewhere carefully attentive to questions of color and visual representation. Both *Le Jardin du roy très Chrestien Henry IV* and *Le Jardin du roy très Chrestien, Louis XIII*, for instance, are collections of engravings of exotic botanical specimens, mostly from Spain, North Africa, and other Eurasian locations, that formed the royal gardens. In his preface to these volumes, Vallet expresses regret that the illustrations were not in color, but then offers precise instructions on how readers could use alchemical waters and dyes to add color to their copies of the book, including ten pages of detail specifying the colors for each figure that will appear in the main part of the volume. For "Narcissus Africanus," for instance, Vallet advises his readers that the leaves surrounding the flower should be a "jaune blassart," the calyx a beautiful gilded gold, and the underside entirely green.[63]

In the *Adventures amoureuse*, by contrast, Vallet tends to discourage his readers from seeing color in his text. Vallet's epitome is organized much like an emblem book with an argument, an illustrated plate, and two quatrains devoted to each of what Vallet took to be the romance's central episodes. Ordinarily, each episode has its own image, but when he arrives at the account of the conception and birth of Charikleia, Vallet instead repeats the illustration of the birthing scene, using it for both scenes. This image depicts a group of serving women clustering around to wash the baby while in the background Persinna lies in the birthing bed (33^r, 34^r). Vallet goes further than Dubois by including a small, somewhat obscure picture of the naked Andromeda in the background, but the accompanying text does not explain what happened and instead refers to Charikleia's birth rather elliptically as "un accident de sa conception" (33^r). At birth, Charikleia is "d'une coleur contraire" (33^r) and, when recognized later by her father, as being of "tient different" (III^r). Charikleia is marked as different, rather than explicitly described as fair-skinned, in part to avoid identifying other characters as dark skinned. Elsewhere in the volume, Vallet uses cross-hatchings to depict the darker skin tones of "un jeune Indien" (23^r). In this scene, where Persinna and the baby are intended to be of "une coleur contraire" from each other (33^r), Vallet does not use cross-hatchings or include other visual details to suggest that Persinna's complexion is any different than her daughter's. Likewise, in the recognition scene, Vallet again reuses the same illustration (III^r, II2^r) in ways that limit his reader's ability to see what Persinna has seen. If Vallet's dedication suggests that Louis XIII can in some sense bring Heliodorus' characters to life in ways that would seem to repeat Persinna's acts, the text itself delimits that possibility by ensuring that Louis XIII and Vallet's other readers can only see through the kind of perspective provided by King Hydaspes.

Early modern visual representations of this narrative, particularly these first "readings" of the romance that are most directly and closely tied to Amyot's translation, tend to eliminate the questions about aesthetic and racial genealogy that are connected with the text. In making these choices, such artists read only part of the *Aethiopika*, and they tacitly decline, for either themselves or their audiences, to become versions of Persinna. In his anti-Homeric romance, Heliodorus imagines what might be described as a kind of female gaze: seeing offers an aesthetic act through which the reader, like Persinna, can create race and identity. In general, Renaissance readings of Heliodorus follow Tasso in de-emphasizing the recognition scene as a way of refusing to pursue the text's questions about racial and aesthetic genealogy.

Heliodorus appealed to Amyot because he was looking for fiction that conformed to Aristotle's understanding of the relationship between matter and form, and was a product of the mind rather than the body. Whatever Amyot said, though, the *Aethiopika* was about how art might be produced by the mind *through* the body since, for Heliodorus, mind and body were not separate, but hybrid. Indirect proof of Heliodorus' claims can be found not in early modern fiction but in early modern natural philosophy and theology. It is here that the logical consequences of the alignment between Aristotle's *Poetics* and his *Physics* are most fully evident. Aristotle himself might not have dismissed Charikleia as a fiction: in texts such as *On the Generation of Animals* and *On the Movement of Animals*, Aristotle outlines the possible natural causes that might indeed produce this kind of anomaly of birth. Aristotle would have classified Charikleia as a monster insofar as her birth represents a thwarting of the proper teleology of human creation. This subject was of interest to early modern natural philosophers and theologians who, as Lorraine Daston has suggested, had a commitment to separating the preternatural and supernatural from the natural.[64]

It is perhaps not surprising, then, that a number of early modern philosophers and theologians cite the *Aethiopika* as evidence of the power of the maternal imagination. Antoine Fouquelin's decision to use examples from the Amyot translation to illustrate his commentary on Peter Ramus' anti-Aristotelian *Dialectique* gives some indication of how early modern readers associated Heliodorus with Aristotelianism and tended to regard this romance text as a part of a larger philosophical argument. In his Aristotelian work on monsters and marvels, the surgeon Ambrose Paré includes Charikleia as a key example of monsters produced by the imagination: "because of the appearance of the beautiful Andromeda" that her mother "summoned up in her imagination, for she had a painting of her before her eyes during the embraces from which she became pregnant."[65] Andrew Willet attributes Heliodorus' story to "the Hebrewes" in order to use this pagan fiction as an exegetical source: "The Hebrewes report of an Aethiopian, that had a faire childe, and a Rabbin being asked the reason therefore showed the cause to be a white table that was in her sight at the time of conceaving."[66] Martin Luther similarly tells of "a queen who gave birth to a child with the form and face of an Ethiopian as a result of a strong mental image of an Ethiopian painted on a tablet near her bed."[67] Thus, whereas Cervantes might imagine that lovers emulate romance, it is scientists and natural philosophers that imitate and draw on Heliodorus. If the *Aethiopika* is a book about art becoming life, then when natural philosophers and theologians cite Heliodorus as a "fact" to prove their argument, they indirectly replicate and even confirm the aesthetic premise of Heliodorus' story.

Seeing these double contexts for Heliodorus – the twinned genealogies of literary and biological creation – may help explain why the *Aethiopika* finally did not change how Renaissance romances were read. The implied understanding that race is marked by visual apprehension and genealogical reproduction explains why Heliodorus' treatment of the recognition scene is so crucial and evasions of it like Tasso's so telling. Heliodorus sets up the recognition scene in Book 10 in which Charikleia proves her "true" identity so that even while the narrative seems to move the reader toward a safely patriarchal conclusion that would logically depend on the recognition of the father, the narrative actually works to make the reader a version of the mother. The tension between those two possibilities – the mother's instinct versus the father's need to look at the portrait in order to know – is not really a choice between epic and romance, as it may appear. Rather, it presents the possibility for what I would call an othered epic in the sense that the father's recognition is anti-Homeric. That is, the recognition of Charikleia produces a return at the end of the story but the return is to a place that is not Greece. The return involves the securing of a descent line, but only through the transformation of the quintessentially Greek Theagenes into the spouse for the Ethiopian Charikleia. The main, or father-based, narrative takes a Greek storyline but displaces it to Ethiopia. The *Aethiopika* is a narrative about descent, lineage, and national identity, but one that suggests that the Greek epic is transportable.

The maternal narrative that Persinna extends to readers of the romance, by contrast, seems potentially more radical because it involves overturning the relationship between identity and culture. Rather than imagining that culture is a consequence of identity – you make epics or pictures because you have a certain identity – Persinna's narrative implies that culture creates identity and does so through the power of the aesthetic imagination. You can make Charikleia because you have a picture of Andromeda. The mother's narrative does not merely say that other, non-Greek peoples may have their epics too but also perhaps that we, as readers, are created by our identity stories. This is a radical possibility because what Persinna imagines for us – that one may move from white to black, or black to white – is not bound by the understanding of genealogy that defines epic. Renaissance readers recognized the threat posed by the visual component to this narrative that is both racial and aesthetic. I would suggest that although Heliodorus was popular among Renaissance readers, none of his admirers could imagine or complete a truly Heliodoran narrative that successfully integrated the romance interested in origins with the epic interested in descent. Despite Amyot and Tasso, no one in the Renaissance achieves a narrative which accepts Amyot's challenge for a new way of reading romance in the strong terms that Heliodorus' story implies.

CHAPTER 3

The conversion of the reader: Ariosto, Herberay, Munday, and Cervantes

Jacques Amyot presented his translation of Heliodorus' *Aethiopika* in part out of his concern about what might happen to those who read romances such as *Amadis*. Despite Amyot's efforts, sixteenth-century readers of *Amadis* were many. As different versions of the *Amadis* cycle circulated across Europe and into the New World, in hundreds of editions, large numbers of readers encountered these volumes: Marian Rothstein estimates as many as 500,000 sixteenth-century readers for the French editions alone.[1]

The impact that the *Amadis* cycle had as it was introduced into print culture by Montalvo and then adapted and transmitted into other vernacular contexts was considerable. Winfried Schleiner characterizes the *Amadis* cycle as "the most influential work of prose fiction of the sixteenth century."[2] Publication details and physical states of existing copies make clear that these volumes were among the most widely published and read texts of the period. It is likely that a version of Books 4 and 5, which represent Montalvo's most radical reworking of the manuscript materials that he inherited, was printed first, before the other parts of the cycle, sometime in the 1490s. It is not until after Montalvo's death, though, that we see a strong and constant demand for new editions in the Spanish markets: between 1508, the date of the earliest extant edition of the first four books, and 1540, the date of the first Janot edition in France, there are almost a dozen Spanish editions. Most of these were folio editions of the first four books of the cycle and published in Seville, but editions also appeared in Salamanca, Saragossa, and Medina del Campo, as well as in Venice and Rome.

The material features of the *Amadis* cycle became central to its dissemination into France and, from there through second-level translations and adaptations of the Herberay editions, into England, as well as into Germany and the Netherlands.[3] In France, the Herberay translations of the cycle dominated secular French fiction from the 1540s through the

1560s. These editions were read avidly in ways that cannot be separated from the new physical formats in which they were published. In *Le premier livre de Amadis de Gaule* (Paris, 1540), the Parisian printer/bookseller Denis Janot re-imagined the romance by replacing the traditional black-letter gothic scripts that had been associated with earlier romances with an elegant Garamond font, a paper-rich single column format, modern punctuation, and prolific illustrations with woodblock prints.[4] Virginia Krause has argued that the self-conscious commitment to serialization in the Herberay/Janot editions changed literary production across Europe. For Krause, the unprecedented popularity of these volumes "reflected new publishing practices and reading habits."[5]

As a probable result of the way in which the Amadis romances dominated sixteenth-century secular reading and the book market, *Amadis* became closely associated with the reading practices that it seemed to have generated. As Rothstein suggests, many treated *Amadis* "as a kind of exemplar," insofar as reading it was understood, by both its proponents and detractors, to have powerful effects on its readers.[6] As they left Spain, the Amadis volumes became a kind of trope for the consequences to reading and, as I will suggest here, one of the key concerns involved responses to Montalvo's arguments about the relationships among faith, birth, and identity.

Scholars working in the history of reading have identified both romance as a whole and the different Amadis volumes, in particular, as important test cases for understanding the transformation of early modern reading practices. This chapter will follow some of those contemporary readers of *Amadis* whose likely activities worried Amyot, Juan Luis Vives, and other sixteenth-century moralists. In the first portion of this chapter, I will be looking briefly at three contemporary responses to Montalvo that, in different ways, reject the new model of identity (transformative rather than fixed, based on belief rather than birth) that Montalvo integrated into his rewriting of the *Amadis* story and do so in ways that self-consciously express their attitudes toward conversion, racial identity, and reading. These are first, Ariosto's rewriting in *Orlando Furioso* (1516) of the madness of Amadis/Beltenebros in his own racially inflected version of the madness of Orlando; second, the French translations of the *Amadis* and *Esplandián* volumes (1540–44) done by Nicolas de Herberay for the court of François I; and finally, the English translations that Anthony Munday (published under both his own name and under the pseudonym Lazarus Pyott) did of the first five books of the cycle (1590–1619) that were themselves later read by writers such as Lady Mary Wroth. In the final section of the chapter, I will turn to arguably the century's greatest reader of *Amadis*, Cervantes' Don Quixote.

As readers of Montalvo, Ariosto, Herberay, and Munday all reject, along racially-demarcated lines, his model of conversion and the assumptions about identity that underpin that model. When readers, editors, and translators take race back out of their versions of the *Amadis* cycle, they are not just being more or less racist than Montalvo. What is at stake is not simply the way that the kinds of identity structured by desire are for Ariosto more powerful than those of descent, race, or faith; or the fact that the specific intensity of blood laws in the Spanish context does not carry over to the court of François I, or the different cultural value associated with "fair" skin or with conversion for English readers. Readers also resist these conversion narratives because they want to remove the instability of identity that these racially-inflected conversion narratives brought into Montalvo's texts. That is, I am not so much concerned with the narratives fates of Calafia or Frandalo as with how readers may resist the narratives that are implied by their presence in the romance. As the comments of Norandel suggested, conversion may begin as a political and theological subject it becomes a poetic practice because it is so centrally concerned with the creation of readers' identities.

Before turning to Montalvo's readers, though, it seems useful to begin with his anticipations of those readers. Throughout both his revisions of Books 1–4 and his writing of the original Book 5, Montalvo demonstrates that he is strongly attuned to the kinds of responses that his text would generate in readers. Book 5 as a whole arguably stands as Montalvo's attempt to provide a first "reading" of his version of the *Amadis* cycle as a way of anticipating and structuring the activities of would-be readers of his text. Montalvo's interest in defining the importance of the act of reading and its relationship to the theological questions that are at the heart of his vision for romance after the Fall of Constantinople is probably most explicitly signaled in the birthmark that he imagines for his Christian hero, Esplandián. Montalvo inherited Amadis, but Esplandián is his character and Montalvo imagined his identity in ways that highlight the acts of reading that Montalvo hoped readers would bring to his text.

When the story of Esplandián's birth is told in Book 3, Oriana's ladies-in-waiting notice that the infant is marked in a wondrous but mysterious way:

they saw that he had some letters as white as snow under his right nipple, and under his left nipple there were seven letters as red as live coals; but they were not able to read either set of letters, nor did they know what they said because the white ones were in a very obscure Latin, and the red ones were in very incomprehensible Greek.[7]

Like the scar on Odysseus' leg or the black band that encircles Charikleia's arm, the birthmarks engraved on Esplandián's chest become not simply marks of identity but, more fundamentally, the material sign of the act of recognition that the romance demands from both its characters and its readers. This act of recognition is central to Montalvo's depiction of the new theological character of romance after the Fall of Constantinople. Equally importantly, though, it is also central to his understanding of the new forms of reading that characterize post-Gutenberg romance.

This double birthmark, which becomes legible gradually over the course of Books 4 and 5, suggests the ways in which reading has taken the place of recognition in the structure of Montalvo's model for romance. When the hermit Nasciano baptizes the foundling baby, he is able to read the white set of marks, but not the colored ones:

Reading them he saw that the white ones in Latin said, "Esplandián." Thinking that must be his name, he gave it to him; but, despite all his effort, he could not read the red ones, nor could he understand what they meant.[8]

For most of Book 5, the meaning of this second set of birthmarks remains significant but unknown. When the infanta Leonorina first met Esplandián, she already knew of these marks, but "in her extreme agitation, she forgot to look at the letters that the knight had on his chest."[9] The narrative, however, suggests that Leonorina would not have been able to read these letters even had she remembered to look at them. Midway through this book, Esplandián and his knights capture the infidel sorceress Melía from Persia and bring both the sorceress and her library of books, "with their magnificent bindings covered in gold and silver" (382), back to Constantinople. When Esplandián comes to claim Leonorina from her father, the Emperor insists that if Leonorina is to be his, then she must be able to read the marks on Esplandián's chest for he knows from the prophecy "that the name who belongs to him appears on his left side, and that the letters of her name are to be revealed by her alone" (500).[10]

In the first test of Esplandián's identity, baptism transforms him in a way that now makes it possible to read his identity. Yet, Esplandián's identity does not just arise out of belief or faith; it is also conferred by texts and in particular by these printed ones, with their magnificent bejeweled bindings. In this second scene, it is not love or identity itself that enables Leonorina to claim her beloved: it is instead an act of reading.

When she sees the red letters on Esplandián's chest, Leonorina is able to match them up to the characters she has seen in one of Melía's books, "which showed these seven red letters just like the ones on Esplandián" (501).[11] When Leonorina brings the volume to her father and the court, they too are able to read it:

> The emperor and all those lords read them and saw clearly that they did not vary one jot from the ones on Esplandián. Then they looked at the caption, which read thus: "The blessed knight who will win the sword and great treasure that I enchanted will be the one who has his name and his amie's name written on his chest. Because the seven red letters will be very obscure, and because there will be no one learned enough to decipher them, I have decided to inform those who will come after me that the red letters spell the name of Leonorina, daughter of the great emperor of Greece." (501)[12]

Leonorina must be able to read the text of Esplandián's identity, and she is only able to do so because she is able to produce the original and non-classical text (what Melía imports and translates into Christian Constantinople is not *The Odyssey* or even *Aethiopika*) for other would-be readers.

Reading the text and seeing Esplandián's identity become versions of one another. Montalvo transforms the classic romance recognition scene theologically by shifting emphasis away from genealogy (the birthmark as the fixed sign of one's birth) to baptism and conversion (that mark only becomes legible through the transformation produced by faith). At the same time, though, Montalvo also insists through the figure of Leonorina that readers are necessary to process of creating the identity that they find. In the classical versions of Homer and Heliodorus, recognition produces identity; in this post-print version, it is reading that produces it.

One might here usefully contrast Esplandián's birthmark with the appearance of the character Feirefiz in Wolfram von Eschenbach's thir-teenth-century romance, *Parzival*. In *Parzival*, Feirefiz is the son of the Christian knight Gahmuret and Belcane, the black queen of Zazamanc. In a gesture that points to the sense that this character is a kind of figure for the genre of romance, Feirefiz is also identified as the future father of Prester John. In a key recognition scene, Feirefiz's skin is described as being like "a written-on leaf of parchment, black and white, here and there."[13] Wolfram and Montalvo share the traditional romance under-standing of the body as a text whose identity must be read to be recog-nized. In addition to moving from parchments to books, Montalvo also suggests that the text that is the body can only be understood by com-paring what may be inscribed there to other, non-metaphorical, texts. In the case of Esplandián, what connects these double revisions to the classic recognition scenes of romance is Montalvo's commitment to a transformative model of identity for both his readers and his characters. As we shall see, it is this transformative model of identity – both racial and textual – that subsequent readers of Montalvo will most consistently reject.

Conversion is in *Esplandián* a form of poetics and one that has implications not just for what stories romances tell but for the manner in which romances could be read. It thus makes sense to turn to the question of how contemporary readers responded to the conversion narratives that Montalvo used to conclude his romance. This question is an especially important one because the primary goal of reading in this kind of romance is the creation of identity. In one sense, the reading of identity is clearly literal: Esplandián's identity is actually inscribed on his chest and must become legible for his fate to be achieved. But the need to read identity is also true in a more pervasive way: the genealogical model of identity that defined Books 1–4 of *Amadis* was itself an expression of the idea that not only was identity visible but, indeed, it was the reader's job to recognize and comprehend identity in the knights that they encounter as readers.

My argument has been that how romances represent racial difference is important not simply for its own sake but because of romance's commitment to creating social identities that allow its readers to know who they are through the reading practices by which they know who and what the white knight, the tawny knight, or the black knight means and are. Following the trajectory of this argument I will here look at what happens to these conversion narratives as they are incorporated, transformed, and omitted from contemporary responses to and adaptations of Montalvo's works. Because romance is predicated upon the assumption that readers use a model of legibility to construct their own identities, it is important to pay attention to what readers do when confronted with those moments, like religious conversion, which explicitly and directly challenge romance assumptions about the nature of identity.

One of Montalvo's earliest and most notable readers was Ludovico Ariosto. As a reader, Ariosto recognized and rejected the racial implications of Montalvo's arguments about conversion. Ariosto's response to Montalvo's understanding of identity emerges in his rewriting of the key scene of the hero's melancholic passion. In Montalvo's version, Amadis' love-sickness provides an occasion for Montalvo to begin revising the model of descent-based identity that, as we have seen, defined Books 1–4 of *Amadis*. When Amadis becomes mistakenly estranged from Oriana, he abandons his armor and identity. Taking on the name Beltenebros, he is also transformed physically, becoming unrecognizably dark and ugly: "his face was very gaunt and dark [descarnado y negro], much more so than if it had been disfigured by some great sickness; so that there was no person who could recognize him."[14] It is in this form, as the darkly shadowed Beltenebros, rather than as the fair and handsome Amadis, that Montalvo's hero expresses the key sentiment that "the hearts of men, and not their good appearance, accomplish good things" (2.527).[15] This moment in Book 2 anticipates the transformation of Montalvo's attitude toward the nature of identity. As we have seen, Books 1–4 consistently understand physical appearance as an infallible mark of both moral worth and family identity. Beltenebros' comments about "good appearance," by contrast, point toward Book 5's assumption that religious conversion creates new forms of identity that overwrite the traditional familial and racial identity that defined Books 1–4. Appropriately, it is thus during this liminal moment when Amadis is no longer himself that Montalvo can express a perspective that argues for a different understanding of how you might know a person's identity and establish their worth.

This transformation of the fair Amadis into the dark Beltenebros informs both Ariosto's imagining of the madness of his hero, Orlando, and, as I suggested in the Introduction, will also prompt Cervantes' imagining of the consequences to reading such stories of madness. Whereas Montalvo embraces conversion as the basis for a faith-based form of identity that transcends both family and race, Ariosto rejects such transformations. He signals this rejection in part by inscribing physical race, African blackness, rather than the complective but not strictly racial melancholic "darkness" of black bile, into his version of how Orlando is transformed by the sickness of love. After being rejected by the fair Angelica, Orlando becomes mad in a way that follows but then goes beyond that of his literary predecessor Amadis: Orlando first falls into rages of emotion that "obfuscate and darken all his senses" in a manner commensurate with Amadis' madness.[16] Abandoning his armor and his clothing (24.4.3), Orlando soon becomes inhuman as he wanders naked through the narrative, eating raw food and hunting humans with a "savage relish" (24.13.8).[17]

The most extreme moment of Orlando's self-degradation, and the one that most fully engages and rethinks Ariosto's source in Montalvo, occurs when the crazed Orlando glimpses Angelica on her way back to the East with her new lover. Angelica does not see him ("of his presence unaware," 29.58), but the reader does:

> Beholding him, she would not think this man
> Could be Orlando, he was so much changed,
> For ever since his malady began,
> Quite naked in all weathers he had ranged.
> He was as burnt and black as if Aswan
> Or where the Garamanths their gods avenged
> Had been his birthplace, or the mountains where
> The sources of the river Nile appear. (29.59)[18]

Here, Ariosto explicitly racializes Montalvo's image. Orlando is not just "darkened" in his emotions: this hero whose enchanted skin marks his identity as the Defender of the Faith (34.63) has become as "burnt and black" in complexion as Ethiopians, Egyptians, or Libyans, as dark as those who worship Aswan or the gods of the Nile. In John Harington's 1591 translation, the naked Orlando is "sunne burnd and parcht," "[i]n face like death, in hew like an Egyptian."[19] Presented in racialized terms, Orlando's estrangement is the culmination of a movement away from the Christian cause that begins when he first sets off in pursuit of Angelica. Abandoning the defense of Paris and his duties to Charlemagne, Orlando puts aside his familiar white armor with its crimson quarterings and replaces it with a black surcoat, "a trophy he had from an emir won" (8.85).[20] That black surcoat of the African Almonte is in turn shed, leaving Orlando with only his naked, blackened skin.

In Orlando's blackness, we should see more than just another instance of the culturally prevalent association of blackness with savageness, sexual jealousy, or moral depravity. Ariosto is in part drawing on Ficinian ideas of melancholy to depict the furor of love as a change in physical complexion.[21] At the same time, though, Ariosto also makes it clear that we must take this transformation of Orlando's complexion, at once pallid and yet also burnt and blackened, seriously in both racial and religious terms. He repeatedly stresses the astonishing fact of Orlando's nakedness (24.4, 28.8, 29.59, 31.45, 34.63, 39.44, 39.60). In much the way that we learn about the black skin of the Sultan of Damascus in *The King of Tars* only at the moment of his transformation, here it is not until Orlando has been transformed by the madness of love that we learn that Orlando's skin is enchanted and must be read as a mark of his religious identity. Medoro thus cannot harm Orlando because he "had skin so hard … his enchanted body was like steel, impenetrable, suffering no ill" (29.62).[22] As St. John explains later, Orlando is more than just a Christian Achilles: he cannot suffer any wound in his body because God has made him the Defender of the Faith (34.63).

The mad Amadis becomes dark and gaunt in his melancholy; the mad Orlando becomes black in his savageness. Why this difference? For Montalvo, the central insight of Amadis' madness prepares the way for his narrative in Book 5 about how conversion produces a Christian faith that must transcend any more worldly racial and geographic differences. Ariosto, by contrast, makes the madness of Orlando part of a narrative whose ultimate endpoint is a denial of the kind of conversion that Montalvo envisions. He incorporates religious conversion into *Orlando Furioso*, but he does so in ways that consistently reaffirm, rather than challenge, the power of familial identity and, through that, the insurmountability of racial difference. As a reader, Ariosto rejects the implications of Montalvo's theological claims and does so in part by reasserting racial difference within his romance. Orlando's savage blackness becomes a way for Ariosto to supplant the types of conversion that Montalvo had in *Esplandián* made a centerpiece of both church policy and romance plotline.

Ariosto makes Orlando black so that he can baptize him, at least symbolically, as a way of anticipating the actual and related baptism of Ruggiero. Orlando becomes, for a time, black – he is sunburnt and dirty, he is mad with jealousy, and he is transported to Africa (30.15). The narrative leaves him at the depth of his madness on the way to Africa, where when we later find him he is among "a dark-skinned host," "vast and unending as infinity" (30.15).[23] Orlando's madness ends in a baptismal washing that takes away his blackness. Astolfo instructs, "wash him seven times / And seven times immerse him in the waves / So that the filthy coating that begrimes / His brutish face and limbs the water laves" (39.56.1–4).[24] Sunburnt skin and everything it signifies now become no more than dirt.

The restoration, the salvation, of Orlando provides the turning point in the victory for the Christians; it allows for the bringing together of the paradigmatic hero of traditional chivalry (Orlando) with the larger military force (Astolfo's black army vast enough to defeat seven Africas) that post-Fall of Constantinople romance suspected was necessary. These plot reasons notwithstanding, what is most importantly at stake is Ariosto's refusal of the kinds of conversion upon which the Iberian romances that we have seen depended.[25] For Ariosto, there are no mass conversions to create armies of the newly faithful: the converted Marfisa, for instance, proposes to forcibly convert her whole kingdom, but the narrative does not rely upon that conversion and it is not included within the text (38.18); in contrast to Tirant's Ethiopians or Montalvo's Californians, the Emperor of Senapo's people are already converted.[26] Indeed, Ariosto subtly aligns them with Orlando by suggesting that, however black, they carry their own mark of Christian identity on their skin that parallels his, but one that confirms rather than requires their baptism: "if I mistake not, here they brand / The neophyte upon his brow, as well / As using water – or so travelers tell" (33.102.6–9).[27]

Equally importantly, Ariosto does not give us the kinds of individual conversions Montalvo saw as the hope for both Christianity and romance: were Montalvo writing *Orlando Furioso,* for instance, the truth of the romance and the defeat of the infidel threat would have been secured by the conversion of a character such as Rodomonte, Agramante, or Mandricardo. The "black knight," Brandimarte, himself converted to Christianity by Orlando in Boiardo's *Orlando Inamorato*, brings us closest to this possibility when he attempts, unsuccessfully, to convert Agramante (41.38–39).[28] What we do not get in *Orlando Furioso* is the conversion of a pagan or a Muslim, an African or Tartarian, someone whose religious identity could be understood to begin in some instance of ethnic difference that conversion then overcomes in a manner that testifies to the efficacy of conversion and the power of faith (and with it, romance) to create new forms of identity.

The washing clean of the already Christian Orlando, a baptism that transforms him from a black savage back into the chief of the European Christians, a hero whose very skin is heralded as a confirmation of his Christian identity in terms quite different from Esplandián's, is instead designed to supplant the more racially dangerous conversions that drove Montalvo's revisions to *Amadis*.[29] This symbolic baptism anticipates the parallel conversion of Ruggerio and the related death of Rodomonte at the end of *Orlando Furioso*. As a (not really) black (not really) savage in Africa (only temporarily), an inhuman beast who is only converted in the sense that he returns to his original identity, Orlando is the perfect model for the much more limited kind of re-conversion that Ariosto's romance can accommodate.[30] Orlando's trajectory through Africa, away from the both sexually and spiritually infidel Angelica and back to the true faith, provides a template for Ruggerio's conversion to Christianity. Ruggerio converts to Christianity but that conversion bears no resemblance to those of Frandalo, Escariano, and Calafia, or, in a historical register, to that of Leo Africanus. Ariosto's readers do not need to believe in a kind of faith that can truly change identity, in the kind of conversion that can do away with perceived racial and cultural differences, to arrive at a commonality based on (the always very hard to see) truth of faith alone.

What Ariosto's readers get in Ruggerio is instead a conversion that involves a return to family or kin – and thus to genealogical forms of identity. Ariosto's repeated paralleling of Orlando and Ruggerio (travel to North Africa, washing in the waves, real and symbolic baptism as a means of return) is designed to show that while Orlando breaks faith in his passion for Angelica, Ruggiero instead returns to the faith through his love for Bradamante. Writing dynastic history for the House of Este, Ariosto transforms a narrative that was a traditional romance focused on Orlando into a genealogical and heraldic epic about Ruggiero.[31]

At the same time, Ariosto is also resisting certain kinds of arguments about conversion, prominent in both Montalvo and Boiardo, which are not compatible with the epic movement that Ariosto wants to associate with Ruggiero. Under this heraldic premise, it must be blood, not belief, that defines identity in Ruggiero. At the same time, Ariosto also recognizes that however venerable Ruggiero's blood is from some perspectives ("the ancient blood of Troy," "commingled from two purest strains," 3.17), too much attention to Ruggiero's blood could make him racially suspect (he is also the grandson of Agolante of Africa, the son of the converted Galiciella). In order to overcome any possible taints to Ruggiero's blood, Ariosto thus introduces racial language into the symbolic conversion of Orlando as a way of removing them from the actual conversion of Ruggerio.[32] In the same way that Orlando is only apparently black, Ruggerio is only apparently a pagan. His conversion is not a transformation of the kind that Montalvo's romance holds out. Rather, it is the reassertion of a fundamental identity, one that returns him to the great identities of his father's line ("his father, his grandfather and all that side / Of his great race were Christians," 22.35.4–5),[33] one that brings both faith and love (Charlemagne and Bradamarte), and reunites him with his family (Marfisa, having accepted baptism immediately and without hesitation).

The racialized madness of Orlando has a second consequence, which some of Ariosto's own readers seem to have recognized. The movement of Orlando back into Christian society provides the model for Ruggiero's change in faith; at the same time, his position outside that society, outside all humanity, becomes the pattern for Rodomonte's increasing estrangement during this section of the romance and his death at the end of the romance. The African Rodomonte takes the place of the "burnt and black" Orlando. Defeated first by the sacrifice of Isabella and by the sword of Bradamante, Rodomonte becomes increasingly savage, mad, and estranged from humanity. He returns, unexpectedly, in the final scenes to challenge Ruggiero's conversion: he denounces him as both an apostate traitor, for "Your change of faith is not to be denied" (46.106.2).[34] When Rodomonte breaks in on the last day of the wedding feast to challenge Ruggiero, their fight and Rodomonte's ultimate death is the challenge that confirms the validity of Ruggiero's baptism.

Indeed, Rodomonte's utter difference (racial, religious, and geographic) confirms Ruggiero's conversion and the power of Christianity as a whole. In a generic sense, Rodomonte must die for the epic component (and, with it, the genealogical identity that tacitly affirms racial difference) of Ariosto's narrative to win out over the romance elements (of universal desire and transcendent faith). Rodomonte is African, and he comes to embody the characteristics that the "black and burnt" Orlando showed in his madness. While Ariosto's Rodomonte is never explicitly black, later readers nonetheless saw him in the terms that Ariosto used to describe the mad Orlando. In the manuscript continuation of her *Urania*, Lady Mary Wroth creates her Tartarian king Rodomandro as a literary descendent of Rodomonte. Rodomandro's black skin ("but for the coleur of it, itt plained shewed the sun had too hard kissed it") is, as we shall see, a key component of his identity and a legible mark of the personal estrangement that he represents for Wroth.[35]

As the "burnt and blackened" Orlando is re-converted and returned to the Christian side, Ariosto washes away the powerful race-overcoming forms of conversion that Montalvo had advocated in *Esplandián*. When Nicolas de Herberay translated the *Esplandián* volume into French, he had to confront Montalvo's changes to the main line of *Amadis* much more directly than did Ariosto. In 1540, Herberay began publishing a series of translations of the Spanish *Amadis* volumes, apparently at the request of King François I, who was first introduced to the Spanish romances of chivalry while he was being held by the Spanish as a prisoner of war after his loss at the Battle of Pavia. Although Montalvo's books were popular, Herberay's translations of them were even more widely read and more influential. For most contemporary readers, Amadis meant Herberay's *Amadis*. Herberay completed his translations of the Montalvo portion of the cycle with *Le cinquiesme livre de Amadis de Gaule* (1544). As studies of Herberay's work have made clear, Herberay's translations of the 1540s became the literary text of the ideals and aspirations of the French royal court.[36] The Herberay *Amadis* was designed as a fiction of social identity: these romances gave aristocratic readers, Herberay's first and primary audience, a chance to return nostalgically to a heraldic past that glorified their virtues and confirmed their identities. In *Orlando Furioso*, the only dark-skinned person who is "converted" is the already Christian and originally fair-skinned Defender of the Faith, Orlando. In *Le cinquiesme livre de Amadis de Gaule*, there are no dark-skinned peoples and almost no conversions of any kind.

As we have seen, Montalvo in Book 5 replaces what had been an ethnos-based model of identity in which the "tests of true belonging," to use Ivan Hannaford's phrase, were decided on "the purity of language, color, and shape"[37] with a common identity produced through a universal, Christian faith. In Montalvo's *Esplandián*, the physical appearance of the beautiful and fair Esplandián does not serve as a test of his identity, a sign of who and what he is, but as a mark of his ability to transform the religious identities of characters such as the also beautiful but black Califía. Or, put another way, Montalvo uses new forms of racial and ethnic difference (the black pagan Califía, the giant Turk Frandalo) as a means to reject the traditional models of racial identity (the fair Amadis and his equally fair brothers Florestan and Galour) that had defined the earlier volumes of the series. Either way, conversion and the shared identity of faith suggest a potentially unbounded realm in which you are what you believe, not what you look like or who you are born of. This possibility runs counter to the forms of both traditional genealogical and emerging proto-racialist identity. As a reader of Montalvo, Herberay wants to return to traditional genealogy and its heraldic, aristocratic identities. To do so, he must not just remove the religious narratives that Montalvo had introduced into Book 5; he must also remove the new forms of visible racial difference that Montalvo had used to create his narratives of conversion. Herberay's changes to *Esplandián* arise out of religious and nationalistic attitudes, but, importantly, those changes are expressed through the way that he rewrites Montalvo's arguments about the relationship between physical appearance and identity. Even more so than Ariosto, Herberay recognizes and consistently rejects the implications of Montalvo's attitude toward conversion and the model of faith-based identity that it implied.

The idea that you can discern who and what someone is by looking at them is a powerful possibility. As we have seen, this idea is, as a literary possibility, at the heart of traditional romances (such as Books 1–4 of *Amadis*). As a political ideology, this idea also drives the emergence of racialism (whether this is the desire of the authorities of the Inquisition to uncover and make visible the hidden identities of *conversos* or the desire of early modern ethnographers to impose proto-racialist systems of classification onto the peoples of Asia, Africa, or the New World).

The idea that looking at others might fundamentally change who *you* are is a different thing. Montalvo's representation of Esplandián as a sign of God and a physical force for conversion introduced this disturbing and unsettling possibility into the *Amadis* cycle. In his revisions of *Le cinquiesme livre*, Herberay works to remove this possibility.

Herberay consistently de-emphasizes Montalvo's attention to religion and especially to religious conversion. Frandalo initially joins the side of the Christians after an interview with the Emperor of Constantinople. In Montalvo's version, the Emperor demands that Frandalo must follow God in turning "bad works into good ones" by abandoning the infidel's "evil and perverse sect" (192).[38] In the Herberay version, Frandalo changes sides, but for reasons of money and convenience: Herberay transforms Montalvo's act of religious faith into a gesture of political fealty ("je ... vous jurant sur ma foy ... que vous aurez en moy un serviteur qui avecq le temps vous donnera à cognoistre par effait combien j'estime cette grace").[39] When Norandel decides to abandon the old practices of traditional chivalry to follow Esplandián's new form of religious crusade Montalvo presents that decision in terms of a religious experience (he has been "changed and converted from the old ways into seeking that by which, risking the death of my body, I can win glory and eternal life for my soul," 206).[40] In Herberay, Norandel meets up with Esplandián and decides to stay with him rather than go back to England as he had planned, but there is no sense that the decision is a significant one or that Norandel has in any way experienced a transformative change in what he believes ("puis que fortune nous a ainsi assemblez je vous prie soiez content que je ne vous habandonne sans occasion," 44[r]).

The conversions of Frandalo and Califía were so integral to the construction of Book 5 that Herberay may have felt unable to remove them entirely. Even there, though, he does what he can to de-emphasize these events. In Montalvo, for instance, Frandalo's conversion is described in detail and then later referred back to often because Frandalo's decision to join the Christian forces is the reason that they are able to defeat King Armato and the Turks. Frandalo makes it possible for the outnumbered Christians to infiltrate the Turkish defenses because of his experience with the battle tactics of his former master, through knowledge of the language, the dress, and the countryside, and even through use of his own relatives as spies and advance scouts. Frandalo's ability to infiltrate and overcome the Turks from inside is a fictional trope for what Montalvo saw as the possibilities of religious conversion for achieving military crusade: as Frandalo himself recognizes when he first sees the famed Esplandián, "merely seeing and hearing the knight were enough to convert not only him but all pagans" (219).[41] In Herberay, Frandalo does still convert, but there is no account of the event or how it happens. Indeed, one of the few references to Frandalo's conversion ("je suis maintenant Chretien et Chevalier de Jesuschrist," 48ᵛ) occurs in a conversation in which King Armato questions his motives and impugns the validity of the conversion.

Montalvo's model of religious conversion ran counter to the assumptions about racial and ethnic identity that dominated early modern culture. Once Esplandián's appearance becomes a mark of religious truth, that is, it changes the identity of the fair Amadis as much as it does that of the black Califia. Herberay's rewriting of Montalvo's conversion scenes thus necessarily also involves a consistent suppression of the forms of physical appearance that Montalvo had used to underwrite his conversion narrative. Montalvo used Esplandián's appearance as a narrative trope for the power of religious conversion to transform identity: Herberay eliminates this emphasis in his translation of *Le cinquiesme livre*. In Montalvo when Esplandián and Frandalo have an audience with King Armato, the king understands Frandalo's decision to go over to the Christian side as soon as he sees Esplandián: seeing Esplandián's physical beauty, Armato immediately recognizes that the god of the Christians must be more powerful than is his god (235). When Herberay's Armato meets Esplandián, there is no emphasis on the knight's physical beauty. Instead, Armato sees only Esplandián's youth and imagines that Frandalo mocks him ("le voyant si jeune & san un seul poil de barbe, eut fantasie que Frandalo disoit cella pour s'excuser," 48ᵛ). In the French versions the damsel and Queen Calafie still recognize the handsomeness of Esplandián but the fervor of apocalyptic religious language that Montalvo had brought to those encounters is now gone.

For Montalvo, the key to the conversions was the way that God's truth manifested itself in Esplandián's physical appearance. In Frandalo's case, seeing and hearing him is powerful enough, he imagines, to convert all pagans (219); in Calafia's, the beautiful black lady-in-waiting makes it clear that no one could believe he existed unless they saw him for "if he belonged to our religion, we would certainly believe that our gods had made him, and that they had used all of their creative power and knowledge to produce such a masterpiece from which they left nothing out" (477).[42] Herberay does not seek to convert his characters or transform his readers: both of these key passages and the assumptions that drive them are carefully cut from the image of Esplandián that he creates for his readers.

This rewriting of the meaning attached to Esplandián's physical appearance is part of Herberay's larger project of creating for his readers, beginning with the king and extending to the courtly aristocrats who were his intended audience, a visual experience in reading the text that used romance to confirm a heraldic, genealogical identity. (These courtly, heraldic impulses were also underlined by the very elegant physical state of the Janot editions.) Within this context, any visible appearance that confirmed the power of religious conversion or that ran counter to heraldic nostalgia would be inconsistent with that goal. Herberay thus eliminates visible racial difference from the romance.

Africa thus has no part in *Le cinquiesme livre*. In Montalvo, King Armato's lands are the bulwark between the Christian and pagan nations. As we have seen, the army that Armato brings together reflects the racial, geographic, and religious diversity within these pagan lands ("a horde of barbarian kings from white and black nations," 315).[43] Many and disparate, Armato's allies are alike only in their opposition to the Christians. Herberay, by contrast, resists the implications of this mass of divergent peoples and nations (more peoples than ever since the time of the giant Nimrod [410]) and transforms it into a single, Turkish threat. The threat to the Christians is now flattened out into a single enemy, one that opposes the Christians not for racial reasons but out of religious and political difference. Armato's letter calling for aid is now sent only to the East, to the "seigneurs du levant" (93ʳ). It is not the black and white nations (imagined by Montalvo as aggregated inversions of the converting knights Calafia and Frandalo, pagan Africa and Muslim Asia) who aid Armato: it is simply an army of the princes and potentates of the East.

In keeping with these changes, Herberay eliminates the blackness of Califia and her messenger that had been so much stressed by Montalvo. The Spanish Califía is black and beautiful, the French Calife is simply beautiful (104ʳ), while the English Califie becomes both fair and beautiful.[44] Herberay likewise transports her homeland from Africa, near the earthly Paradise, to a land somewhere in Tartaria ("un pays tres opulent & fertile, qui confine à la source du fleuve Boristenes, pres le descent des montagines Riffées," 103ᵛ). In part, Herberay's changes tend to contain a politically topical warning against French alliances with the Ottoman empire. Certainly, Herberay's tendency to unite all the infidels into a single enemy goes hand in hand with his increased emphasis that this enemy poses a danger to all of Christendom, one that extends even as far as France and England (94ᵛ). Nonetheless, these political concerns are ultimately less important to Herberay than the larger but equally political goal of creating in his romance a visual culture of identity.

In sixteenth-century England, by contrast, attitudes toward conversion were in some sense the obverse to the situations in either Spain or France. These differences are reflected attitudes toward romance and the kinds of impact it was imagined to have on readers. Writers from Montalvo to Cervantes argue for the power of conversion in a manner that develops directly out of experiences with the Jewish and Moorish conversions and explusions. In England, what was at stake were intense lived conflicts of the sixteenth century over repeated changes of doctrinal practice and identity within the nascent Church of England. Recent scholarship has done much to challenge neat binarisms between Protestant and Catholic during this period. Nonetheless, English writers and readers of romance – whether Protestant activists like Philip Sidney and Edmund Spenser or more ambiguous and perhaps crypto-Catholics like John Harington and Anthony Munday – have direct personal experiences with changes in religious faith in ways that Montalvo's original readers did not necessarily. In some sense, England was a nation of converts, and the way in which Iberian romances were imported into England reflects that fact.[45]

In general, the Iberian romances offered readers a mythic plot that, as Donna Hamilton describes it, centered on "the conversion of Constantine to Christianity" and "celebrated a world in which the unity of Christendom defined, co-existed with, and was identical to Catholicism."[46] As we have seen in the resistance to Montalvo and the vexed history of attitudes toward the efficacy of conversion, the "conversion narratives" in these romances were never simple. When these romances arrived in England, Sidney, Spenser, and to some extent Mary Wroth worked to rewrite this Catholic narrative that centered on conversion into a new pan-European narrative that also imagined Christian unity for Europe but through a new and racially-inflected Holy Roman Empire of Protestants. Sidney and Spenser, in particular, rejected the Catholic narratives that they found in their sources and were able to adapt them into new generic forms to coincide with their political and theological assumptions.

As Hamilton points out, though, the translations of these romances were by contrast often associated with crypto-Catholic circles. In the translations, the unity of (Catholic) Christendom might read as an evocation of a lost past, while narratives that centered on the power of conversion might become a hoped-for path back to that past. From a crypto-Catholic perspective, that is, it is not just that the Iberian romances might allow readers to remember and re-live the past, but indeed that the act of reading might itself become a force for conversion. This possibility was one that Catholics may have hoped for; it was certainly one that Protestants feared.[47]

Here, I would like to consider this idea by looking briefly at a notable literary encounter between one of the prominent Hugenot military leaders, François de La Noue (1531–91), and the chief translator of the English editions of the *Amadis* cycle, Anthony Munday (1560–1633). Munday, who also published under the pseudonym Lazarus Pyott, was the primary source for the importation of romances into England in the sixteenth century. Although a number of influential English romance writers read and worked directly from the Herberay translations, Munday's translations were both popular and influential during this period. Having first written an original romance, entitled *Zelato* (1580), Munday then undertook translations of the first five books of the *Amadis* cycle (1590, 1595, 1598, 1618), as well as *Palmerin of England* (1595, 1602), *Palmerin d'Oliva* (1596), and the first and second books of *Primaleon of Greece* (1595, 1596).

In his preface to *Palmerin of England* (1596), Munday includes a dedication to Frances Young in which he defends romances and romance readers. This defense is notable because it responded to complaints that La Noue made in his influential *Discours politiques et militaires* (1587). Munday was clearly familiar with La Noue's work and had translated La Noue's *The Declaration of the Lord de la Noue, upon his taking armes for the just defence of the townes of Sedan and Jametz* (1589).

La Noue's *Discours* was primarily a military and political treatise, but as part of his attention to the proper training of soldiers, La Noue also critiqued what he saw as the dangers that could be caused by reading *Amadis* and other romances. His arguments contain an explicit statement of the humoral theory that underwrote sixteenth-century accounts of reading. La Noue's arguments give a clear indication of how romance as a genre became a trope for the dangers of reading as a whole. La Noue includes reading among the non-naturals that could alter the body's humoral balance and thus regards different kinds of books as food, physic, or poison. For La Noue, the *Amadis* romances, in particular, seemed to be a form of "sustenance," but one that engendered only "evil humours that distempered the soules" of those that read them.[48] Readers of *Amadis* became gluttons: "their teeth watered, so desirous were they even to taste of some small morsel" of these books. Even those who were able initially to resist reading these volumes, ultimately, "having once tasted of them, made them their continuall foode" (48). Romances had the sticky sweetness of sugar. Sugar was understood to be "subtle" because it tempered foods and preserved medicines, but in romances those same qualities became poisonous, "so subtil and penetrative, that to eschue harme thereby, we must first use very good preservatives" (48). Romances are, for La Noue, "bad drugs" (53) that inject themselves into the minds and onto the bodies of readers: "for having once redd them, they cannot afterward so cleanse themselves, but still there will remayne some spottes to staine their conversations" (52).

La Noue's damning sense that to read *Amadis* was to swallow poison was not shared by Munday. In his preface to *Palmerin of England*, Munday begins by telling a story of the illness of King Alfonsus of Naples. Sick and having tried every possible type of medicine prescribed by his doctors, the king ultimately "determined with himself to take no more medicines."[49] Telling his physicians to "feast me no more with Galene and Hippocrates" (A3ᵛ), the king instead turns to historical fictions. When he heard these stories read, "he conceived such wonderfull pleasure, as nature gathered strength by it, and chased away the frowardnesse of his disease" (A3ʳ). While in its original form, as I suggested in the Introduction, this story was primarily about the therapeutic difference between reading/seeing stories and having them read aloud/hearing them, Munday instead takes the conclusion that reading historical fictions and romances, such as his *Palmerin of England*, may change the humoral balance of those who enjoy them and they can thus become a kind of medicine: "to read Histories, which in the judgment of the wise are esteemed as healthful to the mind, as Physick is accounted holsom for the bodie" (A3ᵛ). In this preface, Munday reverses the arguments that Amyot and others made about the dangerous consequences of the strong responses that many readers had to romance. Whereas romance was often charged with inciting the passions and thus upsetting the humoral balance of readers, Munday suggests that that quality is precisely what makes romances a form of physic. Romances may surpass medicine precisely because "the sodain inwarde conceit of delight ... may sooner breake and qualifie the extremitie of a painful disease, than the long and laborsom applying of Physicall recipes" (A3ᵛ).

La Noue, more thoroughly than Sidney or Spenser perhaps, rejected romances outright and did so because he was troubled not just by their content, but by the forms of reading that these books seemed to promote. He believed that the act of reading, rather than just what was read, was likely to harm the souls and even bodies of Protestant readers. For Munday, by contrast, romances become a curative, a form of physic, able to cure diseases, both mental and physical. Munday's insistence that romances are worthwhile because they provoke passions that could transform the minds and restore the bodies of readers informs his translations of *Amadis* and other romances into English. The differing opinions of Munday and La Noue turn on more than just differing assessments of the moral and physical consequences to reading. La Noue must reject Montalvo's *Amadis* in large part because he rejects Montalvo's conversionary narrative and the transformative model of identity and reading that this narrative implies. Montalvo, as we have seen, saw identity as transformative. He embraced the idea that faith and practice, not belief, conferred identity. As a result, he adopted conversion as both a religious practice and a narrative possibility. Montalvo's commitment to faith and conversion will imply very different reading practices to Cervantes, who returns us to reading and conversion in Counter-Reformation Spain.

The century and a quarter that separates the publications of *Tirant lo Blanc* and the second part of *Don Quixote* saw almost unimaginable historical developments. Written in the aftermath of the Fall of Constantinople, the first of the Iberian romances were part of a culture that experienced increasing domestic conflict over the status of New Christians, conflict that gave way to the orders for the expulsion of the Jews in 1492. The conquest of Granada, several months earlier that year, was not the end to this kind of conflict; the 1565 *morisco* rebellion led eventually to the expulsion of the *moriscos* in 1609. This period was one of intense attention to questions about faith, identity, and genealogy. The developments that led from the expulsions of 1492 to those of 1609 coincide with an important transition in the practices of the Inquisition in Spain. Barbara Root argues that at the beginning of this period religious orthodoxy largely centered on questions of belief. Over the course of the sixteenth century, however, the Inquisition turned its attention away from proofs of belief to matters of ethnic custom and then to genealogy itself.[50] Commitment to a new "national" identity produced a situation in which "religious orthodoxy in Spain came to be defined in terms of genealogy or blood": once the "proof of faith" was "genealogy," then "orthodoxy, heresy, dissimulation were all collapsed onto the physical body, into the ethnicity that could not be changed by any action or belief."[51] Barbara Fuchs likewise comments on how this shift created a new culture in Counter-Reformation Spain. Increased emphasis on defining faith through birth and blood produced a world that demanded that identity reveal itself in some visible manner, "as though past religious or ethnic affiliations really did equal a manifest physical difference," and that became "obsessed with identifying difference through outward signs."[52]

Although this attention to visual identity may have been a largely new feature of the culture of the period, it was importantly not new to romance. The sustained emphasis on the legibility of identity that is at the heart of romances such as *Amadis* has a deep affinity with the culture that, as Fuchs puts it, had an "obsession with transparency and genealogy." It should not be surprising that this historical period, characterized by such intense cultural interest in questions of visible identity and invisible faith, is framed by the romances of conversion. The period begins with *Tirant lo Blanc* (1490) and the *Labors of Esplandián* (1510); it ends with the publication of *Don Quixote,* Parts 1 and 2 (1605, 1615). Yet, despite these affinities, the shift from genealogy to conversion that we have seen in romances such as *Amadis*, *Esplandián*, and *Tirant lo Blanc* runs directly counter to the inverse movement from faith to genealogy that dominates the larger culture of sixteenth-century Spain. It is in *Quixote* that we will see both the conclusion of this history of romances of conversion and also, perhaps more importantly, the consequences of romance's movement away from the new culture of race that defined Counter-Reformation Spain.

It should not be a surprise that the culmination of this history of responses by readers to the Iberian romances of conversion comes in Cervantes' *Don Quixote* (1605). Whatever one may say about Quixote's reading skills, Cervantes is unquestionably the great interpretive reader of romance: *Tirant lo Blanc, Amadis, The Labours of Esplandián, Amadis of Greece*, and *Orlando Furioso* fill the shelves of Quixote's library; they provide the text to his adventures. It is not just, as Cervantes proclaims in his "Prologue," that "all of it is an invective against books of chivalry."[53] Rather, the narratives of conversion that drove Martorell's and Montalvo's fictions constitute a central and largely overlooked part of Cervantes' response to chivalric romance. Insofar as Cervantes brings Quixote as a reader into the text of his fiction, his novel is both a last instance and a theorization of how readers respond to the questions about faith, genealogy, and ethnicity posed by the romances that dominated sixteenth-century Europe. As we have seen, Ariosto and Herberay recognize that narratives about conversion, which necessarily involve the introduction of racial difference, challenge romance's commitment to visible identity. Cervantes instead embraces those consequences.

Carlos Fuentes has described Quixote as "a knight of the faith" in the sense that he believes in what others cannot see; Miguel de Unamuno has likewise seen Quixote as the founder of "the Spanish religion," Quixotism.[54] I will suggest, though, that Don Quixote sees the world differently, not so much or simply as a knight of faith, but as one who is also a *converso*. To be a *converso* is in some ways always to put into question the nature of the relationship between appearance and reality. After the expulsion of the Jews and Moors from Spain, there are no longer Jews, Muslims, and Christians; there are only more or less real, more or less authentic, more or less accepted, Christians. This period in the history of conversion introduces the possibility of hidden differences, qualities and beliefs that cannot be seen.

It is out of this possibility, as we have seen, that the assimilation of Jewish *conversos* into Christianity produced racialism. More than just a recognition of the impact of *conversos* and *moriscos* on the culture of early modern Spain, this difference is also one of genre and its possibilities. Earlier romances carefully place their converts on the edges of the narrative world, but Cervantes arguably tells his whole story from this perspective, and it is ultimately this perspective that splits appearance apart from reality and that makes windmills into giants and sheep into armies. This loss of the visible truth that defined romance in turn fractures the genre itself and fundamentally changes the act of reading that it implies. This argument engages a dominant biographical reading of Cervantes but does so through the literary context provided by the conversion narratives that appear in the romances that Quixote, and with him Cervantes, had been reading.

From a biographical perspective, there has long been the argument that Cervantes was himself a New Christian. The central role that New Christians played in the remarkable literature of the period is almost impossible to overestimate. The case for Cervantes being among the New Christian writers, an argument put forward by Américo Castro, among others, has not been definitively provable but is widely accepted as likely.[55] Michael McGaha summarizes the available evidence that points to Cervantes' descent from Jewish ancestry: the Cervantes name is included in the relator Fernán Díaz de Toledo's 1449 list of families with *converso* origins;[56] his father and his family worked in professions and businesses historically dominated first by Jews and later by *conversos*; Cervantes himself was denied appointments and promotions in ways that are perhaps otherwise hard to explain.[57] There is much to be said about how Cervantes' own status as a probable *converso* inflects and structures the fiction of *Don Quixote*: such impulses appear in the pervasive sense of alienation and dispossession from everywhere except the realms of the mind, the mocking and yet anxious depictions of the officers of the Holy Brotherhood, and the dismissals of lineage and idealizing of virtue, as well as in the ambiguous reflections on the shocking contemporary expulsion of the *moriscos* in Part 2.

My discussion here, though, will focus not on Cervantes as a possible *converso* but on his imagining of Don Quixote as one. Alonso Quixano, an impoverished noble who has no claim to present himself as an Old Christian but who was "once called the Good" (935),[58] is perhaps a *converso*; the metafictional character Don Quixote is certainly one. More than just the righting of wrongs and the defense of maidens, what Quixote takes from the pages of chivalric romance is also his own idiosyncratic but powerful understanding of Montalvo's argument that true chivalry must itself be transformed into a means of religious conversion and a weapon against the infidel. This experience is one that he understands primarily through and in his acts of reading, of both texts and the world. Montalvo's *Esplandián* was in part about the religious conversion of individual pagans and infidels; perhaps almost as importantly, it made a call for the conversion, the transformation through religious faith, of the old order of Christian chivalry and, with it, of chivalric romance as a genre. It is in this spirit, as a heeding of this call, that Quixote wants to revive and convert chivalry into contemporary practice and meaning. Writing Part 1 at what turns out, by the time of the publication of Part 2, to have been the last possible moment for a romance of conversion, Cervantes offers his readers through the conversion of Quixano into Quixote the final chapter in the Spanish romances of chivalric conversion that began with *Tirant* and *Esplandián*.

Cervantes initially frames his engagement with Montalvo's arguments about conversion in the famous Inquisition of the Books in Chapter 6. In this scene, the barber, the priest, and the housekeeper undertake a public trial to examine the books in Quixote's library and determine which "deserve to be burned just as if they had belonged to heretics" (44).[59] The first set of books that the barber picks up is a collected edition of *Amadis*, Books 1–4, the format in which that romance was first published. *Amadis* is immediately identified by the priest as having been the first chivalric romance published in Spanish; as this text is the originator of all subsequent romances, he regards it as "the proponent of the doctrine of so harmful a sect" (46).[60] Unexpectedly, however, *Amadis* is not burned. Instead, it is *Esplandián*, "the legitimate son," that goes into the flames and starts the fires in which all of the other sons and grandsons of *Amadis*, the subsequent volumes in the cycle, are also burned: "let it be the beginning of the pile that will fuel the fire we shall set" (46).[61] Within Montalvo's fiction, the character Esplandián may or may not have been the legitimate son to Amadis, a question that depends on historically evolving attitudes toward the validity of clandestine marriage. Cervantes, though, emphasizes the question of descent as being at the heart of the relationship between the two books and at the heart of the judgment being rendered by the priest.

What distinguished *Esplandián* from *Amadis* is not a change in religion but rather a change in the understanding of chivalry as an expression of faith and an instrument of conversion. *Esplandián* is the more obviously Christian, the less potentially heretical, of the two volumes. Yet, the arguments that Montalvo puts forward about conversion, while in keeping with and expressing the policies of late fifteenth-century church doctrine, run counter to the assumptions and practices that emerged in the Inquisition over the course of the sixteenth century. With several limited exceptions, the Inquisition did not place secular romances on the Index of Prohibited Books.[62] Neither *Amadis* nor *Esplandián* were books that the Inquisition identified as harmful or suspect. As this episode may suggest, though, the Inquisition was in certain ways harmful to romance in the sense that it ran counter to the ideals and aspirations expressed by romances. The burning of *Esplandián* is in part a burning of the story about the possibilities of conversion that Montalvo had told and that the Inquisition had in essence ended by denying the validity of the conversions of Jews and Muslims. At the same time, though, Cervantes' insistence on the "descent" of *Esplandián* underlines how the Inquisition is, as Netanyahu argues, about who you are rather than what you believe, about searching out those of the wrong descent rather than simply those of the wrong faith. The more obviously religious *Esplandián* is burnt while the more secular *Amadis* is not. *Esplandián* is burnt as a "legitimate son" in Cervantes' sly fictional recognition that no matter how much faith one has, descent may be enough to consign one to the flames.

It is against this frame of the burning of the romances as heretics that Cervantes effects Don Quixote's transformation into a chivalric knight. A case can perhaps be made that we should understand Alonso Quixano as being of *converso* descent. Sancho repeatedly assures us that he is an Old Christian, but we have no such assurances about the man who becomes Don Quixote. His name may be Quexada (19), or Quixada (23), Quijana (42), or Quixano, the Good (935). He insists that he comes from a "known lineage, with proprietary rights to an ancestral home, and entitlement to a payment of five hundred *sueldos*" (160),[63] but Sancho's Teresa questions his nobility ("I certainly don't know who gave him a *Don*, because his parents and grandparents never had one," 488).[64] He is of a "more than moderately dark" complexion (669).[65] He mistakes and kills sheep as armies of infidels, but he recognizes pigs as pigs and will not fight, kill, or presumably eat them (128, 904). He is a member of a class that, unlike the peasant classes that comprised largely "Old Christians" like Sancho, saw high rates of intermarriage.

Despite such intimations, Cervantes nonetheless does not give us a story about a New Christian. If there is such a story here it is effaced and displaced by what Cervantes presents as the more significant conversion: that of someone who identifies himself as just an ordinary gentleman (894) into a Christian knight of chivalry. Cervantes presents the transformation that defines his fiction as a conversion (he takes a new name to reflect his new identity [23]; he cleans the rusty armor of his great-grandfathers [22]; he has himself knighted by the script of the straw purchase order book [34]). This transformation is, like Esplandián's, imagined as a conversion of the practice and identity of chivalry itself, for "in him errant chivalry would be reborn" (55).[66] Quixote accepts chivalry as both a religion and an act of faith; contravening it becomes for him a heresy (508, 428).

Just as Don Quixote is converted by his faith in the truth of romance, so *Don Quixote* as a text is subject to a similar conversion. At the start, Cervantes makes it clear that this text is not his, or ours: he is only the "stepfather," and we are neither "his kin nor his friend" (3).[67] Whereas other writers disingenuously dismiss their creations as illegitimate offspring, Cervantes insists that neither he nor we are related to his text: this book is descended from another race and lineage. Cervantes here introduces the language of baptism as a way to suggest that one can create new and generically specific identities for one's literary progeny: the narrator's friend thus suggests that he might write his own laudatory sonnets, for "then you can baptize them with any name you want, attributing them to Prester John of the Indies or to the Emperor of Trebizond" (5).[68]

The text that we are reading becomes itself a kind of recently converted New Christian through Cervantes' typically allusive account of Cid Hamete and the *morisco* translator. Beginning in Chapter 9, Cervantes presents his text as a translation of an Arabic history that he found among some notebooks and old papers that a boy was selling to a silk merchant (67). Cervantes imagines for us a series of transformations: from one language and one religion to another, from Arab historian to *morisco* translator to Spanish fiction writer. At the same time, though, other possible conversions shadow this act of transformation and translation. The Alcaná market was in the old Jewish quarter of Toledo. Before the riots, massacres, and forced conversions of 1391, and, again, 1412–18, this was the heart of perhaps the largest and most vibrant Jewish community in late medieval Europe. Even earlier, during the *convivencia*, Toledo was home to the most renowned school of translators in the world, a school that was distinguished in relying on precisely the model of oral, collaborative translation (written Arabic was verbally translated into the romance vernacular by a Moor, while a second translator, either Jewish or Christian usually, would then retranslate that verbal text, again aloud, so that it could be transcribed back into Latin) that Cervantes depicts being effected by Cid Hamete, the *morisco* translator, and himself as a transcriber into Spanish. Under the Christian Alsonfo VI, Toledo became the repository that housed many of the books dispersed from the renowned Arabic libraries of Cordoba.[69] By 1605, the Jews and the Moors are long gone. They have been converted, as have their places of work and worship.

Cervantes, though, remembers the history of these earlier conversions and integrates them into his fiction. When he comments that it would not have been hard to find a translator not just of Arabic but of "an older and better language" (67), he suggests that everything in this place, and in this text, has a whole history of conversions behind it: behind every *morisco* is a Moor, behind every Christian perhaps a Jew.[70] When Cervantes, as the narrator, finds a *morisco* to translate, he goes with him to the "cloister of the main church, and ask[s] him to render the journals, all those that dealt with Don Quixote into the Castilian language, without taking away or adding anything" (67–68).[71] It is appropriately but also ironically in and through the church, itself likely a converted synagogue and a polychronic image of the history of conversions that defined seventeenth-century Spain, that Cervantes imagines this Arabic history becoming a Christian fiction.

Cervantes mocks, in the ways that readers of *Quixote* immediately recognize, the consequences of too great a commitment to the truth of the chivalric histories, consequences that are expressed in the madness of reading. Importantly, though, he also plays out the implications of the turn toward conversion that dominated the works of Montalvo, Martorell, de Silva, and other fifteenth- and sixteenth-century romance writers. There are two key implications to the introduction of conversion into these romances: in a theological register, conversion produced a controversial distinction between race and faith; as a literary consequence, this distinction created a divide between appearance and reality. Both of these carry over into Cervantes' imagining of *Quixote*. In the first case, we have seen that Montalvo, for instance, imagined Esplandián as a figure for how faith could create new and universal Christian identities that would, in a social sense, transcend the fact of birth and, in a literary one, rewrite the genealogical narratives of traditional chivalric romance.

Cervantes uses Sancho and Quixote to resituate this debate, these ideals and their limitations, within the social and political realities of Counter-Reformation Spain. Sancho, for instance, offers us a comic version of the bitter truth that, by 1605, many political and religious offices were only open to those who could document the purity of their blood. In arguing that he should be given his governorship, Sancho declares, "I am an Old Christian, and that alone is enough for me to be a count" (161),[72] as if to suppose that one form of blood purity (Old Christian) might create all others (membership in the nobility). He takes this claim even further later: "though I am poor, I'm an Old Christian ... and because I'm a man I could be a pope" (411).[73] Even as Sancho is confident that being an Old Christian is enough to underwrite even the wildest of his ambitions, Don Quixote worries, "I do not know how it can be discovered that I am of royal lineage, or, at the least, a second cousin to the emperor" (160).[74]

Quixote's imagination seems boundless and unchecked, but, importantly, it does not extend to conceiving a different lineage for himself. The fact of his birth is perhaps the one immutable thing for Quixote. Nonetheless, Quixote does not assume that your identity, your ability to become who and what you want, is limited by your birth. In supposing that you can become what you imagine (even a chivalric knight), Quixote takes seriously Montalvo's argument that faith is enough to transcend race and birth. Faith is powerful enough to convert identity. It is clearly an act of faith that drives Quixote's confidence that he is a chivalric knight. When his neighbor Pedro Alonso insists that he is only "an honorable gentleman, Señor Quijana," Don Quixote explains, "I know who I am and I know I can be not only those I have mentioned but the Twelve Peers of France as well, and even all the nine paragons of France" (43).[75]

Quixote's sense that belief transcends birth to transform identity is so powerful that it extends even to others. In his own case, he suspects that it is only his identity, not his bloodline, that can be converted by his faith in chivalry. With Dulcinea, though, he argues that his belief in her creates her virtue; her worth in turn produces her lineage. The travellor Vivaldi, whom Quixote meets in Chapter 13 and who identifies himself as being of the line of "the Cachopines of Laredo" (91), thus hears Quixote's description of Dulcinea and wants to know Dulcinea's "lineage, ancestry, and family" (91).[76] In Part 2, the Duchess returns to this question. Sancho's description of Dulcinea sifting wheat, she says, makes her question Dulcinea's nobility: "apparently, it was buckwheat, which makes me doubt the nobility of her lineage" (673).[77] Quixote, however, resists such jests as unworthy of Dulcinea. He rejects these and other denigrations of Dulcinea's true nobility and good descent as they are created and confirmed by his belief: "It is enough for me to think and believe ... I imagine that everything I say is true, no more and no less, and I depict her in my imagination as I wish her to be in beauty and in distinction" (201).[78] Whatever he says elsewhere about his ability to create Dulcinea's nobility through his imagination, here he concludes, "as for her lineage, it matters little, for no one is going to investigate it in order to give her a robe of office" (201).[79] In this moment, Quixote suggests that his know-ledge of Dulcinea's true identity would not persuade the officers of the Holy Brotherhood. Faith alone is not enough to satisfy the Inquisition.

From a literary perspective, introducing conversion into romance pro-duces a fracture between appearance and reality. Conversion implies the possibility of imposture, of forms or practices of faith that are only appearance, acts of dissimulation that conceal an inner, unchanged infi-delity. Forced conversion suggests faked faith. It is out of these possibil-ities that one sees anxieties about authenticity. As Fuchs demonstrates, a culture that is committed to making identity "transparent and classifi-able" perhaps inevitably also becomes a culture defined by various acts of hiding, obscuring, or dissimulating identity, a situation that defined not just Spain but much of early modern Europe.

Fraudulent faith was a destabilizing possibility, but the kind of true conversion that changes identity may have been even more dangerous. This possibility is at the heart of *Quixote*, and one that Quixote asks the world to imagine with him. The key shift that Cervantes enacts in this respect is to put Quixote and his conversionary perspective at the cen-ter of his narrative, rather than at the margins, as had been the case in Montalvo and Martorell. As a reader, one may begin with the question of what Quixote looks like to the world, but ultimately the more important question one arrives at is how the world looks to Quixote. It is, I would suggest, a consequence of looking not at Quixote but with and through his eyes that we find a fracturing of appearance from reality that is about the ability to convert the world (not just windmills into giants but skep-tics into participants and in their way believers) to one's point of view.

The way in which Quixote is a *converso* can perhaps best be under-stood by thinking about how his conversion to a Christian knight has changed the way he reads. In the most fundamental way, one could say that Quixote no longer reads chivalric romances but rather reads the world as a chivalric romance. It is for this reason that, with the exception of the moment in the print shop in which he looks at a copy of the spuri-ous continuation to *Quixote*, we never see him actually reading a book

(874). Yet, the shift is not just between the texts and the world, the taking or mistaking of the world for a text. The shift in what Cervantes' knight reads is itself predicated on a more fundamental shift in *how* he reads.

Cervantes' protagonist follows two distinct forms of reading, before and after his conversion, that reflect contemporary understanding of the ways in which reading was imagined to be defined by and to differ across religious faiths. The gentleman who may have been called Alonso Quixano, "once called the Good," the reader of romances, reads like a Jew; Don Quixote, the reader of the world as a romance, reads like a Christian.[80] This distinction is one that emerges out of several hundred years of anti-Jewish polemic. From the late medieval period, Jews were repeatedly condemned by such Christian theologians as Peter Abelard, Peter the Venerable, and the *converso* Petrus Alfonsí for being literalistic readers. As Geraldine Heng notes, "Christian polemists from the twelfth century on increasingly accumulated arguments … depicting Jewish rejection of the Incarnation as evidence of a literality – an incapacity of allegorical and figurative thinking." Heng concludes that Jews were understood as "a race," at least from the Christian perspective, that was "incapable of grasping allegory"; their literal-minded methods of reading became a "defining difference from Christians who [were] expert exegetical readers and manipulators of biblical allegory."[81] It was thus this quality that made it impossible for Jews, as readers, to recognize and understand the true implications of the relationship between the Old and New Testaments. Christians, by contrast, saw themselves as distinctive in having the ability to read allegorically to arrive at spiritual truth. It was this metaphorical, spiritual mode of reading that allowed Christians to recognize, for instance, St. John the Baptist as a theological type, a worldly figuration of the more fundamental spiritual truth that inhered in Jesus and the baptism that went beyond water. In making this argument about the religious quality to Quixote's reading, I do not intend to point to some coded religious subtext to Cervantes' narrative. I am interested here not in making the claim that Cervantes may have imposed a religious meaning, an encoded allegorical subtext, into his fiction, but rather in understanding how and why Quixote imposes one onto his world.[82]

As a reader of romances, Alonso Quixano understands the text of romance in strictly literal terms in ways that align with arguments that theologians such as Peter the Venerable made about Jews. He "spent sleepless nights trying to understand them and extract their meaning, which Aristotle himself, if he came back to life for only that purpose, would not have been able to decipher or understand" (20).[83] He is certain that everything set out in these texts must be true. From this perspective, Amadis was historically and necessarily real; any questions that arise (Should knights carry shirts and money? Can Quixote come to Sancho's assistance when he is fighting other peasants? What does Amadis look like?) can and must be answered by the text. Within the frame of *Don Quixote* itself, though, the transformed Quixote reads the world through the perspective of the convert. Partly, this derives from the way that he reads the world as a text, of course, but the world is a text that can only be understood allegorically. In keeping with the sense that he has converted to the faith of the chivalric romance, Quixote reads the world with all the complex allegorical skill that might be demanded in the most complex of Christian hermeneutics. The sheep are armies, the windmills are Moorish giants, and everything else can be explained as the work of enchanters.

Quixote's famous battle with the armies of sheep provides a particularly good instance of how central the romances of conversion are to Quixote's experience and understanding of the genre. This episode also suggests how Quixote's manner of "reading" allegorically may be that of a Christian knight but it is notably and definitively not that of a Christian reader. In this episode, two flocks of sheep converge and, out of the dust on the plain, Quixote sees a great battle that he describes to Sancho. Because Quixote is at first only an observer, this episode provides probably the fullest account of how Quixote reads the world as a text.[84] Here, the source texts that Quixote draws on are centrally concerned with both conversion and ethnic identity. We have seen how Nicolas de Herberay responded to Montalvo and his romance of conversion by taking race out of his translation, re-imagining the ethnic and geographic identity of the black Calafia. Quixote reads the romance he sees on the plain as a conversion story but, where Herberay removes ethnicity, Quixote instead comically imposes race and geographic difference onto the decidedly domestic scene of the ewes and the rams.

The centrality of conversion to the battle of the sheep can be seen from the start. The story that Quixote tells Sancho initially follows the model of "constance romances," the popular medieval romances about Christian women unwillingly married to infidels who, through faith, were able to convert their husbands and their realms to Christianity.[85] Quixote explains to Sancho that the battle they are witnessing must be between the Emperor Alifanfarón and Pentapolín, the King of Garamantes: "They hate each other because this Alifanfarón, a fierce pagan, is in love with Pentapolín's daughter, an exceedingly beauteous and charming lady, and a Christian, whose father does not wish to give her to the pagan king, unless he first renounces the law of his false prophet Mohammed and turns to her faith" (126–27).[86]

Once Quixote and Sancho move off to the side to review the action more clearly, Quixote draws inspiration from different romance sources, but conversion and ethnicity are again central. He now provides a more detailed description of the combatants on both sides, this time emerging from the great epic battles of the Renaissance romances. As the ewes and rams move forward, they become in Quixote's eyes a parade of troops, an army of "innumerable and diverse peoples" (126):[87]

This host facing us is made up and composed of people from diverse nations: here are those who drink the sweet waters of the famous Xanthus; the mountain folk who tread the Massilian plain; those who sift fine gold nuggets in Arabia Felix; those who enjoy the famous cool shores of the crystalline Thermadon; those who drain by many diverse means the golden Pactolus; and Numidians, untrustworthy in their promises; Persians, those noble archers; Parthians and Medes, who fight as they flee; Arabians, with movable houses; Scythians, as cruel as they are white-skinned; Ethiopians, with pierced lips; and an infinite number of other nations, whose faces I recognize and see, although I do not recall their names. (128)

This passage, with its evocations of Renaissance ethnography, is Quixote's rewriting of the parade of troops that is a prelude to the battles of Virgil, Boiardo, Montalvo, and Ariosto.

As David Quint suggests, Virgil in the *Aeneid* uses this survey of the forces at Actium to characterize the western armies as "ethnically homogeneous, disciplined, and united; the forces of the East … [as] a loose aggregate of nationalities, prone to internal discord and fragmentation."[88] In the Renaissance romances that rewrite this scene from the *Aeneid*, the parade of troops becomes a visual image of what faith fights against. Writers like Boiardo ("Now all the men of Africa / Are stretched around Biserta's walls, / Varied in language, strange of face, / So different in their clothes and arms / That one can sooner count the stars," 2.22.28) create for their readers a panorama that puts the singularity of Christian monotheism against the multiplicity of the infidel (multiple gods, many lands and languages, diverse and disunited peoples). In Montalvo, this moment provides a visual image of what faith must convert: the armies are in their geographical and ethnic and religious diversity precisely what will be transformed by the one true faith of Christianity. Whereas Esplandián's faith converts armies into Christians, Quixote's converts sheep into armies.

Quixote's imaginative transformation of sheep into armies involves changing the domestic and daily into the foreign and exotic, remaking the world as a fiction. In this sense, it is quite clear how and why Quixote experiences the flocks of ewes and rams as an encounter with the "battles, enchantments, feats, follies, loves and challenges" of his books (126).[89] Yet, at the same time, it may be worth approaching the sheep not as "real" sheep but, in keeping with the logic of Quixote's impulses, as more of a text about sheep since that is how Quixote experiences them. Within Christian allegory, sheep are quintessentially the flocks of the faithful, the unity of Christendom. Where others would see such a flock as an image of Christian identity, and even a short-hand for a certain mode of allegoresis, Quixote instead sees Scythians, Ethiopians, and Parthians. Where Herberay took out race and flattened out geography, Quixote re-imposes it onto his world.

It may not be simply that Quixote has in one respect mistaken reality and in another misconstrued the proper terms and iconography of Christian hermeneutics. Taken from a more cynical perspective, Quixote's ability to see to pagan and infidel armies of Scythians, Persians, Numidians, and Ethiopians where others see only variously hued sheep conforms bitterly and ironically to the practice and culture of visible identity that defined Counter-Reformation Spain. For the Inquisitors, the flock of the faithful could never be identified simply by outer appearances. Those who looked more carefully, as the series of edicts that the Inquisition issued over the course of the sixteenth century encouraged good Christians to do, would discern in precisely the most domestic and daily of situations a whole world of racial and ethnic differences, people "varied of language" and "strange of face" whose faith was as suspect as their birth and who might, indeed, on closer examination turn out to be infidels and pagans. As a converted reader of the world, Quixote sees levels of meaning that others miss, but ironically he does so in a way that conforms to the skepticism, the lack of belief or of belief in belief, that increasingly characterized church policy in late sixteenth-century Spain.

Quixote does not simply see the world differently: it is not just that he sees giants where we see windmills. When a traveler demands to see Dulcinea before he will agree to swear that she is the most beautiful of maidens, Quixote responds with a classic, and almost Pauline, call to faith as a demand to believe in that which cannot be seen: "If I were to show her to you," Quixote responds, "where would the virtue be in your confessing so obvious a truth? The significance lies in not seeing her and believing, confessing, affirming, swearing, and defending that truth" (39).[90] As Quixote's answer suggests, he believes not just what we cannot see, but he also believes even when he cannot see. It is thus important to recognize that Don Quixote does not, perhaps, see everything that he says he sees and not just in the Cave of Montesino. In Part 2, for instance, when Quixote is welcomed by the Duke and Duchess, he recognizes and believes that for the first time he has become a true, rather than a fantastic, knight (658). It is not precisely that Quixote has been lying, or even lying to himself. Rather, Quixote's whole model of reading the world is predicated upon and made powerful by the act of faith that his reading demands. Belief is only belief when it is not immediately or easily confirmable by daily reality.

In the episode with the sheep, Quixote had initially responded to Sancho's assertion that the armies are not armies but sheep by insisting, "It is your fear that keeps you from seeing or hearing properly" (129).[91] Afterwards, though, Quixote, bleeding on the ground, seems to recognize that is not just a failure of belief on Sancho's part. He assures Sancho, "If you do not believe me, by my life, you can do something, Sancho, to be undeceived and see the truth of what I am telling you: mount your donkey and follow them, with some cunning, and you will see how, when they have moved a certain distance away, they resume their original form and are no longer sheep but real, complete men, just as I first described them to you" (131). Yet, even as he makes this suggestion, Quixote almost immediately dissuades Sancho from pursuing the army of sheep. In this moment, it is not that Quixote suspects that the sheep will still be sheep, regardless of how far or how cunningly Sancho pursues them. Because Quixote has chosen to believe that they will (soon, again) be armies, he must also take the perspective that seeing them as such would render acts of belief and faith pointless. That is, not seeing becomes for Quixote a confirmation of the theoretical assumptions that underwrite the faith that defines his manner of reading the world.

In Ariosto, Herberay, and Munday, the introduction of faith as a form of identity into romance also bought with it articulations of racialism. In *Quixote*, faith fractures the model of visible identity that had defined chivalric romance and that had made romance such a powerful model for practices of social identity. As a reader of romance, Don Quixote provides a conclusion to the story that began with the romances that initially followed the Fall of Constantinople and does so in ways that are primarily about romance as a genre. I have here been tracing out a history of readers' responses to the way in which, after the Fall of Constantinople, narratives of conversion changed the kinds of social identity upon which romance depended. In this discussion, I have tacitly been treating Quixote as a "reader" of romances. Of course, Quixote is a reader only in the sense that

Cervantes has imagined him to be one, and it is through Quixote that Cervantes is theorizing the kinds of responses that earlier readers, writers, and translators made more directly in their fictions and adaptations. I conclude this discussion by turning attention more fully to Cervantes himself as a reader of these romances of conversion. In Quixote, we see the end in a generic sense of the romances of conversion. In Cervantes himself, I would suggest that we see what in a historic sense may be the last of the responses to Montalvo.

Quixote's "conversion" into a knight of faith is always at once funny and sad, playful and moving. It is a transformation for which Quixote may in his body suffer much, but in the end it is one that Cervantes retracts precisely so that no reader of *Quixote* need worry about the fate of his soul (935–40). The question of how what is a fiction for Quixote is a truth for Cervantes is a complex one, but the Captive's Tale that forms the end of Part 1 offers us what may well be the closest approach to Cervantes' own understanding of the intertwining of faith, identity, and romance.

As María Antonia Garcés, among others, has pointed out, the Captive's Tale is deeply autobiographical. It was probably written before, or at least independent of, the rest of the novel; it emerges out of Cervantes' horrific experiences being held captive in Algiers for five years.[92] Leaving private service in Milan, Cervantes enlisted as a soldier in the *tercio* of Don Miguel de Mancada. In September of 1571, he was on board the Marquesa galley, departing the port of Messina, with the international fleet assembled to take on the Turkish armada. Two months later, Cervantes was wounded in the Battle of Lepanto. With chest wounds and his left hand shattered by gunshot, he recuperated in a hospital in Messina for several months before returning to service, this time in the *tercio* of Don Lope de Figueroa. As a soldier, stationed variously in Sardinia and Genoa over the next several years, Cervantes participated in the failed attack on Navarino and saw the capture, in 1572, and subsequent loss, in 1574, of the North African fortress, La Goleta. It was in September of 1575, discharged from military service and carrying letters of recommendation, that Cervantes left Naples to return home to Spain. Off the coast of Marseilles, the vessel in which he was sailing was captured by corsairs and he and his brother Rodrigo became captives in Algiers. Rodrigo was ransomed three years later, but it was not until 1580, after several remarkable and failed escape attempts, that Cervantes was finally ransomed through the efforts of the Trinitarians; he returned to Valencia in October, more than five years after he had embarked from Naples.

Although this harrowing interlude has been much discussed, here I would call attention to the fact that in transforming personal experience into fiction, the key element that does not come fairly directly out of his own experiences is the conversion story centering on Zoraida. The Captive's Tale brings together Cervantes' experiences and understanding of war and captivity. Through Ruy Pérez de Viedma, we get accounts of the Battle at Lepanto (337), the fall of the fortress at Goleta (339), encounters with Hasan Pasha, the *beylerbey* of Algiers (343), and most importantly, through this retelling, the imagining of a successful escape that would overwrite the many unsuccessful attempts that Cervantes undertook during his years in captivity (345–68).

In this story, though, it is Zoraida rather than the captive Ruy Pérez de Viedma who becomes Cervantes' fictional alter ego. As Garcés points out, Zoraida is first introduced into the story immediately after the most directly autobiographical moment in the narrative, when the captive tells his audience about "a Spanish soldier named something de Saavedra, who did things that will be remembered by those people for many years, and all to gain his liberty" (344).[93] The captive assures his audience that his story, had he time to tell it, would amaze them more than anything he could tell of his own history (344). Zoraida's story thus literally takes the place of the tale that might have been told of Cervantes: the story of Cervantes is not told so that Zoraida's story can be introduced.

Zoraida's story is in many respects the unfulfilled desire, the movement of hope, that structures the final portion of Part 1 of *Quixote*. Like other former captives, Cervantes on returning to Spain needed to document his faith by providing testimonials that he had never wavered in his religious beliefs. Yet, Cervantes in this story is more interested in Zoraida's change of faith than in Ruy Pérez' unwavering belief. The captive's situation follows Cervantes' own experiences of the war and of captivity, but only if you focus on the danger of apostasy rather than on the larger life of being a *converso* in a world that increasingly saw religious transformation as only a threat. Zoraida's tale, as opposed to the captive's, is a conversion narrative and it is, I would suggest, this feature that draws Cervantes' attention.

To understand what Cervantes does with Zoraida and the Captive's Tale, we need to go back to the story of Dorothea since it is her role as the Princess Micomicón that frames Zoraida's appearance in the novel. Dorothea had been living her own real-life romance, one that literally began in and was pursued through the pages of *Amadís de Gaula*. After being found by the priest and the barber in the Sierra Morena, Dorothea removes her boy's disguise. She then enters into Quixote's imaginary romance by assuming the identity of the Princess Micomicón, queen of the kingdom of Micomicón in Ethiopia (244), a fiction she helps invent as a strategy for getting Quixote to return home. A character whose beauty is defined by her remarkable whiteness (her feet were "like two pieces of white crystal" and all who saw them were "stunned by the beauty and whiteness of those feet" and her legs, as she washes them in the stream, "beyond all doubt seemed like alabaster," 228[94]) thus becomes an Ethiopian princess. In the romances that both Quixote and Dorothea have read, the most important of the white Ethiopian princesses is Tasso's Clorinda. As we have seen, Tasso's story of Clorinda ends in a way that suggests that certain people, or certain races and kinds of people, are excluded from the possibilities of conversion. Some version of Tasso's response to Montalvo is in Cervantes' mind when he creates Dorothea as a white Ethiopian princess who is not real and who does not convert as a prelude to Zoraida, a light-skinned Muslim, who does. In some ways Cervantes says that what Tasso gave us is only a fiction, whereas this perhaps most idealized moment of his work is the one he wants to be most true.

Dorothea is Cervantes' white Ethiopian princess. Like Clorinda's, her story is not a conversion narrative.[95] Cervantes uses what does not happen to Dorothea to promise us what will happen to Zoraida. In the final chapters, Zoraida is closely linked to Dorothea. They are both first described and identified by the fairness of their skin. We first see Dorothea as she is washing her crystal-white feet; we are introduced to Zoraida when the captive describes how he and his companions see "an extremely white hand" (345)[96] emerge out of the windows overlooking their prison. But physical appearance is, in the world of *Quixote*, no longer equivalent with or fully revealing of identity in the ways that it had been in Montalvo. The sense that outer appearance is at most only a single part of one's identity is here tacitly suggested by the fact that the fairness of Dorothea and Zoraida does not provide a mark of recognition. Those who see them do not really see them, do not recognize who and what they are; they see not a whole identity but only a single body part (hand, leg, foot), and, having done so, misidentify not just who but what kind of person they are seeing.

The fairness of Dorothea and Zoraida does not, as it would in the world of *Amadis*, produce a moment of recognition but rather perpetuates or creates misrecognition. The barber, the priest, and Cardenino marvel at Dorothea's white feet and legs but nonetheless continue to believe that she is a peasant and a boy; the captive and his companions, seeing in the window opening only the whiteness of a braceleted hand, mistakenly imagine that this must be a renegade Christian.

Dorothea and Zoraida are alike in their fair appearance, but that shared physical appearance is set off by the differences in their blood and race. The question of whether it is blood or appearance that constitutes identity is at the heart of their experiences. The romances in which Dorothea and Zoraida find themselves initially turn on questions of blood and birth. As Dorothea explains to the priest and the barber, she comes from a family of simple people "with no mixture of any objectionable races, what are called the Oldest of the Old Christians" (230).[97] Yet, as an almost necessary corollary, Dorothea's Old Christian bloodline also means that she is not of noble stock, and her situation is thus a consequence of her birth and that of her parents (230). Zoraida, who has of course not yet been baptized, will be the newest of the New Christians. When Dorothea asks whether Zoraida is a Christian or Moor, Ruy Pérez thus must admit that she is a Moor "in body" but asserts that "in her soul she is a devout Christian because she has a very strong desire to be one" (327).[98]

In Dorothea and Zoraida, we see the two often incompatible understandings of the meaning of blood in Counter-Reformation Spain. In both cases, though, Cervantes stresses how stratifications of blood define identity. Cervantes uses the familiar domestic case of blood and genealogy that we see in Dorothea to introduce Zoraida's more fundamental racial difference. In Dorothea's case, what initially seems to be a question that turns on blood as birth and rank becomes one that can only be resolved through an appeal to blood as religious identity. Indeed, the narrative tacitly aligns Don Fernando with Quixote and suggests that, under the terms established by the Inquisition, Dorothea's bloodline is almost certainly theologically purer, if not more noble, than Don Fernando's. At the inn, Dorothea confronts Don Fernando and insists that he cannot have Luscinda because she is already married to Cardenio and because Don Fernando in turn is married to herself (315–19). In her impassioned appeal, Dorothea implores him to live up to her blood, if not to his: she insists that if he is as much a Christian as he is a gentleman, then he must recognize that they are already married (317). Just as Dorothea's faith – and her appeal to Don Fernando – transforms his desire and requires him to live up to the nobility of his own "illustrious blood" (319),[99] so in Zoraida's case we must believe that her faith is enough to transform her into a Christian and thus make her a wife for Ruy Pérez.

At the end of Part 1, Quixote's fictional and fictive conversion as a knight is most fully achieved in Zoraida's real conversion. Because Quixote's faith sustains and enables the fictions of belief that occur wherever he is, he indirectly makes such conversions possible. The intertwined stories of Luscinda, Dorothea, and Zoraida, all of whom enter the pages of *Quixote* like romance heroines, largely displace the comic chivalric romance of Don Quixote from the point at which Quixote and Sancho first find Cardenio's notebook in Chapter 23 until Don Fernando helps the barber and priest contrive the cage that takes Quixote back home in Chapter 47. These narratives of faith, blood, and romance in Part 1 end in optimism. Although we do not witness the baptism of Zoraida and her final transformation into the Christian María, the narrative leaves us confident that Don Fernando's brother will "act as godfather" at the baptism; we feel assured that faith will and has created new identities in each of these inset and interlaced romances (369). When Quixote and his companions part ways with Don Fernando and the other lovers, he offers us the narrative's promise that he will write to the priest to tell him how their stories have turned out and implies that those endings will be happy ones (407).

By the time that Part 2 of *Quixote* was published in 1615, the historic situation is different. The 1609 expulsions of the *moriscos* fundamentally changed life in Spain. In the case of *Don Quixote*, they also changed fiction and, in particular, symbolically put an end to the kind of romance that Zoraida represents. In some way, Cervantes' Zoraida and her story have been expelled from the boundaries of the literary imagination just as much as real *moriscos* had been expelled from the actual lands of Spain. It is no longer possible to write a story that imagines that faith – whether the kind that Quixote, Zoraida, or even Cervantes, who was deeply committed to proselytizing while in the bañios of Algiers, expresses – can change identity by creating Christians through acts of faith rather than through facts of birth when the state said otherwise. Indeed, the events of 1609 rewrite the conversion of Don Quixote to the faith of chivalry as much as they do that of Zoraida to that of Christianity. What we see in *Don Quixote*, Part 2, is that 1605 turned out to be nearly the last possible historic moment at which to write a romance of conversion; thus, a set of responses and rewritings of Montalvo that begins with de Silva, Amyot, and Herberay ends with Cervantes.

In Part 2 the story of Zoraida is replaced by that of Sancho's neighbor Ricote and his daughter Ana Félix, the exiled *moriscos*. In this story, Sancho and Quixote first meet Ricote, a *morisco* shopkeeper who was once

Sancho's neighbor, now disguised and traveling with a group of German pilgrims. Recognizing his old neighbor, Sancho immediately exclaims, "tell me, who turned you into a foreigner" (811).[100] Of course, the answer to Sancho's query is the king, with his proclamation "that threatened the unfortunate members of my race so severely" (811).[101] Ricote, we learn, left Spain for first France, Italy, and finally Germany to find a place where his family could live and remain Christian (813). He has returned to find his wife and daughter, as well as the money that he told his daughter to have buried outside their village (814). His daughter, who had left for Barbary with her uncles, also returns to Spain in disguise. Quixote and Sancho encounter Ana Félix, dressed as corsair, in Barcelona: having assumed man's clothing and captained a brigantine out of Algiers as part of a complicated attempt to rescue her Christian lover, she is captured and sentenced to be executed because of her role in the death of two soldiers. It is at this moment of reckoning that she reveals that she is not a Moor, Turk, or renegade, but a Christian woman (878).

Ana Félix should be a second- or third-generation Zoraida, but in the new historic context of Part 2, she cannot be. We must instead imagine her as a kind of story about what happened to Zoraida after she converted, after conversion turned out not to be the resolution that it had seemed to be even in 1605. Born in Spain and raised in Christianity, Ana Félix is by faith a true Christian, but she is nonetheless of "that nation," the *moriscos* (879). Like Zoraida, she seems to have inherited her faith in and through her mother: "I drank in the Catholic faith with my mother's milk" (880).[102] Ana Félix is pardoned for the crimes that she did not commit when her true identity and situation are made known. Still, what the narrative recognizes but many of the characters evade is that while the identity she reveals may exonerate her from the accusations at hand, in other respects that identity is itself enough to indict her.

As a *morisca*, Ana Félix's fate provides a kind of conclusion to Zoraida's tale. Zoraida's tale had ended with a future of promised baptism – an event that stood as a testimony to the notion that faith can indeed, as Quixote promised and Cervantes hoped, create identity. With Ricote's daughter, though, the ending is more ambiguous. Although Don Antonio Moreno is able to convince the viceroy not to execute Ana Félix, it is not at all clear that he will be able to save her, or her father, from the more inexorable sentence of the king's edict. The renegade, who had helped Ana Félix in her escape, returns to Algiers and is able to achieve a remarkable rescue of Don Gaspar Gregorio (891).

The edict against *moriscos*, however, means that the reunion of the young lovers in Barcelona does not end their story. Whatever that ending will be, it is not one we can know. The viceroy and Don Antonio both believe that there is no reason why "so Christian a daughter and, apparently, so well-intentioned a father" should not be able to remain in Spain (891);[103] Don Antonio thus offers to go to court to try to negotiate on their behalf. While Don Antonio seems optimistic that special dispensations might be achieved, no certainty is possible and the narrative, necessarily unfinished, does not really hold out hope for those possibilities. More importantly, Ricote himself seems to suggest that the king was right to expel them. Ricote thus insists that, however terrible it is to his people who weep for Spain, it was "divine inspiration that moved his Majesty to put into effect so noble a resolution" (813); "a heroic decision by the great Felipe III" (892). Ricote also expresses skepticism as to whether Don Antonio's efforts will be effective and insists that "one must not place hope in favors or gifts" (891).

Cervantes' own opinions are necessarilty difficult to discern. Richard Hitchcock has documented how Ricote's arguments supporting the expulsion of *moriscos* align with those in a large number of texts, religious polemics as well as histories, in the period 1610–15.[104] Throughout Ricote's extended commentaries on the expulsions, the narrative as a whole seems to take the perspective of Ricote rather than that of Don Antonio. It is telling that Cervantes here speaks in the voice of the convert, if only to suggest the implications of his narrative, and not to reveal his political opinions.

I have suggested that in Part 1 the two converts, one literary, the other religious, create the perspectives that best define Cervantes' aspirations in this novel. In their different ways, Quixote and Zoraida exemplify the kind of belief that drives the fiction of Part 1. In Part 2, Cervantes uses Ricote to again ask us to take the perspective of the convert. Insofar as Ricote repeats, in the ways that Hitchcock demonstrates, the claims of contemporary Dominican polemic against *moriscos*, we do not hear anything like a revisionist history.

Cervantes' attitude toward the *moriscos* may ultimately be less important here than his attitude toward belief. In Ricote, Cervantes now gives us a character who encourages us to disbelief, to blood over faith. Ricote is a character who ultimately lacks faith. He may or may not be a good Christian. He himself does not seem to know or be certain: "I know for a fact that my daugher, Ricota, and my wife, Francisca Ricota, are true Catholic Christians, and though I am less of one, I'm still more Christian than Moor" (814).[105] Regardless of what Ricote thinks about God, though, he has no faith in the sense, so crucial to *Quixote*, that he does not and cannot believe the impossible. He insists that they must not hope for gifts and favors because the authorities believe, in ways that he does not entirely dismiss, that "the entire body of our nation is contaminated and rotten .... none of our people can stay behind or be concealed, like a hidden root that in times to come will send out shoots and bear poisonous fruits in Spain, which is clean now, and rid of the fears caused by our numbers" (891–92).[106] He knows, as Quixote refuses to know, that the identity of blood has now overcome that of faith. This conclusion does not mean the end of *Quixote* but it is part of the narrative process that inevitably leads to Quixote's recantation at the end of Part 2.

CHAPTER 4

Pamphilia's black humor: reading and racial melancholy in the Urania

Lady Mary Wroth's remarkable two-part romance, the printed *The Countesse of Mountgomerie's Urania* (1621) and its manuscript sequel, *The Secound Part of the Countess of Montgomerys Urania*, provides a key endpoint to this story about how the practice of reading and the history of racial identity developed within printed romances of the sixteenth and seventeenth centuries. Discussions of race and Lady Mary Wroth understandably often begin with Wroth's performance in Ben Jonson's "Masque of Blackness" at Whitehall in January, 1605, where she, Queen Anne, and ten other ladies of the court played the roles of the daughters of Niger in a controversial and much commented-upon performance. Kim Hall thus sees Wroth as "deeply implicated" in the production of a "persistent presence of a discourse of blackness in James' court" and frames her discussion of the *Urania* through the perspective of Wroth's role in Jonson's masque.[1] Critical attention to the implications of Wroth and the Queen's other ladies performing with "black faces and hands ... painted and bare up to the elbows" are consistent with the dominant theatrically-inflected models for understanding racial difference in terms of embodied encounters that I discussed in the Introduction.[2]

Here, though, I would like to approach the topic of identity and racial difference in the *Urania* as it emerges not out of performance practices but out of reading experiences.[3] Mary Wroth was a reader. As a reader, she had almost unparalleled access to books. When she was nine months old, Wroth's father Robert Sidney was appointed governor of the port of Flushing, but Wroth grew up largely at Penshurst with her mother and siblings and at Wilton House and the other estates of her aunt, Mary Sidney Herbert.[4] The library at Penshurst was extensive: the antiquary Antony Wood marveled in 1671 that for "Seven score years" the Sidneys "have been collectors of books and have furnished such an eminent library that there were 3 thousand folios in it."[5] The Wilton House library was, if anything, even more illustrious. In the 1590s, Mary Sidney Herbert created a vibrant literary and cultural environment by bringing Samuel Daniel, Ben Jonson, Abraham Fraunce, and Thomas Moffet to Wilton House; at the same time, though, John Aubrey described Wilton House as being "like a college" not only for the "many learned and ingenious persons" there but also because of the "noble librarie of bookes, choicely collected in the time of Mary Countess of Pembroke."[6]

Of Mary Wroth's personal library, less is known. David McKittereck's complaint that the "comparative neglect of the history of women's reading and book ownership contrasts strangely with the many projects and publications concerned with women's writing" certainly applies to Wroth. We do, however, know that Wroth's books were important enough to her that when her husband added a codicil of "speciall Legaceys" to his will he specifically bequeathed to her "all her books and furniture of her studye and closett."[7]

While we do not have a library catalogue or commonplace book that might provide more precise material evidence documenting Mary Wroth's personal reading, it is clear that Wroth's *Urania* emerges directly out of an engagement with a central tradition of early modern printed romances, most notably Sidney's *Arcadia*, Cervantes' *Don Quixote*, Montalvo's *Amadis*, and Heliodorus' *Aethiopika*. The printed romances that I have been considering throughout this book were well represented on the library shelves at Penshurst, Wilton, and Loughton halls. While working to improve his Spanish, Wroth's father Robert Sidney wrote to Mary Wroth's cousin, William Herbert, to request that he obtain a copy of "that Spanish *Amadis de Gaule*" for him.[8] In dedicating his 1618 and 1619 editions of his *Amadis* translations to Philip Herbert, Anthony Munday comments on the proliferation and dispersal of these romances: remarking on the "manifold impressions of this history, the Bookes thereof being now come to be five and twentie in number, and printed in places far distant a sunder," Munday thanks Herbert's wife, Susan de Vere, for her help in providing him with "such Bookes as were of the best editions."[9]

Abraham Fraunce, who was closely affiliated with Mary Sidney Herbert, likewise undertook a partial translation of Heliodorus' *Aethiopika* that was included in his *Countess of Pembroke's Ivy Church* (1591), while John Harington's translation of *Orlando Furioso* was read carefully by Robert Sidney.[10] Anne Clifford's Appleby triptych, which is committed to creating a visual document of the intellectual and material lineage she was claiming, captures some of the Herbert family's commitment to romances in this period, including both the Shelton translation of Cervantes' *Don Quixote* (1612, 1620) and a 1593 edition of the *Arcadia*.[11]

Even the *Arcadia*, which initially circulated in manuscript as a "scribal publication," became increasingly a product of print culture under Mary Sidney Herbert's ongoing involvement in the editing and publishing of the composite *Countess of Pembroke's Arcadia*. It is this later, printed version of the *Arcadia*, rather than the earlier manuscript one, that most impacted Wroth's romance: as Josephine Roberts speculates, the publication of the *Urania* in 1621 was probably timed to coincide with a new edition of the *Arcadia*.[12]

Mary Wroth was a reader of printed romances and the *Urania* was written out of her experiences as a reader of these fictions. Roberts and others have traced the literary expressions of Wroth's acts of reading – the textual borrowings, the generic reshapings, the engagements and critiques – that appear within the pages of the *Urania*.[13] In this chapter, I would instead like to approach the *Urania* as a text that suggests how reading – and the reading of printed romances, in particular – might be understood to change not just how and what Mary Wroth wrote but also who she was. In this sense, my goal here is to begin to construct a critical history that is in keeping with my argument that a material history of reading must include not just that which inheres in the physical state of early modern texts, but also that which would have been understood to inhere in the bodies of readers themselves. While we lack the commonplace books and shelf lists that might allow us to construct the first history, Wroth's romance offers key evidence for the second set of inquiries.

As I have suggested, reading impacted identity because it was experienced within the body. Humanists, physicians, and translators made it clear that what you read could change mind, soul, *and* body, transforming how you thought, felt, and even appeared. Throughout this book I have used the critical accounts of Vives, Amyot, La Noue, Wright, and other contemporary critics to construct a phenomenological model to explain how romance reading was understood and probably experienced. Here, it may be useful to set Wroth's *Urania* alongside those accounts, not so much to read Wroth through the perspective implied by their arguments, but as an instance of an allied but ultimately separate phenomenology of reading. When we approach Wroth's work in this manner, we see an account of reading that fractures from this dominant tradition in ways that arise out of shifting understandings of racial identity and out of changing attitudes toward printed romance.

Had they considered the activities of reader like Lady Mary Wroth – and the same conclusions would likely apply to Susan de Vere, Philip Herbert, Mary Sidney Herbert, and probably Robert Sidney – Vives and other critics who warned against romance reading would have been able to make a clear prediction. Reading the kinds of romances that were available in the library at Penshurst, circulated through the coterie at Wilton House, and probably shelved in Mary Wroth's personal closet was a dangerous activity. Readers who were exposed to these kinds of texts were thought to be likely, as we have seen, to become melancholy, black, impassioned, and lascivious.

Mary Wroth's fiction provides a good textual frame against which to read this diagnosis of romance readers. Wroth's fiction is, first, the most autobiographical of the romances that I have considered. The *Urania* is about Wroth. Pamphilia and the other characters who shadow Wroth within the fiction tell us a good deal about her life and loves; they also, I will suggest, tell us a good deal about Wroth's experiences as a reader. Second, Wroth's romance is also arguably the most self-conscious of the romances that I have discussed. While the self-reflexivity of Cervantes' romance arises out of his interest in breaking the genre, Wroth's fiction is self-reflexive in ways that arise out of a quite different desire on Wroth's part to return to a lost genre and the age it seemed to celebrate. Finally, Wroth had a personal interest (and in this she is not unlike Feliciano de Silva and Cervantes) in romance as a genealogical document that might allow her to create literary kinship with the uncle who died a year to the day before she was born and the two illegitimate children whose identities she hoped to have recognized by her cousin and lover, William Herbert, Earl of Pembroke. The *Urania* is thus a meditation both on Wroth's personal experiences and on the genre of romance; indeed, these two are closely intertwined for her.

As I have suggested, humoralism became associated with romance as a trope that seemed to offer a physiological explanation for the consequences that reading had on the body and its passions. Within the texts of early modern romance itself, however, humoral physiology did not typically play as large a part in the construction of character as it did in genres such as drama. Readers of romances were themselves understood to have humoral bodies in the ways that Vives and other humanist critics suggested, but, with some notable exceptions, comparatively few of the characters within those romances did. The emphasis on humoralism within the *Urania* importantly integrates the theory and practices that, as we have seen, were widely associated with romance reading into its fiction. This chapter returns us to the physiological language of the Introduction and it does so because of the degree to which Wroth incorporates contemporary philosophical and cultural concerns about reading romances into her fiction. Like *Quixote*, Wroth's *Urania* marks itself as a late romance in part through its self-conscious attention to the acts of reading that define this genre; Wroth's *Urania* differs from earlier romances in part because of the way that she brings the experience of reading romance into her construction of character and identity.

Speaking of Philip Sidney, H. R. Woudhuysen notes that "the writer, in his works, becomes a fictional character, becomes up to a point, a hero in his own right."[14] A similar claim could be made about Wroth's understanding of the relationship between fictional character and auto-biographical identity. As a character and authorial alter ego, Pamphilia brings Wroth's experiences – both as a lover and as a romance reader – into the text. From this perspective, what is most notable about Wroth's depiction of Pamphilia is how she differs from what Vives and other critics of romance would predict. Pamphilia is melancholy. She is impassioned. She is also, in the terms that critiques of romance reading would suggest, arguably black. In these respects, Pamphilia conforms closely to prevailing accounts of the emotional and physical consequences to reading romances. She is not, however, inconstant or lascivious. Indeed, as I will suggest, Wroth is able to depict Pamphilia's constancy as itself a type of humor and is able to do so in the first part of the *Urania* because she draws on the geo-humoral tradition of black melancholy. This chapter will thus explore how and why Wroth is able create a character who, as a version of Wroth herself, tacitly stands as a refutation of the kinds of arguments that Vives, La Noue, Amyot, Malón de Chaide, and others made about the physical consequences to reading romances.

More so than any other of the romances that I have discussed in this volume, the two parts of Wroth's *Urania* are written across the shift from pre-racial to racial bodies. Competing understandings of humoral and racial complexion informed how Wroth created her characters and imagined herself, and, as I will suggest, they also determined how her romance was published and could be read. In pursuing this argument, I will focus on how Wroth's construction of Pamphilia as a black melancholic in the first part of the *Urania* emerged out of her experiences and understanding of reading. Pamphilia's melancholy is, in part, a story about race and the kind of national "body" identity that aristocratic Englishmen were working to claim for themselves in the early seventeenth century. In the context of romance, though, the fate of Pamphilia is also a story about reading. The Pamphilia of the print *Urania* is imagined in the context of a humoral model of the body and, by extension, of the acts of reading that were implied by that body. The Pamphilia of the manuscript continuation, by contrast, exists as a proto-racial character. In the conclusion of the chapter I will then consider two events that distinguish the manuscript continuation of the *Urania* from the printed first volume: first, how emergent discourses of racialism, emblematized by the publication of Robert Burton's *Anatomy of Melancholy*, changed the meaning of melancholy for Wroth; and second, how William Herbert's designation of his nephew, rather than his and Wroth's illegitimate children, as his heir, changed Wroth's potential readership. Considered together these two events, historical and personal, ended Wroth's hopes for constructing genealogical identity through her fiction.

Before turning to the understandings and practices of reading that are integrated into the *Urania*, though, I would like to begin with an account of two very different contemporary readers of Wroth's romance. The first of these, Sir Edward Denny, was a reader who read Wroth's romance in ways that she had not intended; the second, William Herbert, was a reader who failed to read the romance in the ways she had hoped. When Wroth published the first part of the *Urania* in 1621, she did so in self-conscious emulation of the printed romances that had influenced her work. The results were probably not quite what she had expected: they were almost certainly not what her publishers had hoped for.

John Marriott and John Grismond entered Wroth's romance in the Stationers' Register on July 13, 1621. Three days earlier, they had both been examined about their involvement in the purportedly unlicensed publication of George Wither's satiric poem, *Withers Motto*, which had been refused by the censors but had been published anyway. Wither was imprisoned, not for the first time; Marriott, Grisham, and the printer Augustine Matthews were fined and, in the case of Marriott and Grisham, briefly imprisoned.[15] While the consequences to publishing Wither's overtly vicious (and very popular) satire might have been anticipated, Wroth's publishers and printer probably did not anticipate a similar uproar over her seemingly fictional romance. However, Wroth's romance almost immediately prompted a storm of widely-circulated criticism from courtly readers, most notably Edward Denny, Baron of Waltham; as Roberts has demonstrated, after complaints were made directly to the king, Wroth seems to have withdrawn the volume from sale.[16]

The responses of Denny and other readers are worth returning to here because they turned on questions about a relationship between reading and identity that was understood to be specific to romance. As Roberts notes, the *Urania* was a self-consciously "quixotic romance," and that influence may include not just the narrative structure but the reading strategies that Cervantes introduced to the genre. Roberts suggests that for English readers Cervantes' romance had "suddenly thrown into question how romance can be read and interpreted" and had created a new critical insistence that "women must interpret romances only as allegories, not as texts which might touch on actual experiences."[17] Roberts' suggestion about allegory is worth pursuing since much of the controversy over the volume turned not so much on the actual content of Wroth's romance but on how it was imagined to be read. Was the *Urania* an allegory? Did it, to use more Protestant terminology, "shadow" or "figure" the lives of court readers like Denny? Was it a genealogical document through which Wroth could assert her identity within her family and within the patriarchal structure of the court society? Was it "just" a fiction?[18] Obviously, the *Urania* asks us to consider each of these questions, but how one answers them depends largely on how one understands the relationship between reading and identity.

Within the context in which Cervantes wrote, allegory was a racially and theologically marked form of writing. Almost as clearly as a drop of impure blood, how one read could identify who one was. Paul's injunction that "the letter killeth but the spirit giveth life" (2 Corinthians 3:6) was a central text in a long theological tradition (extending from Augustine to Aquinas, Peter the Venerable, and Petrus Alfonsí) that denigrated Jews as "carnal" readers who could only read literally rather than allegorically.[19] As we have seen, Cervantes invoked and vexed this tradition by creating in Quixote a character who read romances as a literalist (everything printed in the pages of his books had a kind of gospel truth for him), but seemed to read the world itself allegorically (where others saw sheep, he saw armies and evil enchanters). Quixote's reading practices produce rather than reveal his identity in the sense that Cervantes appeals to the theological tradition surrounding supposed Jewish literalism to suggest that what allows Quixote to read allegorically is his faith in romance. Whoever or whatever he was born, Quixote has been converted through his reading into a "true believer."

The issues surrounding Jewish and *converso* reading practices did not apply in Jacobean England, but the questions that *Quixote* raised about whether romances should be understood literally, or whether they pointed toward a higher, hidden truth that only some readers would be able to understand, does carry over into Wroth's romance. Following Cervantes, Wroth also constructs her romance to create what she hoped would be two kinds of readers – ones whose acts of reading might both reveal and confirm their identities. In contrast to Cervantes and in keeping with the generic nostalgia of the *Urania*, though, what might have distinguished those readers for Wroth was not faith, but birth. What she was trying to create in the *Urania* was a fiction that, when read correctly by the proper reader, would become a genealogical document of her (and her children's) identity.

The responses from contemporary readers, however, suggest the complexity of this attempt. In a well-known episode, Sir Edward Denny, Baron of Waltham, responded angrily to what he took to be the scurrilous and only too manifest depiction of his family scandals in the episode involving Sirelius.[20] In a series of widely circulated exchanges with Wroth, Denny expressed outrage at how what he took to be Wroth's allegorical fiction made his identity transparently visible to everyone who read the *Urania*. Denny complained that Wroth had written an "Idell book …" where thou strikes at some mans noble blood"[21] and raged that she had "palpabilie and grossely" traduced him as "the whole wor[l]d conceives me to be ment in one of the weakest and unworthiest passages in your booke."[22] Other readers seem to have read Wroth's romance through the same kinds of generic conventions as did Denny: George Manners, the seventh Earl of Rutland, wrote to her almost twenty years later, apparently having acquired a copy of the *Urania*, asking that she "interpret unto me the names as heere I have begun them."[23]

Wroth herself expressed surprise at the ferocity of these responses and insisted that such readers were wrong, putting "strange constructions" on her book, "contrary to my imagination, and as far from my meaning as is possible for truth to bee from conjecture."[24] She insisted to Denny that she had not intended "one word of that book to his Lordships person or disgrace" and exclaimed that "I never thought on you in my writing, I never meant you."[25] In this heated exchange of letters and insults between Wroth and Denny, Denny had insisted that he was the fictional Sirelius' father-in-law and she was Pamphilia. For Denny, both their identities were, to his mind, equally transparent, palpable, to all.

While Wroth was surprised and upset that a reader like Denny was able to see his identity within the fiction in ways that she had not intended, a more central problem for her was that the romance did not seem to allow her to articulate her own identity clearly enough for the one reader she most obviously wanted to reach with her romance: her cousin, William Herbert, the third Earl of Pembroke. Wroth's cousin and the father of her illegitimate children, Pembroke was the real-life model for Pamphilia's beloved but inconstant Amphilanthus. Equally importantly, Pembroke was also almost certainly the intended reader for Wroth's romance.

The idea that Wroth might want to invoke Pembroke as the central reader for her text is not surprising. Beyond Wroth's personal connections to him, Pembroke was a powerful cultural patron: beginning with William Thorne's dedication of *Ducente Deo* to him in 1592, more published works were dedicated to Pembroke during this period than to any other figure outside the royal family.[26] These included Samuel Daniel's *Defence of Ryme* (1603), Ben Jonson's *Catiline* (1611), and the First Folio (1623, from John Heminges and Henry Condell, jointly with his brother Philip).[27] Michael Brennan notes that a number of romances were dedicated to William's brother, Philip.[28] Leonard Digges, however, included both Philip and William in the dedication to his translation of the Spanish romance, *Geraldo* (1622), which presented itself as "a pattern for lascivious lovers."[29] Pembroke is so consistently invoked in early seventeenth-century dedications that he stands as a kind of figure for the quintessential courtly reader. This attention to Pembroke as a reader was perhaps especially powerful in 1621 in the context of the intense literary nostalgia that surrounded the death of his mother, Mary Sidney Herbert.

Yet, the material state of both the printed and the manuscript versions of the *Urania* are notable for the extent to which they register Pembroke's presence as a reader in only negative terms, through a kind of textual absence. First, in the printed edition, Pembroke is not, as might be expected, the dedicatee for the *Urania*: rather, the 1621 edition begins with an elaborate, engraved portrait title plate but then jumps immediately, without any other prefatory materials, to the beginning of the text on B1r. The paratextual space between the frontispiece engraving and the beginning of the text itself that is missing here – the numbering of the signatures suggest that the printers were expecting as many as eight pages of prefatory materials – was often used by early modern authors to define the reading practices for their works. In the texts on which Wroth modeled her romance, such paratexts created a margin between author and audience, one centrally concerned with negotiating the act of reading. It is impossible to determine precisely why the printers expected but did not receive the usual dedicatory materials to the volume; it is also hard to speculate about parts of a text that are not there, but this material absence is nonetheless notable.

In the manuscript continuation, a similar absence – this time, an excision – may also be connected to Herbert as a possible reader of the text. Wroth uses Pamphilia to present herself as a reader of Herbert's writing when she has Pamphilia sing to Amphilanthus as "one of his owne" (2.30) a poem written by Herbert.[30] In the manuscript, the introduction of the poem into the manuscript is conspicuous: in contrast to a poem like "Why doe you thus torment my poorest hart," which is written in a tiny, cramped hand, the poem from Herbert is very elegantly set off, in the largest, most expressive (even otiose) form of Wroth's italic cursive, with ample spacing before and after the poem as well as between stanzas.[31]

These physical details of the text may suggest not simply Wroth's care in copying Herbert's poem into her manuscript, but the attention with which she seems to have hoped his words might be read. Although Wroth attempts to script Herbert's reading of the manuscript (both, here, through his own words and, later, through such devices as the ciphers associated with the lost princes and princesses), the only material evidence of Herbert as a reader is once again negative: one of the more intriguing textual features of the manuscript is the missing bi-folio in the first volume of the manuscript continuation (bi-folio 10). This section of the manuscript deals with an important moment of separation between Amphilanthus and Phamphilia, one where she notably returned to her home and "lived beeloved," while he becomes involved in the dalliance that leads to their separate marriages. As Suzanne Gossett and Janel Mueller note, the numbering of the folios (which Wroth inserted after she completed the manuscript) make it clear that this bi-folio was probably removed not long after she finishing writing, and they speculate that it was excised from the manuscript by either Herbert or Wroth herself.

Wroth's decision not to publish Part 2 of the *Urania* probably did not arise from the complaints of Denny and other readers that her romance "strikes at some mans noble blood." Arguably, Denny was right, but it was Herbert's blood, not his, that concerned her. Wroth needed Herbert, as a reader, to recognize the identity she was asserting about herself as a constant lover and her children as true heirs. That act of genealogical recognition is at the narrative heart of romances from the *Odyssey* and the *Aethiopika* to *Amadis*, and it is one that Wroth would draw from the pages of the romance and transfer to the readers of that romance. Part 1 was legible to readers like Denny largely because Wroth created a "cipher" that could not be truly private insofar as the identity and truth that she wanted to create – patriarchal recognition – was one that could only be conferred within a public social world rather than within a secret, personal one. Part 2 of the *Urania*, by contrast, is arguably written for a single reader, and Wroth's decision not to finish or publish this portion of the romance is likely connected to Wroth's realization that Pembroke did not intend to legally recognize her illegitimate children as his own. By the end, the identity that Wroth hoped to claim for herself and her children through the acts of genealogical recognition that Pembroke as a reader might have made was no longer possible.

Understanding how and why Wroth's readers responded as they did to her work requires us to assess how she constructed character and identity within her romance. In this context, Wroth's depiction of Pamphilia as a black melancholic is central to the identity she was hoping to create and to the assumptions about reading she was following. Wroth introduces a humoral model of the body into the first part of the *Urania* as a way to describe Pamphilia and, through her, Wroth herself, as a lover and writer. Wroth's Pamphilia is a melancholic character. Pamphilia is not an instance of the "genial" melancholic that writers such as Ficino and Sidney associated with intellectual furor. Rather, Wroth imagines the character of Pamphilia in terms of a racially and geographically marked form of "black" melancholy that writers such as Pierre Charron drew on when they imagined southern peoples as "Little, melancholicke, cold, and dry, black, Solitary" in body but "Ingenious, wise, subtile, opinative" in spirit.[32] Wroth's interest in imagining Pamphilia in these terms should be understood in terms of the larger "discourse of blackness" that Hall has identified as characteristic of James' court.[33] The character that Wroth creates, however, is in several key respects culturally, if not biologically, impossible and generically illegible.

The fullest and most remarkable expression of Pamphilia's melancholic disposition in the *Urania*, Part 1, comes when Pamphilia first despairingly wonders "why was this rare excellent qualitie of constancy alotted thee?" (1.464). Constancy is Pamphilia's defining quality, and, in ways that have not been recognized, that constancy is directly tied to Wroth's depiction of Pamphilia as having a melancholic complexion.[34] Even as Pamphilia questions the origins for her constancy, Wroth insists upon them by connecting Pamphilia in body and imagination to the figure of the black melancholic. Invoking the absent Amphilanthus as the object of her constancy and source of her melancholy, Pamphilia then avers "I would rather wish to be a Black-moore, or any thing more dreadfull, then allure affection to me, if not from you" (1.465).

Wroth's interest in melancholy initially arises out of her need to establish Pamphilia's virtuous constancy in a way that allows Pamphilia to be not just the subject of the narrative but also its source. Pamphilia is not melancholy because she is constant. To the extent that we might imagine in Pamphilia a narrative progression from love to loss in which her sadness is the consequence of being constant in the face of being forsaken, we bring novelistic expectations about change and emotional development that do not apply in the fictive world of the *Urania*. Rather, for Wroth Pamphilia is constant because she is melancholy: by introducing a humoral model of melancholy to identify Pamphilia Wroth draws on the iconographic associations of black melancholy in order to create a character who *is* constant, rather than *becomes* it, in ways that conform generically with romance even as they depart from contemporary cultural and medical assumptions about women's humors and complexions. As an organizing structure and central trope of the *Urania*, melancholy allows in Pamphilia the fictional expression of an identity that both medical science and social morality doubted was possible.

Wroth's attention to melancholy is part of what Gail Kern Paster has called an "affective vogue" within English aristocratic culture in the period 1610 to 1630.[35] English treatises such as Timothy Bright's *Treatise of Melancholy* (1586), Thomas Wright's *The Passions of the Minde in Generall* (1601), and Robert Burton's *Anatomy of Melancholy* (1621) should also be considered in the context of the strong continental interest in melancholy in such works as Juan Huarte's *Examen des ingenios para les sciencias* (Pamplona, 1578), Andrés Velásquez's *Libro de la melancholia* (Seville, 1585), André du Laurens' *Discours … des maladies melancholiques* (Tours, 1594), Pierre Charron's *De la Sagesse* (Bordeaux, 1601), Alonso de Frelas' *Discurso si los melancholicos puedan saber lo que esta por venir* (Jaén, 1606), and Ercole Sassonia's "De Melancholia" in his *Opera practica* (Padua, 1607).[36] The first part of Wroth's *Urania* is published in 1621, alongside Robert Burton's *Anatomy of Melancholy*. A similar attention to melancholy also appears across a wide range of contemporary genres and forms, including Ben Jonson's humoral comedies, Robert Greene's romances, and John Donne's sermons. As we shall see, Wroth's use of melancholy works against this larger early seventeenth-century English appropriation of melancholy as the passion of aristocratic, white, northern men. Wroth will draw on earlier and very un-English images of melancholy – the kind that appear in exotic travelogues and foreign histories such as Richard Knolles' *History of the Turks* (1603) and Pierre d'Avity's *Estates, empires and principallities* (1615) – as well as on the racially and geographically specific accounts of melancholy that prevail in Galenic and geo-humoral texts. Whatever other sources inform Wroth's understanding of melancholy, though, she nonetheless starts with the dominantly Ficinian melancholy of Sidney's sad Arcadian heroes, Musidorus and Pyrocles.

Much critical attention has been paid to understanding how Wroth rewrites the narrative and generic models implied in her uncle Philip Sidney's *Arcadia*.[37] Wroth's rethinking of Sidney's model of melancholy is particularly important because it shapes how Wroth constructs character within the fiction and how she imagines the act of reading outside it. Sidney was central to the introduction of melancholy into English fiction. While Ariosto's knights and lovers suffer from a "mad" passion that is later mocked by Cervantes, Sidney's heroes are wet and sad in their consuming melancholy. Musidorus, Pyrocles, Amphialus, and Philisides are all afflicted with melancholy. Katherine Duncan-Jones comments on how "suffused with melancholy" Sidney's works are and argues that Sidney's melancholy constitutes a key interpretive problem for understanding his works and life.[38] Following Ficino, Sidney understands melancholy as the source of nobility in his male characters and yet also as that which thwarts their realization of those noble qualities in the form of heroic action. When Sidney introduces Musidorus as a melancholy figure at the start of *The Countess of Pembroke's Arcadia*, he sketches out the narrative trajectory that his romance will take as a whole. This opening frame is worth examining because it is one that Wroth rewrites when she introduces Pamphilia as the figure of melancholy in Part 1 of her romance.

The *Arcadia* begins when the shepherds Strephon and Claius fish the naked and bereft Musidorus out of the ocean.[39] The lamenting Musidorus falls into a sustained melancholy when they fail to rescue his companion Pyrocles, and he is carried off by pirates. Seeing that Musidorus has "a sorrowful mind supported with a weak body," his rescuers recognize the symptoms of melancholy in Musidorus:

> knowing that the violence of sorrow is not, at the first, to be striven withal ... they gave way unto it for that day and the next; never troubling him either with asking questions or finding fault with his melancholy, but rather fitting to his dolour dolorous discourses of their own and other folks' misfortunes. Which speeches, though they had not a lively entrance to his senses shut up in sorrow, yet like one half asleep he took hold of much of the matters spoken unto him, so as a man may say, ere sorrow was aware, they made his thoughts bear away something else beside his own sorrow. (*Arcadia*, 69)

This first melancholic episode makes clear that, for Sidney, melancholy may begin as a character disposition but it also becomes a narrative prediction. As Ficino suggests, to be melancholy is to feel rather than to act, to be overcome with a passion that enables one but may also make it impossible for one to act in ways that express that nobility. Melancholy is not a "virtue," at least not in Machiavelli's sense of virtue as having and using the power to act, the ability to achieve oneself as a man and a prince.

This quality of melancholy means that whatever one may say about melancholy as a medical disposition or personal temperament, it is, for a fictional character existing in a heroic world, a flaw. As the defining characteristic of Musidorus, melancholy brings him into Arcadia but also leaves him unable to achieve his aims or those of Sidney's narrative. Indeed, Musidorus recognizes this himself when he later confronts the melancholy that overcomes Pyrocles. Musidorus complains about the change in his friend's temper and disposition:

> whereas you were wont in all places you came to give yourself vehemently to the knowledge of those things which might better your mind, to seek the familiarity of excellent men in learning and soldiery, and lastly, to put all these things in practice .... [but now] you let your mind fall asleep: beside your countenance troubled, which surely comes not of virtue, for virtue, like the clear heaven, is without clouds: and lastly, you subject yourself to solitariness, the sly enemy that doth most separate a man from well doing. (*Arcadia*, 110)

As we shall see, melancholy is a male humor, one that arises out of but is ultimately not fully consistent with male virtue. Here, Musidorus follows Machiavelli's definition of virtue in the *Prince* more than he does Sidney's in the *Defense*. Under these terms, melancholy is not a true virtue – and does not appear as such in Pyrocles' face – because whatever its intentions, melancholy expresses itself as a solipsistic self-indulgence that does not demand acts of "well doing." Musidorus' comments apply to the fiction as much as they do to Pyrocles' disposition: Musidorus' personal frustration seems to anticipate the kinds of narrative frustrations that readers have experienced with Sidney's failure in the *Arcadia* to achieve a heroic epic of "well doing" in the way that the *Defense* had promised. Within Sidney's gendering of heroic virtue, melancholy is an impasse that produces character but impedes narrative.

Wroth takes Sidney's opening melancholy and transposes it onto her central female character, Pamphilia. We see Pamphilia's melancholic passion almost as soon as she is introduced into the narrative, and her humor creates the central emotional depth to Wroth's romance. As soon as we are introduced to Pamphilia, she in a sense pulls us away from the narrative into her private passions: "They gone, Pamphilia alone began to breath out her passions, which to none shee would discover, resolving rather so to perish, then that any third should know shee could be subject to affection" (1.62). Filled from this first moment with "ceaseless mourning," Pamphilia laments that she is full of "broken joyes, blacke despaires, incirkling me" (1.62). Identified as the "melancholy Lady" (1.91), Pamphilia adopts light Tawny and Murrey as heraldic colors that mark the combination of despair and constancy that defines her melancholic humor (1.165). Melancholy drives Wroth's narrative: Pamphilia's humor troubles her dreams, prompts her ceaseless writing, and precipitates her ultimate marriage to the King of Tartaria.

Yet, Pamphilia's humoral disposition – and the constancy that conjoins it – is for most Renaissance thinkers a medical and moral impossibility in a woman. Humoral handbooks address and imply a universal man as their subject: the enduring and often supplemented *Problemes of Aristotle*, for instance, offers answers to "divers questions ... touching the estate of mans bodie."[40] Discussing the range of humors, the *Problemes* concludes that "every one hath his proper place in mans bodie" in a way that is gendered in both practice and theory. Each humor describes a man and men describe the humors: of one, "he is faire and beautifull"; of another, "he is furious and angrie"; of a third, "he is swartie, browne of complexion."[41] When humoral texts include women within their model of the temperaments and humors of "men," they identify women as wet and cold. The only humor that women could "normatively" inhabit, as Gail Kern Paster notes, was the phlegmatic.[42]

Melancholy, by contrast, is the cold, dry passion associated with black bile, with Saturn, with the scholarly genius of men, and with constancy. The cultural meaning and value associated with melancholy changed during this period. Yet, in ways that Wroth's narrative recognizes and confronts, that history of melancholy is always a history of male melancholy.[43] There is no comparative history of women's melancholy to be told. In some fundamental physiological sense, while individual women could be and were often diagnosed as melancholy (though more often under the subcategory of hypochondriacal melancholy), women could not collectively or as a category be melancholy.[44] At most, women might be imagined to be excessively but momentarily sad. Such sadness was not melancholy but a temporary aberration, what later ages could dismiss as a passing "mood swing." This asymmetrical gendering of a universal humoral model – in which each individual man might be disposed to any of the four humors, while women were constrained to a single quadrant in the chart of the humors – denies the full range of emotional expression to women. This model refuses to acknowledge such range by diagnosing emotions "uncharacteristic" of the gender (that is, passions and dispositions that in a man would be comprehended as choleric, sanguine, or melancholic) as instances of the kind of "temperamental" inconstancy (excessive ire, spite, frivolity, sadness) that was understood to be specific to women. Wroth's Pamphilia seems to exist as a refutation of this accepted cultural knowledge. She is not sad or changeable. She is instead both melancholic and constant and, more importantly, her melancholy constitutes the primary mark of her unending constancy.

Given this larger cultural context within and against which Wroth imagines Pamphilia, what makes it possible for her to construct Pamphilia as a figure of constant melancholy? The preliminary answer may be the familial one. Sidney's regendering of melancholy in Book 1 of the *Arcadia* probably precipitates Wroth's appropriation of melancholy. Sidney's understanding of melancholy emerges out of the medical theory of Ficino and the literary tradition he inherits through Ariosto. As we have seen, at the start of the *Arcadia*, Musidorus laments the apparent loss of Pyrocles in a "dolour" (*Arcadia*, 69), a "violence of sadness," that is both expected and apparently comprehensible to all. That very Ficinian melancholy – the loss of a male other who is and is not the self – is nonetheless not the melancholy that structures the *Arcadia*. Once found, Pyrocles is almost immediately lost again, this time not to pirates but to a passion prompted by his having seen Pamela's picture. Falling in quick succession from unbounded love into a melancholy humor and the costume of an Amazon, he has moved beyond what Ficino imagined.

Pyrocles' passion is not just a transposed version of Musidorus'. As a sickness produced by seeing an image of Pamela, Pyrocles' experiences do conform closely to the kind of image-based model of adust melancholy that was also thought to make reading dangerous. Gender is probably the most important component of Pyrocles' humor. Musidorus' loss of Pyrocles conforms to traditional male melancholy – one that verges between solipsistic self-regard and a mourning for the loss of the self. The passion that Pyrocles feels for Pamela, by contrast, intrudes a woman into what Paster characterizes as the "male-only temperament" of melancholy and the result will ultimately be the transformation of the prince Pyrocles into the Amazon Zelmane.[45] It is at this moment that Sidney parts company with not just Ficino but also Ariosto and Cervantes. In Wroth's reading, the humorally mixed and biologically improbable melancholy of Pyrocles/Diaphantus/Zelmane enables the passion of Pamphilia. Wroth recognizes the Ficinian model of melancholy that Sidney adheres to: Amphilanthus insists that Pamphilia was "borne under the fiercest-frowning quarter of Saturnes raigne and must never see more Joyfull days" (2.134). And like Ficino's melancholics, Pamphilia is in her melancholy "a brave and manlike spirit, and wondrous wise"

(1.570). Yet, Pamphilia is clearly not another Zelmane, Pyrocles, or even a new Musidorus.

Whatever medical texts might suggest as a biological fact about melancholy, Wroth in the *Urania* finds that melancholy works for female characters in a narrative sense. Melancholy can be assimilated to female virtue in ways that it cannot accord with male virtue: what are narrative problems for Sidney become authorial solutions for Wroth. Through melancholy, Wroth claims constancy without being compromised by the kind of passivity that emasculates in Sidney. At the same time, by integrating complective melancholy of the type that she found in contemporary travel narratives and ethnographic texts with Ficinian melancholy, Wroth also lays claim through Pamphilia to a virtuous form of writing for herself. Virtue in a woman does not demand what Musidorus demands of Pyrocles – the virtue of "well doing," "of put[ting] all these things in practice" (*Arcadia*, 116). Female virtue instead typically involves restraint and is thus a quality without an act of precisely the kind about which Musidorus complains.

Sidney imagines melancholy as a transformative passion. As the narrative develops, Musidorus and Pyrocles will change everything. Almost wantonly, they alter or abandon gender, name, class, identity, desire, clothing. All this flux, though, begins with their "great alteration" to – or of – melancholy (*Arcadia*, 110). Once Pyrocles has seen Pamela

such a change was grown in [him] that (as if cheerfulness had been tediousness, and good entertainment were turned to discourtesy) he would ever get himself alone, though almost when he was in company he was alone, so little attention he gave to any that spake unto him. *Even the colour and figure of his face began to receive some alteration, which he shewed little to heed.* (*Arcadia*, 109; my emphasis)

The shepherds who bring Musidorus out of his melancholy by relating their own versions and experiences of melancholy follow accepted medical treatments. Musidorus, by contrast, instead tries to reason with Pyrocles, but his attempts only further distemper his friend: with "the oft changing of his face," "his words interrupted continually with sighs ... [were not] knit together to one constant end, but rather dissolved in itself as the vehemency of the inward passion prevailed" (*Arcadia*, 113). Bewailing the changes that have overcome Pyrocles, Musidorus calls out to his absent friend: "Pyrocles, what means this alteration?" (*Arcadia*, 116).

Sidney emphasizes the transformative effect of melancholy – repeatedly characterizing it as an "alteration" – to invoke a previous, now lost, heroic virtue in the implied narrative world that we are asked to imagine having preceded the *Arcadia*. He constructs his narrative against the frame implied by earlier versions of a Musidorus and Pyrocles who had been heroic and virtuous before they wash up in Arcadia. That is, in Sidney melancholy is a humor that allows one not so much to be heroic as, through its genius, to tell stories of past heroisms rather than to achieve new ones.

Humoral theory makes clear, though, that changeability is the keynote of phlegm, not melancholy. What distinguishes cold, wet phlegm from cold, dry melancholy is their different relationships to flux and constancy. In the pseudo-Aristotelian *Problemes*, for instance, this distinction provides the answer to why fevers that arise out of melancholic imbalances last longer than those that are phlegmatic in origin: "fleume, although it be colde, and much of it, yet it is moyst, and moystnes is easily altered and changed," whereas "black choler or melancholy is cold and dry, and therefore is hardly altered and chaunged." The two humors "deceiue therefore with the likenes of cold."[46] The phlegmatic are cold but full of moisture and, because of this fluidity, they are susceptible to alteration. Melancholics, by contrast, are cold but dry. They thus are comparatively impervious to change: as a kind of burned away residue, melancholy is the state after transformation rather than the possibility of it. Unlike Sidney, Wroth recognizes this quality of melancholy in her depiction of Pamphilia. Wroth thus begins with Pamphilia's melancholy by introducing Pamphilia only after introducing her jealous rival, Antissia. Where Musidorus and Pyrocles suffer a "great alteration" that seems to take them from the sanguine to the phlegmatic, Pamphilia is unchanged, as constant in her melancholy as in her love.

Wroth's regendering of Sidney's model of melancholy is enabled by her strategy of conceiving of Pamphilia within a racially and geographically marked version of this humor. In the Hippocratic tradition, melancholy was understood to be a disease produced by the most corrupted and inherently pathological of excess bodily fluids. From at least the time of Plato and Aristotle, melancholy is variously associated with madness, moral insanity, sexual excess, physical heroism, and great intellectualism.[47] Sidney inherits this tradition from Ficino. Humoral theory was more than just a medical model for understanding the human body, though: the influence of Empedocles' theory of the four elements and seasons on the Hippocratic understanding of the humors of the body meant that humoral theory was also a global theory. One's temperament might be produced by the inner fluids of the body but those were, in turn, inseparable from and interdependent with the seasons, climate, and environment.[48] Humoral theory was inherently geographical and climatic: it explained not just what kind of person you were (as an individual disposition), but also indicated where you came from and how that might make you who you were (as a geographic identity and complexion).

Mary Floyd-Wilson recognizes this key feature of melancholy in her work on the geo-humoral character of race and ethnicity in early modern England. She suggests that humoral theory was geographically specific in ways that made it a central expression of racial identity: humoralism is, she concludes, "a form of ethnology."[49] Melancholy looks different within this larger geo-humoral context: in what might be imagined as a global map of the temperaments that was as familiar to writers as it was to cartographers, melancholy was the "southern" humor. Whereas Scythians and other northern peoples were thought to tend toward the phlegmatic, melancholy was the humor of Egyptians, Ethiopians, and Africans. Erwin Panofsky thus traces the history of associations between black bile and black skin: while early writers such as Archigenes of Apamea identify "dark skin" as symptom produced by melancholy, later writers who follow the influence of Hippocratic understandings of climatic humors link the two qualities more directly: Rufus of Ephesus characterized melancholics as "swarthy"; Albertus Magnus likewise describes them as "nigri"; Johann von Neuhaus as "corpus niger sicut lutum." Renaissance compilations clearly attribute this perspective to Aristotle: the *Problemes* simply introduces the melancholy man as "swartie, browne of complexion."[50]

Albrecht Dürer's "Melancholia" represents a new form of melancholy which was "black" only in an emotional or metaphorical sense. As Panofsky makes clear, before Dürer melancholy always had a physically and literally dark face: "The child of Saturn and the melancholic – whether melancholy through illness or by temperament – were by the ancients reckoned swarthy and black of countenance."[51] In this model, interest in the blackness of southerners involved a form of ethnography based on humoral distinctions rather than phenotypes. Pierre Charron's *Of Wisdome* (1612) offers an early modern codification of this strand of cultural knowledge. "Northern people are High and great, phlegmaticke, sanguine, white and yellow" in body; they are "heavy, obtuse, stupid, sottish, facill, light, inconstant" in spirit. Southerners, by contrast, are "Little, melancholicke, cold, and dry, black, Solitary" in body but "Ingenious, wise, subtile, opinative" in spirit.[52] Juan Huarte, drawing on Galen, thus notes that the "melancholicke humour is the author of integritie and constancie."[53] While Sidney's melancholic tradition thus imagines that melancholics tend toward madness and sexual lasciviousness, the broader tradition that Wroth draws on in her depiction of Pamphilia instead associates melancholy with wisdom, constancy, and sexual abstinence.

Pamphilia is the eldest daughter of the King and Queen of Morea in central Greece. In a strictly geo-humoral sense, Pamphilia is a child of the temperate zones and thus ought to have the model temperate disposition (sanguinity) that was associated by Empedocles, Hippocrates, Aristotle, and other Greek philosophers with what they took to be the balanced center of the human world. While proto-racialist models of identity would reassure English travelers that foreign climates could not hurt them or alter their essential "Englishness," humoral theory was predicated on a very different understanding of the relationship between the body and its world. Complexion – as a balance of fluids – by definition could never be fixed or unchanging. In the humoral world, travelers might over time thus alter and adopt the complexion and disposition "native" to the lands in which they traveled. This is what seems happens to Pamphilia: originally from Morea and presumably classically Greek, Wroth's heroine comes to inherit the kingdom of Pamphilia from her childless uncle. After he abdicates his throne to her, she moves to this country in Asia Minor to rule (1.100, 145). In some realistic sense it hardly seems likely that Pamphilia could take on the character of her new country. She has never been there before she is crowned its queen, and her coronation in Pamphilia is a much deferred event that does not occur until fairly late in Part 1. Even once queen, Pamphilia is rarely at home: right after the coronation, she almost immediately leaves for the enchantments on Cyprus, while in Part 2, one of the few state decisions she makes is to flee her country to insure that her enemies attack her rather than the country.

Yet, Pamphilia is as much the place as the person. As Sheila Cavanagh points out, "the person Pamphilia is often difficult to distinguish from the country whose name she shares."[54] For Wroth "Pamphilia" is almost certainly a place before it is a person. Noting that Pamphilia seems to have acquired her name only at the point when she was "named" her uncle's heir, Cavanagh concludes that "her close affiliation with this unknown country destabilizes her identity" in ways that seem to run counter to Pamphilia's defining virtue of constancy.[55] Thinking about the iconography of Pamphilia as a place makes it clear that Wroth names her character precisely as a means of creating a constant and stable identity for her. We should not imagine that "Pamphilia" was something else – had some previous identity or earlier passion – before we began reading the *Urania*. For Wroth the point is that she has always been as she is and cannot be otherwise: her passion and the constancy that goes with it extend backwards as well as forwards. It is important to recognize how Pamphilia differs in this respect from Musidorus and Pyrocles. While their previous, pre-Arcadian identities become a central subject in the inset, retrospective tales that emerge out of their melancholy, Wroth creates "Pamphilia" and marks her identity as created precisely because she wants her readers to experience and understand Pamphilia as always constant.

Pamphilia, the country, is a place Wroth identifies iconographically with melancholy and constancy. As a character Pamphilia embodies those qualities. During Wroth's lifetime Pamphilia was ruled by the Ottoman Turks. Pierre d'Avity thus devotes a long section of his geographic account, *The Estates, Empires, and Principalities of the World* (1616), to the lands in Europe, Asia, and Africa that were subject to the "ambition and crueltie" of the mighty Süleman I, "who is become such a terrour to all Christendome."[56] In Asia Minor, as d'Avity reports, "the great Turke" rules over a "great tract of countrie" that includes the provinces of "Pontus, Bynthias, Asia, Lycia, Galacia, Pamphylia, Capadocia, Cilicia, and Base Armenia."[57] It is for this reason that Bernadette Andrea asserts that "underlying all the movements in Wroth's romance, then, is the powerful subtext of Ottoman imperialism."[58] Wroth's fiction maps contemporary concerns about the geo-political reality that seventeenth-century Europe confronted with Turkish military dominance and religious imperialism. In Part 2, Pamphilia's country remains a sovereign state but is repeatedly attacked and challenged by Turks, Saracens, and other violent infidels who threaten to make her realms into a fictional enactment of what writers such as d'Avity regarded as Pamphilia's real life subjugation to the "ambition and crueltie" of the "great Turk."

In Part 1 of the *Urania*, though, Pamphilia appears as a southern land as much as it does an eastern one. Wroth's sources for her representations of Pamphilia, as a place and person, come out of Pliny, Herodotus, and, most importantly, the Acts of the Apostles. For these writers, Pamphilia is part of the circular geographical perimeter that sweeps south and then west across the northern part of Africa to Egypt and Libya. In a historical sense, Pamphilia is not as Wroth represents it: like other provinces in this contested region, Pamphilia was always being conquered by or intermarried with someone: it was governed or subjected to Alexander the Great, the Ptolemies, the Cilicians, and the Seleucids, among others.[59] Pamphilia is thus a place of mixed races and peoples. Herodotus records that Pamphilia was settled by Achaeans who intermarried with native, non-Greek peoples after the Fall of Troy.[60] In the Acts of the Apostles, Paul's missions spread the Word throughout this region; he ultimately sails over the Sea of Pamphilia only to be shipwrecked on the way to Rome. Here, too, Pamphilia is associated with a larger mixing of peoples and languages: Paul's travels are themselves the geographic consequence of the Pentecostal gift of tongues. The Pamphilians are one among the many peoples gathered in witness of this event: "Parthians, and Medes, and Elamites, and the dwellers in Mesopotamia, and in Judaea, and Cappadocia, in Pontus, and in Asia. Phrygia, and Pamphylia, in Egypt, and in the parts of Libya about Cyrene, and strangers of Rome, Jews and proselytes, Cretes and Arabians, we do hear them speak in our own tongues."[61] The Rhodian Greeks, who did not understand the language of the region, interpreted its name as "pam-phylos," and thus comprehended this to be the "land of all races." The various tribes that come together to form Pamphilia – the Egyptian, the Macedonian, the Phrigian – these are the regions noted for their melancholy dispositions.

For Charron, southerners are "Little, melancholicke, cold, and dry, black, Solitary" in body but "Ingenious, wise, subtile, opinative" in mind. This description of the humoral disposition and complexion of southerners serves as a fairly good template for understanding Pamphilia's character. Melancholic, solitary, black, ingenious, wise, subtile, cold, and opinionate, Pamphilia carries these qualities in her person as if she were a country unto herself. Throughout Part 1, Pamphilia always seems to be traveling, always about to embark on a series of ever-delayed journeys to (and interspersed with rarely protracted visits in) Pamphilia. When Pamphilia travels to the country she reigns over, she follows in the footsteps of Homer's Amphilochus and Calchas and the Acts' Paul. She takes over and claims as her own the disposition that one might ordinarily expect to see in the people of this region. In Part 1, she makes three trips to her new country. The first time, she sails "with happy and pleasant content" (1.149). After that, though, the country's joyousness contrasts sharply with her melancholic humors: on a second trip, "with infinite joy, and troopes of people, shee was received," but Pamphilia herself remains melancholy (1.266); on the next trip, "the people from all parts come to see her, and joy in her presence, while she joyed in nothing" (1.484). In taking on the country's traditional humor along with its name, Pamphilia becomes like her own country. Melancholy is a land that Pamphilia never leaves, wherever she may travel.

Wroth stresses that, despite expectations we might have from humoral handbooks, "change" of place does not alter Pamphilia's humor or change her complexion. In Part 1, Book 3, the always traveling Pamphilia complains to Urania: "'I would,' said Pamphilia, 'we were gone from hence. I hate this Corinth, and long to see Arcadia againe'" (1.458). Urania remonstrates with her and questions, "will your sadnesse end then?" (1.459). Pamphilia admits that it would not: "change cannot nor must not aspire to worke such effect in mee" (1.459). In this conversation, Pamphilia resolutely resists any double meanings to the word "change": change of place does not entail any more fundamental inconstancy. It is out of this refusal that she startlingly identifies change itself as a humor and one that she will not allow in herself: "if I let in that worthlesse humor change, which I can never doe till I change my selfe ... Pamphilia will not change" (1.459). In the fluid model of identity and emotion imagined by Galenic humors, changeability is a part of the basic structure of disposition: indeed, it is the interval between the humors. For Pamphilia, though, change becomes not the interval between humors but a disposition in its own right and one that she refuses.

While Pamphilia is herself a kind of boundless land of melancholy, her geographic namesake seems to lose that humor to her. The country Pamphilia becomes not a place of melancholy, as we might expect, but the cure for it. At the end of Book 4, the admittedly fickle Cauterino meets a fair and wanton Lady. As part of her attempt to seduce Cauterino, the Lady tells a story about a special water to be found in the land of Pamphilia: "I undertooke a journey into Pamphilia, where it is said, there is a water, that will recover all diseases, ease all griefes, especially take away all melancholies" (1.610). Whether a cure or a cause, a land or the person of its qualities, Pamphilia is clearly associated with the "grief" of melancholy but, because of that, not with the humor of change.

These humoral attributes of black melancholy are, in turn, evident in Pamphilia's complexion. Pamphilia is clearly and unexceptionally beautiful, but she is not fair in comparison to her fictional alter egos and in the terms that romance usually expects of its heroines. Amphilanthus' complexion, for instance, is much easier to see and interpret than is Pamphilia's: his appearance conforms to romance expectations even when his behavior does not. Amphilanthus is always identified as "fair," and this quality serves to distinguish him from other characters who try to usurp or emulate his identity. The "false Amphilanthus" is thus castigated as a "fair false man" in terms that might well apply to Amphilanthus (1.299), but in the end Perissus is able to separate the true Amphilanthus from the false one on the basis of physical complexion (1.356). The Ambassador to the King of Candia is a darker-complexioned version of Amphilanthus: "For Complection, haire, and all loveliness soe like Amphilanthus ... Onely beeing neerer the sunn, hee had more hardly used him in roughly kissing then hee had Amphilanthus" (2.58). The Prince of Transylvania likewise resembles Amphilanthus in both his actions and person, but "if well marked" can be recognized as "short of him in stature, more in shape, and colour being blacker, and most in sweetenes, and perfect lovelynes" (1.586). Despite his failures and misjudgments, Amphilanthus always remains the most light-skinned, fair-headed, and white-attired of the knights in the *Urania*.

This same structure of physical identity continues for Amphilanthus in Part 2. Pamphilia encounters a knight in unfamiliar armor with a close beaver, but she nonetheless recognizes Amphilanthus by the color of his hands: "His hands bare, she was soone assured who itt was, for though the strongest and bravest man breathing, yett hee had hands of that delicasie for pure whitenes, delicate shape, and softnes, as noe lady could compare with them" (2.197). The colors "black" and "tawny" are never associated with Amphilanthus as designations for skin color or complexion. Amphilanthus takes on these colors in his armor, but only temporarily in ways that remind Wroth's readers that his first and truest armor was probably his original all white armor (1.99). In the enchantment at the Throne of Love, Pamphilia castigates Amphilanthus for his repeated changes to his colors, asking "do you adde to your inconstancy, as fast as to your colours?" (1.165). As her complaint suggests, Amphilanthus' inconstancy is a color, but it never colors him. Whatever his moral qualities and personal failings, Amphilanthus conforms physically to assumptions concerning the visible manifestation of heroic and noble virtue (the fair are fair, the nobility noble) that had defined romances such as *Amadis*. Equally importantly, Amphilanthus' fairness of complexion allows him to be legible and identifiable as such by both other characters and the readers of Wroth's romance.

Pamphilia is not fair like Amphilanthus, and her identity is less compatible with the conventions of romance identity. Pamphilia is never quite readable as being as black as she might imagine herself when she says that she would rather be a "black-moor," but the narrative repeatedly compares Pamphilia's skin and complexion to those of Philistella (1.263), Antissia (1.37, 1.61), Urania (1.37), Limena, Lindafilla (2.168), and even Amphilanthus. In these comparisons, Wroth depicts Pamphilia's skin as less fair, more dark, or ultimately, in some manner, neither light nor dark in ways that make her person and her emotions harder to read within the traditional terms of the genre.

Pamphilia's complexion and disposition are first introduced relationally through the figure of Antissia. The comparison between Pamphilia's and Antissia's fairness is made in passing by Allimarlus (1.37), but the first moment at which we really have a sense of Pamphilia as a character is when she complains about Antissia's white complexion. When Amphilanthus brings "the faire Antissia" (1.61) to the Morean court, he praises Antissia so strongly that Pamphilia responds by dismissing Antissia's "extreame whitenesse":

For truly my Lord … me thinkes there is not that beautie in her as you speake of, but that I have seene, as faire and delicate as shee; yet in truth shee's very white, but that extreame whitenesse I like not so well, as where that (though not in that fulnesse) is mix'd with sweete lovelines; yet I cannot blame you to thinke her peerelesse, who viewes her but with the eyes of affection. (1.61)

Readers have tended to accept Amphilanthus' interpretation of this scene: Pamphilia is jealous and her attitude toward Antissia expresses the jealousy of a "Womanish disposition" (1.61).[62] Antissia functions within Part 1 of Wroth's narrative as a counterpoint to Pamphilia in that she represents a different model of passion (both amorous and humoral) and, with those, a different kind of writing (good and constant writing which emerges out of melancholy as opposed to the jealousy-driven writing that emerges out of Antissia's dominant choler and which ultimately leads her to madness).[63] These differences in physical and authorial disposition are marked in the text as differences in complexion as well. Jealousy becomes Antissia's signature and, if Pamphilia expresses that disposition here, then it is primarily a way for Wroth to shift that emotion away from Pamphilia and onto Antissia.

This scene is less about Pamphilia's jealousy than it is about her melancholy. Immediately after this conversation, Pamphilia withdraws to her room, "to breath out her passions," to lament to the moon the "broken joyes, blacke despaires, incirckling me," and to write and then immediately destroy the first of many verses about her love and "silly woes" (1.62). In a gesture that marks Wroth's interest in creating Pamphilia within a racially-inflected model of melancholy, Pamphilia's conversation about Antissia's white skin thus leads to the first expression of the black melancholy "which abounded in the Princesse" (1.63).

Throughout the romance Pamphilia's complexion is never itself described in the ways that those of Antissia, Urania, Limena, Lindafilia, or Amphilanthus are. At best, we always see her standing, shadowed, alongside a fairer companion. Pamphilia may be fair and then dark, but the shift between the two is a narrative one, not a character one, a change in how and what we see rather than in how Pamphilia herself is. In contrast to Amadis, Orlando, Quixote, and Pyrocles, Pamphilia does not change. She does not "become" dark in her melancholy. Because Sidney is working within the Ficinian tradition that links Plato's "divine furor" to the pseudo-Aristotelian Problem 30, he necessarily conceives of melancholy as a transformation, a falling away that begins in the mind and soul and then extends to the body. The emotional and spiritual degradation of the once heroic Pyrocles thus expresses itself as a physical darkening of his complexion: "Even the colour and figure of his face began to receive some alteration" (*Arcadia*, 109). Rejecting this fiction of the physically transformative consequences to the passion of melancholy that she inherits from Montalvo, Ariosto, and Sidney, Wroth never suggests that the "color and figure" of Pamphilia is in any way a degradation. By being told that she is fair but then seeing her as dark in the important first scene of Pamphilia's recurring "blacke despaires," we instead are given the constancy of passion without the inconstancy implied by a moment of origin, love without the falling and passion without transformation.

In the same way that Wroth only names Pamphilia at the moment that she inherits her identity, Wroth attributes a darker complexion to Pamphilia from the beginning precisely as a way of protecting Pamphilia from the defects, medical or narrative, that would be associated with intimations of changeability. Her having a dark complexion (being less fair than Antissia or Philistella or Limena) is what enables Wroth to attribute to Pamphilia the humor of melancholy. That is, by associating Pamphilia with the humors and complexional disposition of the "Black-moore" that Pamphilia ultimately but despairingly wishes she were, Wroth makes it possible to construct a melancholic character who embodies her own "spotlesse affection" (1.63), the love that she will later describe to Antissia as "a love more pure, / Then spotlesse white" (1.146).

In suggesting that Pamphilia's alter egos (Philistella, Urania, Antissia, Lindafillia) are all represented as being whiter and fairer than she, my goal is not to trace out a racially-inflected binarism running through Wroth's romance. This would be a mistake for two reasons. First, Wroth generally resists our attempts to impose order onto the multiple and multivalent form of the *Urania*. Second, it is important not to bring what Roxann Wheeler identifies as "our current preoccupation with chromatism" back to Wroth.[64] In this respect, I would reassess Hall's conclusion that Pamphilia differs from the other characters because she tries to transcend or subvert the binaries of black and white that are imposed upon her by a male world. Pamphilia does transcend those categories, but it is not because she somehow anticipates either the emergence of racialism or historically later reactions against it. Rather, Pamphilia is a nostalgic character – one whose melancholy looks back to an older model and the possibilities it implied rather than anticipating the terms of a future not yet staked out. That is, in Part 1 Pamphilia's beauty conforms to a humoral model of complexion but not yet a fully racialist one.

Wroth's uneasy relationship to changing definitions of humoral and proto-racialist identity can also be seen in the interplay between "color" as it appears in complexion and corporeal figure, on the one hand, and as a term that describes armor, device, and attire, on the other. "Color" for Wroth is a fluid marker of both the conventions of literary genre and the historic realities of social, ethnic, and personal identity. Wroth is attentive to descriptions of armor and attire throughout the *Urania*. In keeping with the heraldic and aristocratic sources for romance, her characters are associated with colors that express the ways in which their identities are conceived by Wroth and meant to be construed by her readers. In the *Arcadia*, Sidney uses armorial impressas to signify identity (Philisides, "spotted to be known," for instance): as signs, they must be read. Requiring both interpretation and intellectual deciphering, Sidney's devices mark both social identity and genealogical descent. Wroth, by contrast, uses color alone as a device. Wroth's colors are not so much heraldic devices as they are complective colorings that reveal emotion and disposition. Wroth's devices no longer mark kinship identity in the same ways that Sidney's devices did, but these colors are also not yet complexions that provide ways of categorizing and distinguishing groups of peoples.

The most historically and iconographically distinctive color for the knights and ladies in the *Urania* is tawny. Although a number of characters wear tawny, it is Pamphilia's color. Tawny is Wroth's device for Pamphilia. She wears tawny in her triumphal moment at the Throne of Love and other characters wear it in response to or as "shadowed" versions of her. Wroth's use of tawny as a device to identify Pamphilia provides an example of how changing definitions of race and genealogy intrude into the world of early modern romance, but also marks limits of that process.

The first time we see tawny is on Steriamus. In love with Pamphilia and despairing of it, Steriamus dresses according to his fortune, "in Tawny, wrought all over with blacke" (1.76). Nereana, who vainly loves Steriamus, arrives at the Morean court "attended on by ten knights, all in Tawny, her selfe likewise apparreld in that colour" (1.193). Pamphilia succeeds at the enchantment at the Throne of Love, "appareled in a Gowne of light Tawny or Murrey, embrodered with the richest, and perfectest Pearle for roundness and whitenes" (1.169). Emilina, the Lady who has been deceived by the false Amphilanthus and who is a version of Pamphilia, wears her betrayal in her person and her attire: "so handsome, as one might well see, there had bin excellent beauty, but decay'd, as love was withered to her ... her clothes were of Tawny, cut with Willow" (1.300). Amphilanthus himself ultimately takes tawny as his color in Book 3, when, as Amphilanthus defeats his enemies and is ready to claim his throne and return to Pamphilia, she and the princesses disappear, "the losse of the whole worlds beauty" (1.374). Marked as a loss not just of Pamphilia but of a chance at happiness, Amphilanthus becomes the Lost Man: "making all tawny, as if forsaken, which was but the badge of the Liverie he gave her soone after" (1.376). He later elaborates on those colors, according to his "humors," adopting "Tawny, embroidered with Black and Silver" (1.396).

Nostalgically, Wroth wants to associate tawny with the heraldic meanings that it had in an earlier age. In the early sixteenth century, tawny is a cloth color and, through such usage, enters into heraldic and aristocratic registers. In the Elizabethan romances of the 1570s–1590s, for instance, writers such as Sidney, Greene, Lodge, and George Whetstone follow heraldic usage and use tawny to express forsakenness, abjection and steadfastness in love.[65] Even during the Elizabethan period, though, the term and color "tawny" begins to drop out of heraldry and subsequently out of romance because it becomes associated with kinds and populations of peoples (Indians, Abyssians, Tartars, mulattos) whose seemingly mixed and marked identities re-imagined genealogy and lineage in ways that were not consistent with the genealogical goals of either art form. Wroth, like Mary Sidney Herbert, was particularly attentive to metaphors and images of clothing. Wroth's use of the term "tawny" as a device for Pamphilia is worth setting in its larger cultural context, where it reveals the historic tensions in the model of identity that she constructs for this autobiographical character. Looking back to the outmoded colors of the Elizabethan tilts and romances and resisting the newly racialized meanings that had become associated with "tawny" as a color, Wroth evades the lessons of "The Masque of Blacknesse" and "Beauty."

As I suggested in the Introduction, Eden's 1555 translation of Peter Martyr's *Decades* introduces "tawny" into English discussions of racial difference. This is perhaps the first time that "tawny" is used in print to describe a person, rather than their clothes. In "Of the colour of Indians," Martyr meditates on the "marveylous" variety in the color of the peoples in the Indies and introduces "tawny" as his key term for describing both differences between the Indians and Europeans and Africans, on the one hand, and, on the other, as a standard for differentiating among the Indians themselves. Confronting the bodies of the naked Indians, Martyr figuratively covers them by using a cloth color and thus treating their bare skin as a kind of attire, as a natural livery: neither black nor white nor yellow, the Indians are shades of tawny; they are the "other of other colours, as it were of divers liveries."[66] After Martyr, "tawny" becomes a standard term of visual description in the translations of ethnographic and choreographic works of writers such as Samuel Purchas, Leo Africanus, and d'Avity.[67] In this new generic context, "tawny" becomes almost exclusively a term for complexion; other contemporary uses stand as metaphors derived from this new base meaning.

What is most distinctive about Martyr's discussion of skin color – and what informs his metaphor of skin as a "liverie" – is his sense that complexion and color are "natural":

These colours are to be marveiled at, even so is it to be considered, howe they differ one from an other, as it were by degrees, forasmuch as some men are white after divers sorts of whitnesse, yelowe after divers maners of yelowe, and blacke after divers sorts of blackenesse and howe from white they go to yelowe by discolouringe to browne and redde: and to blacke by ashe colour, and murrey, sumwhat lighter then blacke: and tawney like unto the west Indians which are altogether in general either purple, or tawny like unto sodde quinces, of the colour of Chestnuttes or Olives, which colour is to them naturall and not by their goinge naked as many have thought: albeit their nakednese have somewhat helped thereunto. (310ᵛ)

For Martyr, skin color is importantly not a dis-coloration. Seeing such color demands wonder as a response, in part because there is no narrative (no implied before and after) attached to skin color. Having the same kind of fixed symbolic status as liverie would in a world governed by class stratification and sumptuary laws, skin color is for Martyr a given identity rather than a mark of alteration. Although Martyr's terminology – or Eden's translation of it – is widely accepted, most later writers do not accept his arguments. Interest in treating skin as a discoloring transformation (from what is always assumed to be an originary white to black, yellow, or tawny, through either the burning of the sun or the curse of God) quickly dominates late sixteenth- and early seventeenth-century discussions of the "other" colors of "other" peoples and what those might mean.

Mary Wroth was almost certainly familiar with her uncle's thoughts on what the diversity of the world, and the peoples in it, implied about the status of God. Philippe de Mornay, seigneur du Plessis-Marly, directly confronts the theological implications of the discoveries recorded by Peter Martyr in his *De la verité de la religion chrestienne* (1581). The translation of *De la verité* that was begun by Philip Sidney and later completed by Arthur Golding, or perhaps by Mary Sidney Herbert, as *The trewnesse of the Christian Religion* (1587) records what happens, even by the 1580s, to arguments such as Peter Martyr's. In an essay that is devoted to demonstrating that there is but one God, Mornay responds to what he takes to be an urgent theological challenge posed by the discoveries in the Indies, and elsewhere, of peoples who seemed to fall outside the expectations of the known world. Responding to the kinds of arguments that had informed Martyr's account, he thus introduces a whole series of rhetorical personifications of God's power to create unity out of diversity.

In *The trewnesse of the Christian Religion*, we again find the metaphor of liveries at the center of a discussion of skin color and the order of the world. Here, Mornay argues that when the "many liveries of soldiers" combine to form but one movement on the field, that means that there is a single general in charge. This metaphor, together with one about magistrates and the rule of law, then introduces what is clearly the chief concern of his argument – God and skin color. For Mornay, the sun

> maketh some folkes whyte, some blacke, some read, and some Tawny; and yet is hee but one selfsame Creature, which at one selfsame instant, by one selfsame course, and with one selfsame quality of heates, doth all the say things, not onely diuers, but also contrarie. And hee that should say that it is any other than one selfsame Sunne that maketh the Ethyopian blacke, and the Scotte yellowi[s]h, were not worthy to be answered. No if a creature doth by heate (which is but a qualitie) bréede so divers effectes; what shall we say of the Creator, I meane the infinite Being of GOD, who imparteth himself to all things?[68]

Where Martyr figured skin as a livery because he saw identity as natural and visible, Mornay fractures that model: it is only the soldiers on the field who wear livery. In the face of unexpected diversity and multiplicity, Mornay is committed to articulating an ordered universe with a single God: countering suggestions that the Indians had their own gods and worshipped the Sun, Mornay makes the Sun stand alongside magistrates and generals as a way of transforming worship and divinity into idolatry and worldly authority.

The key point, though, that distinguishes Martyr from Mornay is that skin color is "made," an accidental attribute ("but a qualitie") that is produced by the sun. Mornay's emphasis on complexion as a sign of *alteration* (a physical degradation that will be easy later to see as a moral fallenness) persistently informs the early seventeenth-century linguistic shift from "tawny" to "tanned."[69] Mary Sidney Herbert, for instance, in *The Tragedie of Antonie* (1595), has Cleopatra imagining herself having dominion over a vast empire beyond Egypt of "tawny nations scorched with the sun."[70] Cleopatra's colonized subjects are nations of people who have been made "tawny" by the sun – and that state of transformation is by implication a quality that enables their subjugation to others.[71]

When "tawny" (color) becomes "tanned" (marked), we see a version in small of the larger cultural process by which skin color, separate from complexion, goes from being the sign of a fixed identity to a mark of alteration. "Tanned" is a possibility invoked by Wroth's "tawny" liveries and devices. In using "tawny" as her device for Pamphilia, Wroth is particularly concerned about the connection between darkness and the alteration that this color implies: those who are tawny are not so much dark, as dark *because* changed. While insisting on a heraldic reading of forsaken steadfastness to her tawny ladies, Wroth is also aware that constancy may have its own beginning and ending.

In the inset narrative of Lady Pastora, Wroth registers this possibility that tawny might become tanned, that constancy might produce the mark of alteration. Pastora is a surrogate for both Pamphilia and Wroth, and her story must be read as a warning or a threat about how constancy may lead not only to unhappiness but to self-destruction. Steriamus finds Lady Pastora, alone, on a rock, brushing her hair and lamenting her lost love. Pastora recounts the story of her love for a knight, and how she was constant and how he forsook her. As they talk, Pastora brushes her fair hair and then winds "her hayre in strings of tawny, to shew her chan[g]e; then as if to hide it a little, or rather her selfe from the Sunne, she put a dainty straw hat on head, appearing like Ceres crowned with her own plenty" (1.416). Lady Pastora's story ends with her rescuing her former lover from the sea, nursing him back to health, and then having his new mistress take him away again, leaving Pastora alone on her desolate rock. She is not the fair Andromeda at the start, and she is not the dark Dido at the end. Ultimately, Steriamus and the narrative also leave Pastora behind, "on the Rocke as hard as her fortune and as white as her faith" (1.421). The story of Pastora warns us about the consequence of constancy more ruthlessly and thoroughly than, as yet, Pamphilia's own story does. Lady Pastora wears tawny and is white; but she wears tawny not because of her constancy but because "of her change" and, while still white, risks sunburn and other alterations that will be the consequence of adhering to, rather than deviating from, that constancy.

Pastora is what Pamphilia may become and Wroth herself may already be.[72] Importantly, Wroth uses tawny as a "device" for inscribing, in both a narrative and a heraldic sense, Pamphilia as constant. As the limit case of Lady Pastora suggests, Wroth does so by insisting that, for Pamphilia at least, tawny is a color rather than a complexion. When writing out of the humoral tradition, Wroth describes Pamphilia's complexion and disposition as black in mood and as less than fair in complexion; when drawing on the heraldic and courtly romance, she describes her color, in dress and through the devices of those that serve her, as tawny. In the figure of Pamphilia, these colors and the different forms of visible identity that they imply never collide. Up until the point when Lady Pastora momentarily enters the narrative, Wroth consistently elides any sense that tawny could refer to skin complexion and does so not for what we would understand to be strictly racial reasons but rather to separate Pamphilia from the underlying narrative of alteration, of transformation and degradation, that this complexion implied in the world after Peter Martyr. Through Pamphilia, Wroth looks back toward the fixed identities of both the world of Elizabethan heraldry and the moment when skin color could be understood as a livery.

Considering the *Urania* as a whole, the fair-skinned characters arise out of the old world of romance, while many of the dark-skinned ones also draw on new models of racial difference. In that sense, Wroth's writing articulates an asymmetry that suggests how her work is emerging out of a racially transitional moment. Amphilanthus is always fair-skinned; his heraldic color begins as white and matches his skin complexion. Claramundo, the son of the king of Cilicia, is black and wears black: "without his helme, els compleatly armed, butt all in black … his face likewise bare, and though black yett shewing such a magestick looke, and that with such sweetnes as made the beholders thinke till then they had beeheld noe thing of rareness" (2.240–41). Claramundo does not need to wear a black helmet because his black sorrow appears as its own livery in the color of his face. It is not in any simple sense a fact of geography or biology that makes Claramundo dark skinned ("though black yett showing such a magestick looke"). Wroth does not, for instance, provide any details about the complexion of his father, the treacherous neighboring King of Celcia, because in his case she has no interest in comprehending his emotions: Claramundo, in turn, only appears as a character after and in a sense because of his father's death. Sharing a geographic boundary in melancholy with the country of Pamphilia, Claramundo is black in his mourning because his emotion is one that Wroth understands to be legible in ways that Pamphilia's ultimately is not. Claramundo can be comprehended in largely the same terms as Amphilanthus and in that sense the fair Amphilanthus and the dark Claramundo have more in common with each other than either has with Pamphilia.

Pamphilia's identity emerges out of a racialized and intellectualized model of melancholy in ways that differentiate her from both the other female characters, who are fair, and the male ones, who are not. The sense that identity must be legible in one's skin is at the heart of the well-known episode in which Pamphilia writes her poems and inscribes her emotions into an ash tree. As we have seen, Pamphilia's initial expression of the "blacke despairs" that encircle her follows the pattern of genial melancholy and leads directly to the first of Pamphilia's many moments of authorship: Pamphilia brings into her bed a little cabinet and, dissatisfied with what she reads there, she begins to write, "being excellent in writing" (1.62). In discussing such moments, Gary Waller has described how Wroth works, throughout the *Urania*, to create private spaces which enable her to use "withdrawal as a tactic of self-affirmation for a woman's subjectivity."[73] As a humoral disposition, a complexion that is and is not physically visible, Pamphilia's melancholy is itself construed as a kind of a private space within the narrative of the *Urania*. Despite what seem to be the "secret code" ciphers embedded with the text and in contrast to her sonnets, Wroth's fiction often attempts to disclose and make intelligible to others private experiences and emotions. Introducing the trope of melancholy provides Wroth with one way to create emotional space within the otherwise flat, but legible, world of romance.

Pamphilia writes her first poem on paper, but her next effort is engraved in the "skin" of a tree. Unable to tell Amphilanthus that she loves him and trapped between friendship for Antissia and love for Amphilanthus, Pamphilia finds that her constancy constrains her and makes her "suffer for a vertue" (1.92). Vexed by conflicts between desire and virtue, Pamphilia's melancholy again separates her physically and emotionally from others; she withdraws into a glade. Although initially overcome by despair, Pamphilia's melancholy soon takes a different form:

"Nay," said shee, "since I find no redresse, I will make others in part taste my paine, and make them dumbe partakers of my griefe." Then taking a knife, shee finished a Sonnet, which at others times shee had begunne to ingrave in the barke of one of those fayre and straight Ashes, causing that sapp to accompany her teares for love, that for unkindnesse. (1.92)

As an allegory of melancholic authorship, the image of Pamphilia inflicting pain and inscribing imitation into her readers is a startling one: Mary

Ellen Lamb has thus suggested that this scene is about the angry "heroics of constancy" that are motivated by "dual forces of sexuality and denied anger."[74] Certainly, Lamb's reading is consistent with the Ficinian tradition that connected creative genius (Pamphilia as a melancholic author) with mad fury, jealousy, and sexual excess (cutting into the tree in an act of rage, sexual frustration, and revenge).

Pamphilia's melancholy expresses itself in Ficinian terms, but the emotions that produce that expression also align themselves with the alternative geo-humoral tradition that associated melancholy with constancy and wisdom. What Pamphilia writes is not a simple expression of fury and sexual excess: rather, like the black melancholic, Pamphilia's emotions begin in constancy. They are ones that she tries to comprehend through reason and self-knowledge: "for all these disorderly passions, keepe still thy soule from thought of change ... let me rather hate my selfe for this unquietnesse; and yet unjustly shall I doe too in that, since how can I condemne my heart, for having vertuously and worthily chosen?" (1.92). It is only when she realizes that her emotions cannot find expression in the world, in her body ("delicate without as she was faire, and dark within as her sorrows"), that she shifts to the rage of melancholic authorship. Her command, "Keepe in thy skin this testament of me" (1.92), is in part an expression of her, and Wroth's, frustration at how difficult it is not to maintain but to express constancy in her own person. Writing is aggressively physical and yet it does not seem to capture her complexion: what she writes in the "skin" of the tree is the expression of her own complexion that somehow escapes her body.[75] It is not so much that it is difficult for Pamphilia to say that she loves Amphilanthus; rather, it may be that the very act of saying it contravenes it and, indeed, almost as soon as she writes this poem, she denies it to Antissia.

The desire to make her melancholy legible to others is also at the heart of the dream that leads Pamphilia to wish – and despairingly fear – to be a blackmoor. This scene in the *Urania* needs to be read alongside a related moment in Sonnet 22 in "Pamphilia to Amphilanthus." During the opening section of the sequence, Wroth figures emotional suffering and despair through a series of abstract, incorporeal, and, as Jeff Masten notes, privative images.[76] She initially calls out to Night as a kind of companion in the blackness she feels: "I love thy count'nance" (15/P17.9) and "Come, darkest night, becoming sorrow best" (19/P22.1). She ultimately dismisses the deprivation of light that is night as only a temporary kind of absence, incomparable to hers: "Nor could black darkness ever prove soe badd / As paines which absence makes mee now indure; / The missing of

the sunn awhile makes night / But absence of my joyes never sees light"
(20/P23.11–14). Having dismissed this neo-Platonic conceit, Wroth shifts
from the "countenance" of black darkness to the complexion of "Indians
scorched with the sun." This shift from classical Petrarchan neo-Platonism
to contemporary encounters with other races is achieved in Sonnet 21 by
an uncharacteristic invocation of the absent Amphilanthus. Prior to this
moment, Amphilanthus has been absent not just from Pamphilia but
from the sequence itself: as Elizabeth Hansen notes of this moment, "his
beauty is never blazoned, his actions are never described, he never bestows
or withholds favor, he never tempts the lover to sexual transgression, he is
never named, he is not there."⁷⁷ Yet, in Sonnet 22, Pamphilia does invoke
Amphilanthus, willing him to be there: "Pity my loving, nay of conscience give / Reward to me in whome thy self doth live" (21/P24, 13–14),
and, with this, the sequence momentarily moves out of the abstract and
into the corporeal.

Having suggested in Sonnet 22 that her devotion goes beyond love to
a kind of idolatrous worship (to "thine Image," her "faith is such," 21/
P24.2, 9), Wroth shifts from idolatry to Indians in Sonnet 23. Darkness is
no longer a deprivation and absence but, through the burning rays of the
sun, a mark of presence and, importantly, one ultimately to be desired for
its clarity:

> Like to the Indians, scorched with the sunne,
> The sunn which they doe as theyr God adore
> Soe ame I us'd by love, for ever more
> I worship him, less favors have I wunn,
> Better are they who thus to blacknes runn,
> And soe can only whitenes want deplore
> Then I who pale, and white ame with griefs store,
> Nor can have hope, butt to see hopes undunn;
> Beesids theyr sacrifices receavd's in sight
> Of theyr chose sainte: Mine hid as worthles rite;
> Grant me to see wher I my offrings give,
> Then lett mee weare the marke of Cupids might
> In hart as they in skin of Phoebus light
> Nott ceasing offrings to love while I Live.
>
> (22/P25)

Where Mornay is troubled by the theological threats posed by pagan
idolatry, Wroth follows Sidney in integrating it into the fiction of her
love. Sonnet 22 contains Wroth's responses to Sidney's depiction of love
in "Astrophil and Stella" as a sunburn, scorching his mind and his body
in ways that enslave him. In Sonnet 1, Astrophil wears "the blackest face

of woe" and complains of his "sunburnt brain"; by Sonnet 47, he wonders "Can those black beams such burning marks engrave / In my free side? or am I born a slave?"[78] For Sidney, what is at stake in "Astrophil and Stella" is implicitly a question of authorship and its relationship to subjugation, imagined at such moments as both enslavement and disfiguration. Is Astrophil being written (and constituted) by Stella's burning eyes, which brand into his body, into his skin, the marks of his enslavement? Or, and perhaps equally troublingly, is his brain "sunburnt" not by Stella but by the enslaving forces of bad poetic imitation?

Wroth's "sunburnt" poem is not about poetic imitation: indeed, her chief complaint is that no one can understand, let alone emulate, what she feels. Even though Sidney worries that perhaps his susceptibility to love is proof that he was "born a slave" (47.3), he nonetheless uses the language of race in his sequence as part of his characterization of love as a fallenness, as a form of degradation and entanglement in corporeality. Wroth, by contrast, aligns herself with Indians as an image of devotion and constancy. She begins, "Like to the Indians scorched with the Sun," but in contrast to Sidney, her complaint is actually that she is not enough like them: the sun burns and blackens the Indians who worship it. Sunburn becomes a mark that means that they are answered by their gods as she is not by hers: Wroth does not yet wear the mark of her devotion and she remains "pale, and white" with grief. Masten points out how as a whole this "relentlessly private" sequence "articulate[s] a woman's resolute constancy, self-sovereignty, and unwillingness to circulate among men,"[79] but Sonnet 22 uncharacteristically expresses deep frustration at the limitations to that kind of privacy.

Wroth laments the disparity between her emotions and her (or their) complexion, between what she feels and what she shows, between what she writes and how it (and she) is read. As one "pale, and white ame with griefs store," she seems jealous of those "who thus to blacknes run." She wants to be as visible as they are: whereas the Indians worship their sun openly, she punningly finds that her acts of devotion and poetry are hidden away as "worthles rite." The sestet closes with the request to be more like the Indians: she appeals to wear the mark of her devotion and to do so in a manner that is legible (still invisible but nonetheless readable, "In hart as they in skin"). She wants her rites and writing to be both meaningful and apparently so; she already has the burning heart in her breast; now she wants the mark of it. If this poem is about writing in ways that we would expect from her sources in Sidney, then it is a gesture of inadequacy – a desire for legibility but a frustration of that possibility. While

Wroth does close the poem with the idea that she will continue offer-ings for as long as she lives, Sonnet 22 is unexpectedly not about con-stancy. Rather, it makes an appeal to be changed; racial difference enters that appeal in ways that carry over into Pamphilia's related dream in the *Urania* of her blackness and despairing wish to be a blackmoor.

Wroth's Sonnet 22, "Like to the Indians scorched with the sunne," is a lyric version of the romance lamentation "I would rather wish to be a Black-moore" that appears midway through Book 3 of the published *Urania*. Importantly, both the sonnet and the romance are structured as invocations and imperatives that call for some physical alteration. Wroth has Pamphilia make the same request in each: to be made black (in heart, in melancholy) as the text of her love and devotion. Alone and question-ing her own being – "why was this rare excellent qualitie of constancy allotted thee" (1.464) – Pamphilia despairs:

> I wish I were so fit, as you might ever love, and such an one as all the world might thinke fit for you, then I know you would be just: nor wish I this for any bene-fit, but for your love; for else in the comparison of other gaine unto my selfe, or any other then your loved selfe, I rather would wish to be a Black-moore, or any thing more dreadfull, then allure affection to me, if not from you; thus would I be to merit your loved favour, the other to shew my self purer, then either purest White of Black: but faith will not prevaile, I am forsaken and despised, why dye I not? (1.465)

This episode is the close of a long sequence in Book 3 that should in some sense be the end of the romance and, because that is not achieved, is instead the moment at which it becomes clear that the romance can-not, either in the published or the unpublished version, ever reach that end. This section of the book also concludes Wroth's ability to depict Pamphilia as a melancholic character in what are increasingly historically anachronistic and personally impossible terms.

At the beginning of Book 3, many of the strands and impediments to personal and political happiness come together. On a political level, Amphilanthus and the other princes are successful in their wars and bring peace (1.373); after the death first of his own father at the end of Book 2 and of the Emperor in Book 3, Amphilanthus learns that he has been elected the Holy Roman Emperor (1.440). On a personal level, Antissia, previously a rival for Amphilanthus, is married to Dolorindus (1.397), and Leandrus, who had sought Pamphilia's hand in marriage and might have been understood as an impediment to marriage with Amphilanthus, sud-denly dies of pleurisy, a tragic case of humoral excess (1.463). Yet, just at this moment, as the princes are ready to return to Corinth where their loves await them and, for Amphilanthus, "all happiness appeared ready to embrace him" (1.375), Pamphilia, Urania, Philistella, and Selarina inexplicably wander off on a boat and, in part through Pamphilia's desire for knowledge, become imprisoned in the enchantment of the magic theater (1.371–73).

The ostensible narrative purpose of this segment of the book is to explain why, at the end of the enchantment, Amphilanthus goes off to be crowned as Emperor but Pamphilia remains alone ("when as all the lovers should be made happy with their long desired loves in marriage ... onely Pamphilia was unpromised, for she was her owne," 1.457). To the extent that Wroth resists allowing us to take an allegorically moralistic reading of the princesses' decision to get in the boat that takes them into the storm that leaves them on the island, ultimately the fundamental cause of this disruption in the narrative is Pamphilia's melancholy.

Wroth seems to lack a way to write a happy conclusion not because she cannot imagine one, but rather because she conceives of happiness as impossible within what Pamphilia herself refers to as her "composition" (1.470) insofar as doing so would bring change to Pamphilia's breast and, with it, its own kind of inconstancy. In some respects, the sense of forsakeness and lost possibility that Wroth previously attributed to Pamphilia as a character disperses out into the narrative itself in an unusual number of narrative injections: it is now the story that is forsaken, that takes on the attributes of excessive regret and despair that previously were associated with and within Pamphilia. For reasons that Wroth does not and perhaps cannot explain, this divergence fundamentally breaks apart the possibility of a happy ending for Pamphilia as a character and for the romance as a narrative.

This break also leads to the most sustained depictions – and interrogations – of Pamphilia's melancholy humor. The scene in which Pamphilia wishes to be a Black-moor is the culmination of this questioning and arguably the last moment in the romance at which melancholy is distinctively hers. Unlike the first enchantment on Cyprus which is designed to stage Pamphilia's constancy, this second enchantment becomes a tableau vivant for depicting her melancholy. As various male lovers try the enchantment, the marble theater is filled with pairs of lovers, but Pamphilia remains alone: amid the couples, "still Pamphilia sits leaning her cheeke on her hand, her eyes lifted upwards as asking helpe, at her feete lay Leandrus gazing on her, and as much imploring pity from her, as she begged it from another" (1.421). Pamphilia takes on the distinctive pose of Dürer's Melancholia. And like Melancholia, the swarthy face of melancholy that went hand in hand with constancy and wisdom has in some way now become metaphorical. In an indication that there has been a shift that has material consequences, Pamphilia now actually wears black (1.461) and for the first time her complexion and appearance are described as being subject to change and loss (1.442, 461, 463). In a series of discussions between Urania and Pamphilia, Wroth raises the possibility that constancy is not a virtue: Urania castigates Pamphilia for lack of discretion, for allowing herself to be made subject to love in ways that challenged her ability to rule over others, for idolatry and self-enslavement, and for failing to preserve her beauty – all in the name of constancy (1.458–9, 467–71).

Pamphilia's lamentation to the absent Amphilanthus that she would be black, "or any thing more dreadfull," rather than be attractive to others does in part refute Urania's complaint that pursuit of emotional constancy is altering her physical appearance. It is in that sense that Hall argues that this scene is about Pamphilia's desire to challenge the way that the binary between black and white plays into the gendering of contemporary standards of physical beauty. Yet, I would also stress that it is also the moment at which Pamphilia – and through her Wroth – despairs of making the humor of black melancholy, with its complexion of wisdom, chaste passion, and constancy, visible to others. Pamphilia complains, "You knew my love, you seemed to cherish it, *all eyes saw it too, for my face shewed it, I strove for nothing more then meanes to declare it*" (1.464, my emphasis). Pamphilia does not just wish to embody a physical type that, as Hall demonstrates, was the implied antithesis to Jacobean standards of beauty. Rather, Pamphilia wants to show herself purer than either white or black, to be spotless and clear in her purity.

As Wroth suggests in Sonnet 22, Pamphilia is despairingly willing to let constancy change her (make her even black) if only that will make it possible for her devotion to be physically manifest. Earlier, Wroth had introduced the complective differences between Pamphilia and characters such as Antissia and Philistella in ways that suggested that she was confident that complexion was both physical and moral. The intrusion of a racialist attitude toward the possibility of being truly black (and the denigration, "or anything more abhorrent") is a response to the breakdown and failure of the traditional geo-humoral model of complexion that she had relied upon in imagining Pamphilia as a character. As in Sonnet 22, blackness represents some kind of imaginative boundary. It is not so much or simply that new versions of race insinuate themselves into Wroth's story. Rather, what remains unimaginable for Wroth is a solution to the problem of trying to create – and make readable to others – in one's person a story of constancy and true passion.

Pamphilia's melancholy becomes impossible to sustain as such by the end of Part 1. The unfinished manuscript continuation of the *Urania* marks important changes in Wroth's personal situation. The interval between the writing of the two parts of the *Urania* also coincides with a larger historical re-evaluation in which black melancholy was increasingly being displaced by a white, courtly melancholy that indirectly worked to racialize earlier forms of melancholy. In the final section of the chapter I will trace how, in Part 2, the inability to sustain Pamphilia's black melancholy calls into being – within the logic of Wroth's story and the cultural context against which Wroth is writing – her marriage to Rodomandro, the dark-skinned King of Tartaria. She says "I would rather wish to be a black-moor" in Part 1; she marries Rodomandro in Part 2. Rodomandro is, in part, an alter ego to Amphilanthus and one whose secondary and supplemental quality is marked, in part, through his racial difference.[80] Rodomandro is a fictional expression of the romance consequences of Pamphilia's complexional disposition (melancholy) and key virtue (constancy).

Indeed, it is because Rodomandro is in some sense authored by Pamphilia's creative melancholy that he is so carefully marked as an invented, not quite "real," character throughout Part 2. In that respect, Pamphilia's marriage should not be understood simply as an autobiographical writing out of Wroth's marital compromises: instead, she seems wed to constancy in ways that prevent the much-awaited marriage to Amphilanthus. The appearance of Rodomandro as a character is historically nostalgic to the degree that he looks back to a humoral theory that is increasingly displaced by what will become the twin models of universal emotion and racialized identity that dominate later seventeenth- and eighteenth-century culture. As such, Rodomandro thus both emerges out of Pamphilia's melancholy and yet marks the end of the possibilities that Wroth imagines for Pamphilia and, through her, for herself as an author and lover.

In this extended sequence, Wroth takes us from Pamphilia, sitting on the island as the figure of Melancholia, forgotten and forsaken in the midst of love, to her late-night abject desire to be black and pure in her desire. This section of the romance is concerned with questioning the limits and possibilities to Pamphilia's black melancholy. There are two chief consequences for Wroth. First, in Book 2, melancholy is no longer distinctively Pamphilia's. Melancholy is reclaimed as a masculine humor in ways that conform to the historic emergence of melancholy as a northern, white, and largely aristocratic complexion in early seventeenth-century England. Second, Pamphilia does not become a blackmore, but she does marry the dark-skinned King of Tartaria, Rodomandro. These two events are connected in that they suggest how melancholy is no longer a complexion available to Pamphilia – how that humor and the qualities associated with it have been claimed by men on the one hand and how Wroth in turn registers that loss (emotional constancy, wisdom of the self, and authorial genius) through Pamphilia's marriage outside the Holy Roman Empire and away from Amphilanthus.

In Part 2, melancholy is reclaimed as a masculine affliction. In Part 1, the only male characters who are depicted as being melancholy are Philarchos, whose humor is primarily a sign of kinship with Pamphilia (1.199), and Curardinus, "the dainty melancholy" (1.556). In Part 2, by contrast, melancholy becomes the dominant complexion of the male characters. Wroth initially reopens her story with a description of the disastrous melancholy that consumes Selarinus after his wife, Philistella, dies in childbirth (2.1–10, 22; 2.303–6). This opening frame indicates how melancholy will drive the narrative line of Part 2. Following this introduction, Wroth regenders the humor and complexion of melancholy by imagining it as constitutive of masculine identity. The Duke of Austria, Salamino, falls into a "deepe melancholy" over his love for the married Celia and disguises himself as a woman to pursue her (2.15, 18). We are introduced to both Floristello and his cousin Verolindo, two of the second generation of princes, as "the most brave Melancholy" and "the sad knight" (2.93, 95).

Although Floristello worries when his "passionate discourse" is discovered that his "effeminancie showld outrun my manhood," Wroth herself stresses that the experience of melancholy will be what makes them men: when Floristello finds Verolindo, just as he himself had been found by others, he is "a knight of most beautifull face and complexion … His face and yeers might bee equall with our knights, nature nott yett having dunn them the honor by a beard to show either of them of what sex they were" (2.95). Philarchos, whose melancholy previously seemed to be a familial extension of Pamphilia's, remains "ever melancholy" (2.118), but his melancholy is more fully developed on its own terms: "my self beeing no thing butt thoughts, and thos soe disjoined as made me fitt for no expression but an od thing, a mass of confusion, wanting an new creation to bee a man againe, from the Chaos of my noe beeing, as I ordered the matter" (2.118). Melancholy is a passion that disrupts identity and, with it, narrative; at the same time, the cure for melancholy is also its own telling. Yet, as Philarchos' comments suggest and these examples confirm, in Part 2 of the *Urania* melancholy has become largely a man's story rather than a woman's.

The melancholy of Part 2 of the *Urania* (male characters with dark moods and fair complexions) conforms closely to the passion that Robert Burton describes in his *Anatomy of Melancholy*.[81] As we have seen, 1621 is a shared publication date for the *Urania* and the *Anatomy of Melancholy*. Wroth is aware of the Ficinian understanding of genial melancholy that emerges out of pseudo-Aristotle; this model informs her construction of Pamphilia as an author and is where she is most strongly responsive to Sidney. In a more fundamental way, though, Wroth also looked back nostalgically to the Hippocratic geo-humoral tradition that construed melancholy as a black complexion to establish an amorous constancy for Pamphilia. As recent studies of the history of the passions have made clear, Burton takes a different tack. In Part 2, Philarchos, Selarinus, Floristello, Verolindo, and most especially Amphilanthus appear almost as characters drawn out of the pages of Burton: they exemplify and inhabit his types of melancholy in ways that suggest how Wroth's manuscript continuation to the *Urania*, written several years after the *Anatomy*, involves a fictive engagement with the intellectual shift Burton's work represents. More importantly, Wroth's response to Burtonian melancholy sharply delimits the possibilities for Pamphilia as an author and a lover and, with them, Wroth's as well.

The Anatomy of Melancholy is exhaustive in the typology it offers – as Burton himself often characterizes it, the book is a catalogue of "tedious" details that seemingly include every imaginable possibility and category of melancholy. Nowhere in the encyclopedic *Anatomy*, though, is there a version of Pamphilia. Departing from the assumptions that informed Wroth's integrated understanding of melancholy, constancy, complexion, and authorship, Burton does not understand melancholy in humoral terms. Burton does recognize and refer to the traditions that supposed that melancholy is black and that blacks are melancholic: among those affected by melancholy, he lists blacks (110); he cites Bodin's assertion that "hot countries are most troubled with melancholy, and that there are therefore in Spain, Africa, and Asia Minor, great numbers of mad men" (155), as well as Ercole Sassonia's conclusion that those who are naturally melancholy are of "a leaden colour or black" (261). Despite those acknowledgements, Burton nonetheless qualifies them in ways that give melancholy a face that is much more like his own.

Distinguishing between artificial and natural melancholy, Burton departs from the Greek model of temperature and complexion: rather than seeing northerners as a mirror image of southerners (both equally distant from the classic temperate complexion, but one phlegmatic and the other melancholy), he insists that northerners and southerners are equally likely to be melancholic: "cold air in the other extreme is almost as bad as hot … But these cold climates are more subject to natural melancholy" (156).[82] In addition to redrawing the map of the temperaments, Burton at the same time works to universalize melancholy by arguing that all men, all societies, and even all creatures and beings suffer from the black humor of melancholy (39, 43). In concluding that "All places are distant from heaven alike … to a wise man there is no difference of climes" (406), Burton inverts classic humoral theory, takes the local and asserts it as a universal.

The narrative structure that Burton gives to melancholy provides a way of understanding what happens to race, constancy, and authorship in the second part of the *Urania*. Of all the kinds and possibilities for melancholy, Burton privileges heroic melancholy: "gallants, noblemen, and most generous spirits are possessed with it" (490). This is precisely the tradition of melancholy that, within the register of romance, takes us from Amadis and Orlando to Pyrocles. The heroic virtue to Burton's melancholy differs from Pamphilia's virtuous constancy: heroic melancholy is indeed given to men who are great of heart and desire. "Inconstant they are in all their actions," the heroic melancholic is "prone to love and easy to be taken … quickly enamoured, and dote upon her, *Et hanc, et hanc, et illam, et omnes*, the present moves most, and the last commonly they love best" (257–58).

Amphilanthus embodies Burton's version of heroic melancholy: in name, the lover of two, he also becomes in fact the husband of two. In the "happily ever after" interlude with which Part 2 begins, he insists that his "humor is constancy" (2.37), but this claim is disrupted first by the return of his former love Antissia (2.29), his dalliance with the Queen of Candia (2.58), and his ensuing marriage to the King of Slavonia's daughter (2.131). Even as he pursues love, Amphilanthus now also suffers melancholy. His inconsolable despair thus becomes a major topic throughout Part 2 (2.111, 118–19, 136–38, 141, 172, 182–84, 193, 256–57, 388–90) and, like the magic boat that carries him away on this new passion (2.184), his melancholy moves the narrative line. Re-imagining Amphilanthus as inconstant and melancholy also changes Pamphilia. In Part 1, Amphilanthus' passion was part of a narrative defined by Pamphilia's constancy. As he wandered and returned, she remained the narrative center. While her constancy stood as a boundary against which he defined himself as a character, it was also the means through which Pamphilia created herself as an author. In Part 2, by contrast, what had been distinct – Amphilanthus' passion and Pamphilia's melancholy – are largely conflated onto Amphilanthus. His melancholy, like Burton's, is universal in ways that pre-empt that possibility for others.

Burton provides the framework through which we can understand an important and overlooked consequence to the shift from complective melancholy to a purportedly universal heroic melancholy. In Burton's long section on "Love-Melancholy," the universalization of heroic melancholy brings with it the racialization of lust. Whereas complective melancholy imagined, as Charron and earlier humoral handbooks made clear, that blackness and constancy were different features of a single category, Burton's insistence on a heroic melancholy that is inconstant, but nonetheless strangely dispassionate, leads to a compensatory displacement of lust, lasciviousness, and jealousy onto Africans, southerners and blacks. Burton thus draws on Leo Africanus: "in many parts of Africa (if she be past fourteen) there's not a nobleman that marries a maid, or hath a chaste wife" (647). He likewise follows Jean Bodin who "ascribes a great cause to the country or clime, and discourseth largely there of this subject, saying that southern men are more hot, lascivious, and jealous, than such as live in the north; they can hardly contain themselves in those hotter climes, but are more subject to prodigious lust" (630) and, again from Bodin, "your hot and southern countries are prone to lust and far more incontinent than those that live in the north" (504). Although Burton supposes that women are not ordinarily subject to melancholy, when black men are involved that is no longer the case: "A little soft hand, pretty little mouth, small, fine, long fingers … Though in men these parts are not respected; a grim Saracen sometimes, – *nudus membra Pyracmon*, a martial hirsute face pleaseth best; a black man is a pearl in a fair woman's eye" (517).

In the first two parts of the *Anatomy*, Burton had created the possibility of universal melancholy in part by adding "northern climes" to traditional descriptions of southern humors; in this last book mostly devoted to "Love-Melancholy," Burton creates a tacitly northern "heroic melancholy" in part by splitting them apart again and redescribing southern passion in newly sexualized and racialized terms. That is, in Burton we see how the shift away from complective humors to purportedly universal passions created an intellectual space that enabled incipient racialism.

What does it mean for Pamphilia to wish she were a blackmoor rather than to be attractive to anyone else and then find that not only is she attractive to someone else but that that someone is a version of the blackmoor she imagined as the outer limit of her desires, the test of her constancy and melancholy? In Burton, one consequence of universal melancholy is the racialization of lust. In Wroth, the inclusion of a similar heroic melancholy leads to the appearance of Rodomandro and Pamphilia's subsequent marriage to him. It would be possible to read Wroth's story of Pamphilia marrying Rodomandro in Burton's terms, but Wroth instead uses Rodomandro to register the gendered and authorial consequences of universal emotion and the forms of racialization that they imply. Unlike many contemporary ethnographic accounts of the Tartars, Rodomandro is dark skinned, and his complexion is described in detail: "for the couler of itt, itt plainely shewed the sunn had either liked itt to much, and soe had too hard kissed itt, ore in fury of his delicasy, had made his beames to strongly to burne him … though black, yett hee had the true parfection of lovlines" (2.42). Wroth's Rodomandro is not the black man who is a pearl in a fair woman's eye; he is not, that is, a fictional embodiment or expression of passion or lust in Pamphilia in the ways that Burton encourages us to see.

At the same time, though, Rodomandro is also not the cold, dry, black figure of wise and constant melancholy that Charron described and whose qualities had defined Pamphilia in Part 1 of the *Urania*. In Rodomandro, and in Part 2 more generally, Wroth is giving us neither the new racialism nor the old humoralism. To understand Rodomandro we must also recognize that humoral theory is not consistent with modern understandings of the self as fixed, bounded, and impermeable. This inconsistency expresses itself in literary terms in Part 2 not just in the traits that Wroth attributes to individual characters (the many male melancholics), but in a rethinking of the possibility of character as such.

If we take seriously the premise of a fluidity within and among bodies, passions, and environments, we can see Rodomandro as a creation of the combined humors of Pamphilia and Amphilanthus. The narrative clearly insists that Rodomandro is not a "real" character. In his initial appearance, Rodomandro reads, in ways that none of the other characters within Wroth's romance have, as a kind of figure of romance drawn from the pages of *Sir Gawain and the Green Knight*, *Amadis*, *Quixote*, or the *Arcadia*. Pamphilia and Amphilanthus miss his entrance because they are off hunting a stag that is "for couler and greatnes" as strange as the Great Cham himself. Pursuing a remarkable beast that is "cole blacke, horns and all, and a big as two ordinary ones were, onely one white spott on the left side in shape of an arrow," Pamphilia and Amphilanthus find that they are strangely unable to bring down the bayed animal for when they shoot at it, they find that they have "shott only against a shadow" (2.43). After his marriage to Pamphilia, Rodomandro's existence remains equally shadowy: after he marries Pamphilia (2.74), he almost immediately leaves the court, first with Urania (2.278) and then on an adventure (2.282); he ends up being imprisoned by a giant (2.317), and is rescued and released so that he can attend Amphilanthus' wedding (2.324, 329 351); later recaptured, he is freed again and returns to Pamphilia but only to leave again almost immediately (2.367). Indeed, he dies, only perhaps by accident, and then almost immediately is brought back to life again. His initial appearance is precipitated by how the return of Antissia to the narrative challenges Amphilanthus' new claim to constancy; his continuing presence manifests the conflicting emotions and dispositions that are at stake in these debates. Although referred to as "the Great Cham" and "the Great Tartar," Rodomandro is not so much an exotic stranger intruding into the world of the *Urania*, mysteriously entering the narrative from a distant land of difference, as he is a character created from within the fiction. Constructed by the irreconcilable passions of Amphilanthus and Pamphilia, Rodomandro emerges out of the conflict between personal emotion and social identity that romance expresses.

The new challenges that Wroth sees in making emotions a visible part of social identity are most explicitly expressed in Wroth's treatment of the black deer that Amphilanthus and Pamphilia are hunting when Rodomandro first appears at the Morean court. The deer – the narrative's demand that its hide be read – models the acts of reading that Wroth wants her reader to bring to Rodomandro. The deer is "cole blacke," but is marked with "onley one white spott on the left side in shape of an arrow" (2.43). Pamphilia shoots at the deer but she is not able to hit him not because she misses but because she has "shott only against a shadow" (2.43). She cannot shoot him because he already has been. Complexion – the mark of passion, that of the lovers, not the deer – is inscribed in his skin. In a similar way, their passion is also inscribed in the skin of Rodomandro. Importantly, though, this moment puts both Pamphilia and Amphilanthus into a new position: they no longer inscribe their emotions and passions as authors (into their own skins, onto the skins of trees, leaves of paper, or into the world itself). Instead, in ways that reflect the larger shift between Parts 1 and 2 of Wroth's romance, they have now become readers: whether in the white arrow on the deer's skin or in Rodomandro's complexion, they now read the history and identity of their passions.

The deer is not the only one whose complexion is marked by a passion that needs to be understood as a form of social identity because many of the lost princes and princesses in Part 2 have birthmarks. The birthmarks that are a conventional romance device from Homer and Heliodorus to Chretien de Troyes and Montalvo are signs of genealogical identity and social standing. While such birthmarks promise that identity emerges out of a past that persists and can be "read" on the body, Wroth instead records not past origins but future destinies. Like the deer's white spot, Wroth's birthmarks return us to Peter Martyr's image of skin color as a form of heraldry. Thus Floristello has not a single spot but an elaborate "figure most perfectly framed of a lyoness in bloody couler, as it were ramping to pray upon his bleeding hart strooke with loves dart" (2.97); Floristello takes his name not from his family but from the "delicat, curious flower within a starr" that he mistakenly believes his beloved will have on her breast (2.97). Parselius' son, Trebisound, is recognized by a red spot like a strawberry on his neck (2.219). His daughter, Candiana, also unknown, has a "delicate mole on her left breast resembling a hart, with a dart shott thorough itt" (2.219). Most importantly, Faire Designe, who seems to be but is not yet recognized as Amphilanthus' illegitimate son and who is never named as Pamphilia's son, has "a sipher on my hart" that encodes the name of his beloved as she, he believes, has the matching cipher of his on her heart (2.297).

In each case, these marks do little to clarify origins; if they secure paternity, it is only indirectly. Rather, they express or anticipate passion and in that sense they are complective. The birthmarks are thus a sign of both the new understanding of racial identity as skin color that structures Part 2 and, at the same time, Wroth's own resistance to this new form of identity. Importantly, though, they do not reveal the hidden secrets of individual passion (what, for instance, Candiana does or might herself feel). Rather, Wroth imagines – or hopes – that one's body might express another's passion, rather than one's own. (Whereas Amphilanthus in Book 1 made the cipher his armorial device in Part 1 to signal himself, his son ciphers not himself but his beloved.) This is not just a shift in Wroth's understanding of emotion but more importantly of reading as an act that constitutes that emotion. In Part 2, all of these figures and ciphers demand and depend on an act of reading.

Wroth's desire for legal recognition of her own illegitimate children is at the heart of these stories about the identities, passions, and complexions of the lost princes and princesses. Part 1 seemed to create possibilities for multiple readers: hence the ciphers embedded within the text and worn by the central characters encouraged contemporary readers, like Denny, to suppose that there were ciphers that connected the text to the world that they imagined that it described. Amphilanthus was the Knight of the Cipher, while Pamphilia and others carved ciphers of her love into the bark of trees. It was this sense of shadowed identities that led contemporary readers to write asking Wroth for a copy of the "key" to the ciphers hidden in the text. This interpretation of Wroth's romance emerges in part out of the difficulties that Wroth found in trying to make emotion and meaning visible. Part 2, by contrast, is ultimately structured around a single reader. In Part 1, the various ciphers (on trees, on armorial devices, in sonnets) are expressions of personal passion that are also texts of self-authorization: the characters (and through them Wroth) hope to make the cipher of their passions legible to others. These are texts with possible audiences because at this point Wroth's private passions still have not just personal but also social consequences. If the ciphers are – or can be – misread, it is in part because they are about making emotion and disposition known beyond the self within a public, social world of the kind that romance had always imagined.

In Part 2, by contrast, the focus has narrowed. The ciphers are now inscribed as birthmarks on the bodies of the second generation of princes and princesses. In their very persons, the princes and princesses are of course the physical consequences of expressions of passion. Yet, notably, Wroth's romance continuation does not focus on the past – at least not in the sense of genealogical inheritances. Rather, these new ciphers are only nostalgic to the extent that they work to attribute humoral qualities to William Herbert as a reader. These ciphered bookmarks are not self-authorizing: they are not about Wroth. Rather, they mark and predict reciprocal passion. In that sense, Wroth ultimately uses the birthmarks – however optimistically – to engage and script Herbert's passions. In a literary and emotional sense, Wroth's hope is that, in reading, Pembroke will follow and participate in the quest to find the lost princes and princesses. The acts of interpretive recognition that this search demands stand as fictional versions of the acts of legal recognition that she would have him pursue in giving identity to their shared children. Indeed, Wroth's commitment to securing the rights of paternity for her illegitimate children ought to ally itself well with the genealogical assumptions of traditional romance. What we find, however, is that the form of reading that Wroth hoped to shape for Herbert was not achievable. Pamphilia shoots at shadows; Floristello is mistaken about his love; we never know whether or not the true Sophie has the cipher of Faire Design on her. However unknowable the biographical details finally are, the manuscript *Urania* ultimately ends not because it has no ending, either biographical and literary, because Pembroke, with the possibilities he represents, has stopped reading.

In Part 2 the usurpation of Pamphilia's melancholy and her marriage to someone other than Amphilanthus leads to a breakdown in romance legibility. A key question for Part 2 is thus who its imagined readers are. Does Wroth truly construct any reader for this unpublished manuscript other than her own Amphilanthus, William Herbert, the Earl of Pembroke? The Rodomandro episode is in some way about authorship; Faire Designe and the birthmarks bring complexion back to the subject of readership. In these episodes, Wroth is searching for a way in which new definitions of "complexion" can also imply a new model for reading romance. Just as the birthmarks do not acquire their true meaning or confer identity until the right lover appears to interpret them, the text as a whole suggests a new model of identity that is premised on William Herbert's reading of this manuscript. If the appearance of Rodomandro thus marks the end to Wroth's imagining of the possibilities for authorship, then the birthmarks in a way represent a last, but basically futile, hope for some promise of readership.

Notes

INTRODUCTION

1 Thomas Wilson, *The Arte of Rhetorique* (London, 1560), A5ᵛ.
2 Philip Sidney, "Astrophil and Stella," *Sir Philip Sidney: A Critical Edition of the Major Works*, ed. Katherine Duncan-Jones (Oxford University Press, 1989), p. 153.
3 Thomas Hobbes, *Leviathan, or the matter, forme, and power of a common-wealth* (London, 1651), p. 1.
4 Ania Loomba, "'Delicious traffick': Racial and religious difference on early modern stages," in Catherine M. S. Alexander and Stanley Wells, eds., *Shakespeare and Race* (Cambridge University Press, 2000), p. 201.
5 It may be helpful to provide a word about terminology here: the limitations and usefulness of "race" as a category of inquiry or term of discussion in the early modern period has been much debated. As Peter Erickson notes, "I know of no other area of scholarly investigation in which the overall interpretive stance and conceptual framework so directly and completely hinge on the status and legitimacy of a single word. It is not too much to say that the very existence of race as a valid topic in Renaissance studies depends on the outcome of a definitional crisis concerning the term race" ("The Moment of Race in Renaissance Studies," *Shakespeare Studies* 26 [1998], p. 27). While some critics have understandably wanted to push critical discussion toward making more precise or historically accurate distinctions about this term, Kim F. Hall recognizes the ways that this gesture may be self-defeating to the extent that it has the unintended effect of cordoning off certain kinds of critical scrutiny under the otherwise desirable goal of avoiding various forms of anachronism: "I hold onto the idea of a language of race in the early modern period and eschew scare quotes so popular in contemporary writing" (*Things of Darkness: Economies of Race and Gender in Early Modern England* [Ithaca: Cornell University Press, 1995], p. 6). In a similar vein, Jonathan Crewe has argued against too narrow or too historically precise a notion of what race meant: "it seems to me that prevailing historicist and/or cultural-studies categories make it difficult to precipitate the issue of 'race' in Shakespeare or in Renaissance studies as a whole broadly or fluidly enough to do justice to the phenomenon ... Without denying the sensitivity of the issue, I do not believe that these forms of constriction do any good" (Jonathan Crewe, "Out of the Matrix: Shakespeare and

Race-Writing," *Yale Journal of Criticism* 8.2 [1995], p. 13). In this project, I try not to use the term "race" in an anachronistic sense, but I also recognize that more neutral terms may not always sufficiently capture what may be at stake in these texts, either for us or for contemporary readers. I also recognize, as the following chapters will make clear, that different categories are very hard to keep separate: matters that may seem to be questions of faith quickly turn into issues of genealogy and ethnicity, whereas geo-humoral medical assumptions can easily be absorbed into arguments about Catholicism or conversion.

6 Geraldine Heng, *Empire of Magic: Medieval Romance and the Politics of Culture Fantasy* (New York: Columbia University Press, 2003), p. 14; Mary Floyd-Wilson, *English Ethnicity and Race in Early Modern Drama* (Cambridge University Press, 2003), p. 1; Gary Taylor, *Buying Whiteness: Race, Culture, and Identity from Columbus to Hip-Hop* (New York: Palgrave, 2005), pp. 59–64.

7 Notable exceptions to this pattern of almost exclusive interest in drama are: Hall, *Things of Darkness*; Peter Erickson and Clark Hulse, eds., *Early Modern Visual Culture: Representation, Race, and Empire in Renaissance England* (Philadelphia: University of Pennsylvania Press, 2000); and Sujata Iyengar, *Shades of Difference: Mythologies of Skin Color in Early Modern England* (Philadelphia: University of Pennsylvania Press, 2005).

8 Mary Floyd-Wilson, "Moors, Race, and the Study of English Renaissance Literature," *Literature Compass* 3.5 (2006), p. 1045; 10.1111/j.1741-4113.2006.00366.x.

9 A. C. Bradley also made similar claims earlier, but his statements were not in proximity to the appearance of racial studies as a central part of the field.

10 Andrew Hadfield, ed., *Routledge Literary Sourcebook on William Shakespeare's Othello* (New York: Routledge, 2003), p. 66. Hunter's essay was initially given on April 19, 1967, and published first in *Proceedings of the British Academy* 53 (1968), pp. 139–63, and republished as "Othello and Colour Prejudice," in Hunter's *Dramatic Identities and Cultural Traditions: Studies in Shakespeare and his Contemporaries* (New York: Barnes and Noble, 1978), pp. 31–59.

11 Hunter, "Othello and Colour Prejudice," pp. 31, 59. For recent histories of scholarship on race in the Renaissance, and in Shakespeare studies in particular, see Floyd-Wilson, "Moors, Race, and the Study"; Emily Bartels, "Shakespeare's 'Other' Worlds: The Critical Trek," *Literature Compass* 5.6 (2008); 1111–38; 10.1111/j. 1714–4113.2008.00571.x; and Margo Hendricks, "Surveying 'Race' in Shakespeare," in Alexander and Wells, eds., *Shakespeare and Race*, pp. 1–36.

12 Because of Shakespeare's power as a conveyor of cultural values, attention to race has transformed performance studies in compelling ways. The scholarship here is extensive, and includes work on Anglo-American literature, postcolonial theater, and film. For a collection that brings together important recent work in the field, see Ayanna Thompson, ed., *Colorblind Shakespeare: New Perspectives on Race and Performance* (New York: Routledge, 2006).

13 Dympna Callaghan, "What's at Stake in Representing Race?" *Shakespeare Studies* 26 (1998), p. 23.

14 Dympna Callaghan, "'Othello was a White Man': Properties of Race on Shakespeare's Stage," in *Alternative Shakespeares*, ed. Terence Hawkes, vol. II (London: Routledge, 1996), p. 193.

15 Callaghan, "'Othello was a White Man,'" pp. 194, 211.

16 Barbara Fuchs, *Mimesis and Empire: The New World, Islam, and European Identities* (Cambridge University Press, 2000), p. 4. See also Daniel Vitkus' model of "imitative receptivity" in *Turning Turk: English Theater and the Multicultural Mediterranean, 1570–1630* (New York: Palgrave, 2003) for a related example of the benefits to this kind of approach.

17 Fuchs, *Mimesis and Empire*, p. 1.

18 Stephen Greenblatt, *Renaissance Self-Fashioning from More to Shakespeare* (University of Chicago Press, 1980), p. 3.

19 Jacob Burckhardt, *The Civilization of the Renaissance in Italy* (1860; New York: Barnes and Noble, 1999), p. 81.

20 Greenblatt, *Renaissance Self-Fashioning*, p. 9.

21 Edward W. Said, *Orientalism* (New York: Random House, 1979), p. 63. See Bartels, "Shakespeare's 'Other' Worlds," p. 7.

22 Susan Stanford Friedman, "'Border Talk,' Hybridity, and Performativity: Cultural Theory and Identity in the Spaces between Difference," *Eurozine* (www.eurozine.com), 2002–06–07, 5/14.

23 Mary Thomas Crane, "What was Performance?" *Criticism* 43.2 (2002), p. 169.

24 Crane, "What was Performance," p. 171.

25 Stephen Greenblatt, ed., *The Norton Shakespeare* (New York: Norton, 1997); further citations will be from this edition. See Donald Foster's lexical database, SHAXICON, for the possibility that Shakespeare may have played this role. This possibility, while speculative, is interesting to think about in the context of *both* reading and performance memories (http://shakespeareauthorship.com/shaxicon.html). For a provocative application of Foster's performance attributions to understanding Shakespeare's possible relationship to racial impersonation, see Imtiaz Habib, "Racial Impersonation on the Elizabethan Stage: The Case of Shakespeare Playing Aaron," *Medieval and Renaissance Drama in England* 20 (2007), pp. 17–45. Habib argues for a strong version of the relationship between drama and emergent racialism, tending to see drama as a powerful *causal* force in creating racialism (p. 17). Habib's work is influenced by the post-colonial performance models of Michael Taussig, and he thus is concerned to document the physical presence of black Africans in London in the pre-slavery period. (See also his *Black Lives in the English Archives, 1500–1677: Imprints of the Invisible* [Aldershot: Ashgate, 2007].) Here, I would note that Foster stresses that SHAXICON provides a tool for seeing how Shakespeare's work is "mnemonically 'structured'" not just by his possible performance roles but also by his reading practices.

26 Callaghan, "'Othello was a White Man,'" pp. 195–96; Virginia Mason Vaughan, *Performing Blackness on English Stages, 1500–1800* (Cambridge University Press, 2005), pp. 9–12; Farah Karim-Cooper, *Cosmetics in Shakespearean and Renaissance Drama* (Edinburgh University Press, 2007), pp. 144–45.

27 Richard Eden, trans., *The Decades of the New World or West India* (London, 1655), 310ᵛ. See Chapter 4 for a discussion of the publication history of this essay and its impact on English readers.

28 Robert S. Miola, *Shakespeare's Reading* (Oxford University Press, 2000), p. 2. Miola problematizes older models of source study (pp. 164–69), but he is primarily interested in presenting a clear account of how Shakespeare transformed what he read, "the book on the desk that Shakespeare read and revised" (p. 35). My goal throughout this study is to think more about how readers were transformed, both intellectually and physically, by both what and how they read.

29 Hall, *Things of Darkness*, pp. 94–5, 100.

30 Margo Hendricks, "Surveying 'Race' in Shakespeare," in Alexander and Wells, eds., *Shakespeare and Race*, p. 1.

31 See Elizabeth L. Eisenstein, *The Printing Press as an Agent of Change* (1979; Cambridge University Press, 2008), pp. 25, 220–21; Alfred W. Crosby, *The Measure of Reality: Quantification and Western Society, 1250–1600* (1997; Cambridge University Press, 2007), p. 231; Michael Clapman, "Printing," in Charles Singer *et al.*, eds., *A History of Technology* (Oxford University Press, 1957), III: 377.

32 Heng, *Empire of Magic*, p. 7.

33 Heng, *Empire of Magic*, p. 14.

34 Heng, *Empire of Magic*, p. 70.

35 Benedict S. Robinson, *Islam and Early Modern English Literature: The Politics of Romance from Spenser to Milton* (New York: Palgrave, 2007), p. 4. See, among others, Fredric Jameson, "Magical Narratives: Romance as Genre," *New Literary History*, 7 (1975), pp. 135–63; David Quint, *Epic and Empire: Politics and Generic Form from Virgil to Milton* (Princeton University Press, 1993); Joan Pong Linton, *The Romance of the New World: Gender and the Literary Formation of English Colonialism* (Cambridge University Press, 1998), pp. 13–38; Brian C. Lockey, *Law and Empire in English Renaissance Literature* (Cambridge University Press, 2006), esp. pp. 4, 8, 17–46.

36 Eisenstein, *Printing Press*, p. 170.

37 On the print history of the various versions and portions of the *Amadís* cycle, see Chapter 3.

38 Edwin Place, "Preface," in Edwin Place and Herbert Behm, trans., *Amadis of Gaul: Books I and II* (1974: Lexington: University Press of Kentucky, 2003), p. 9.

39 Irving A. Leonard, *Books of the Brave: Being An Account of Books and of Men in the Spanish Conquest and Settlement of the Sixteenth-Century New World* (1949; Berkeley: University of California Press, 1992), pp. 124–39.

40 The *Amadis* cycle is unusual in that at least the first four books were translated into Latin (Venice, 1533), but none of the later books ever were and this translation was not republished.

41 Fynes Moryson, *An Itinerary Written by Fynes Moryson, Gent., … containing his ten yeeres travell* (London, 1617), pp. 56–57.

42 See Chapter 4 for a fuller discussion.

43 See, especially, Barry Ife, *Reading and Fiction in Golden-Age Spain: A Platonist Critique and Some Picaresque Replies* (Cambridge University Press 1985), pp. 1–23 and Shadi Bartsch, *Decoding the Ancient Novel: The Reader and the Role of Description in Heliodorus and Achilles Tatius* (Princeton University Press, 1989).

44 Ife, *Reading and Fiction*, p. 3.

45 Ife, *Reading and Fiction*, p. 3.

46 Janice Radway, *Reading the Romance: Women, Patriarchy and Popular Literature* (Charlotte: University of North Carolina Press, 1984). For an early modern example of readers who lived these fictions, see Barbara K. Lewalski, *Writing Women in Jacobean England* (Cambridge: Harvard University Press, 1993), pp. 45–65.

47 This question has been a central one since at least Eldred Jones' important *Othello's Countrymen: The African in English Renaissance Drama* (Oxford University Press, 1965), p. viii. See also James Walvin, *The Black Presence: A Documentary History of the Negro in England, 1555–1860* (London: Orbach and Chambers, 1971), pp. 61–63; F. O. Shyllon, *Black People in Britain* (Oxford: Clarendon, 1977), p. 3; Peter Fryer, *Staying Power: The History of Black People in Britain* (London: Pluto Press, 1984), p. 12; Emily Bartels, "Too Many Blackamoors: Deportation, Discrimination, and Elizabeth I," *SEL* 46.2 (2006), p. 306; Habib, "Racial Impersonation," pp. 22–23; and Habib, *Black Lives*, pp. 19–120. For important parallel arguments about the numbers of *conversos*, crypto Jews, and other "false Christians" living in England, see James Shapiro, *Shakespeare and the Jews* (New York: Columbia University Press, 1996), pp. 43–88.

48 Lucien Febvre, *The Problem of Unbelief in the Sixteenth Century: The Religion of Rabelais*, trans. Beatrice Gottlieb (Cambridge: Harvard University Press, 1988). Febvre's formulation, as many critics have pointed out, is at the heart of Marshall McLuhan's *Gutenberg Galaxy*. Febvre's "age of the eye" – what printing did – should perhaps be set alongside Michael Baxandall's notion of the "period eye," which involves an early version of what has since become the field of sensory history. See Mark M. Smith, "Producing Sense, Consuming Sense, Making Sense: Perils and Prospects for Sensory History," *Journal of Social History* (Summer 2007), p. 842.

49 *The Decades of the New World of West India*, trans. Richard Eden (London, 1555), 310$^\mathrm{v}$; see Chapter 4 for discussion of the publication history of this essay and its impact on English readers.

50 Carlo Ginzburg, *The Cheese and the Worms: The Cosmos of a Sixteenth-Century Miller*, trans. John and Anne Tedeschi (1976; New York: Dorset Press, 1980), p. 88.

51 Valerie Traub, "Mapping the Global Body," in Erickson and Hulse, eds., *Early Modern Visual Culture*, p. 46.

52 And Stephen Gosson was not entirely wrong to complain that much of the matter appearing on the Renaissance English stage had been "ransacked" from "the *Palace of pleasure*, the *Golden Asse*, the *AEthiopian historie*, *Amadis of Fraunce*," and the other printed romances (*Playes confuted in five actions* [London, 1582], D5ʳ).

53 Robert Greville, Baron Brooke, *Catalogus librarum ex bibliotheca* (London, 1678).

54 Elizabeth L. Eisenstein, *The Printing Press as an Agent of Change* (1979; Cambridge University Press, 2008), p. 227.

55 See, for example, Roxann Wheeler, *The Complexion of Race: Categories of Difference in Eighteenth-Century British Culture* (Philadelphia: University of Pennsylvania Press, 2000), p. 2; Valerie Traub, "Mapping the Global Body," in Erickson and Hulse, eds., *Early Modern Visual Culture*, pp. 44–45.

56 For an overview of the history of reading as a field, see, among others, Heidi Brayman Hackel, *Reading Material in Early Modern England: Print, Gender and Literacy* (Cambridge University Press, 2005), pp. 2–5, 17–68; Leah Price, "Reading: The State of the Discipline," *Book History* 7 (2004), pp. 303–20; Jennifer Andersen and Elizabeth Sauer, "Current Trends in the History of Reading," in Andersen and Sauer, eds., *Books and Readers in Early Modern England* (Philadelphia: University of Pennsylvania Press, 2001), pp. 1–22. For an account of the methodological goals of the field, see Robert Darnton, "First Steps Toward a History of Reading," *Australian Journal of French Studies* 23 (1986), pp. 5–30, and "History of Reading," in Peter Burke, ed., *New Perspectives on Historical Writing*, 2nd edn. (1991; Cambridge University Press, 2001), pp. 157–86; and Roger Chartier, "Texts, Printing, Readings," in Lynn Hunt, ed., *The New Cultural History* (Berkeley: University of California Press, 1989), pp. 154–79.

57 Robert Darnton, "What is the History of Books?" *Daedalus* 111.3 (1982), p. 65.

58 See, for examples, William H. Sherman, *John Dee: The Politics of Reading and Writing in the English Renaissance* (Amherst: University of Massachusetts Press, 1997), pp. 79–114; Lisa Jardine and Anthony Grafton, "'Studied for Action': How Gabriel Harvey Read his Livy," *Past and Present* 129 (1990), pp. 30–78; William H. Sherman, *Used Books: Marking Readers in Renaissance England* (Pennsylvania: University of Pennsylvania Press, 2008), pp. 127–48. See also Darton, "History of Reading," pp. 142–47, for assessment of the different results produced by macro- and micro-historical approaches.

59 Jardine and Grafton, "'Studied for Action,'" p. 40. See also Anthony Grafton, "The Humanist as Reader," in Guglielmo Cavallo *et al.*, eds., *A History of Reading in the West* (Amherst: University of Massachusetts Press, 1999), pp. 179–212.

60 Sherman, *John Dee*, pp. 65–66, 79–112. See also Sherman's overview in "What Did Renaissance Readers Write in their Books?" in Andersen and

Sauer, eds., *Books and Readers*, 119–37; and Anthony Grafton, "Is the History of Reading a Marginal Enterprise? Guillaume Budé and his Books," *Papers of the Bibliographic Society of America* 91.2 (1997), pp. 139–57.

61 Roger Chartier, *The Culture of Print: Power and the Uses of Print in Early Modern Europe*, trans. Lydia G. Cochrane (Princeton University Press, 1989), p. 3.

62 Brayman Hackel, *Reading Material*, pp. 58–69. See also Peter Lindbaum's examination of the Folger copies of Sidney's romance ("Sidney's *Arcadia* as Cultural Monument and Proto-Novel," in Cedric C. Brown and Arthur F. Marotti, eds., *Texts and Cultural Change in Early Modern England* [Basingstroke: Macmillan, 1997], pp. 80–94).

63 Brayman Hackel, *Reading Material*, pp. 157–58. Sherman finds that, across all categories, about 20 percent of early modern books have "significant" marginalia and inscriptions by early modern readers (Sherman, *Used Books*, p. 73).

64 Brayman Hackel, *Reading Material*, p. 8.

65 Owen Gingerich, *An Annotated Census of Copernicus' De Revolutionibus (Nuremburg, 1543 and Basel, 1566)* (Leiden: Brill, 2002). See also his autobiographical account of this book adventure, *The Body Nobody Read: Chasing the Revolutions of Nicolaus Copernicus* (New York: Walker and Company, 2004).

66 See, for example, Sherman, *Used Books*, pp. 151–78; Gingerich, *The Book Nobody Read*, pp. 202–19; and Jeffrey Todd Knight, "Making Shakespeare's Books: Assembly and Intertextuality in the Archives," *Shakespeare Quarterly* 60.3 (2009), pp. 304–40.

67 Price, "Reading," pp. 212–13.

68 Roger Stoddard, "Looking at Marks in Books," *The Gazette of the Grolier Club* (2000), p. 32; cited in Sherman, "What Did Renaissance Readers Write," p. 122.

69 Helen Hackett, *Women and Romance Fiction in the Renaissance* (Cambridge University Press, 2000), p. 6. The question of precisely who read romances has been a critically persistent one, particularly with respect to issues of gender and class. Recent critical work has emphasized the often rhetorical, ideological character of prefaces and other paratexts, while work in the history of reading has provided new evidence regarding historical readers: see, among others, Louis B. Wright, *Middle-Class Culture in Elizabethan England* (Ithaca: Cornell University Press, 1935), p. 110; Hackett, *Women and Romance Fiction*, pp. 3–19; Lori Humphrey Newcomb, *Reading Popular Romance in Early Modern England* (New York: Columbia University Press, 2000), pp. 1–20; Steve Mentz, *Romance for Sale in Early Modern England: The Rise of Prose Fiction* (Aldershot: Ashgate, 2006), pp. 17–18; Brayman Hackel, *Reading Material*, pp. 153–56. On recreational reading, see Jacqueline Pearson, "Women Reading, Reading Women," in Helen Wilcox, ed., *Women and Literature in Britain, 1500–1700* (Cambridge University Press, 1996), pp. 80–99.

70 On sensory history and history of the senses, see Smith, "Producing Sense"; Patricia A. Cahill, "Take Five: Renaissance Literature and the History of the Senses," *Literature Compass* 6/5 (2009), pp. 1014–30; 10.1111/j.1741.4113.2009.050656.x; on historical phenomenology, see Sean McDowell, "The View from the Interior: The New Body Scholarship in Renaissance/Early Modern Studies," *Literature Compass* 3/4 (2006), pp. 778–91; 10.1111/j.1741-4113-.2006.00346.x; and Bruce R. Smith, *The Key of Green: Passion and Perception in Renaissance Culture* (University of Chicago Press, 2008), pp. 28–29, 40.

71 Bruce R. Smith, *The Acoustic World of Early Modern England: Attending to the O-Factor* (University of Chicago Press, 1999), p. 28.

72 Adrian Johns, *The Nature of the Book: Print and Knowledge in the Making* (University of Chicago Press, 1998), p. 386.

73 See Guglielmo Cavallo *et al.*, eds., *A History of Reading in the West* (Amherst: University of Massachusetts Press, 1999) for an overview of the 2,000-year history by which reading became separated from the physical body. For the overlay of residual humoral and emergent mechanistic models of reading in mid-seventeenth-century debates, see Johns, *Nature of the Book*, pp. 380–443; for arguments that stress the extent to which monistic vitalism and Paracelsianism influenced models of reading in the seventeenth century, see Michael Schoenfeldt, "Reading Bodies," in Kevin Sharpe and Steven N. Zwicker, eds., *Reading, Society and Politics in Early Modern Society* (Cambridge University Press, 2003), pp. 215–43; and Elizabeth Spiller, "The Physics and Physiology of Reading: Milton's Apple and the History of Reading," unpublished essay.

74 On the history of Galenism and Galenic physic in the Renaissance, see especially Temkin, *Galenism*; on Galenic dietaries and the humoral body, see Ken Albala, *Eating Right in the Renaissance* (Berkeley: University of California Press, 2002) and Michael C. Schoenfeldt, *Bodies and Selves in Early Modern England: Physiology and Inwardness in Spenser, Shakespeare, Herbert, and Milton* (Cambridge University Press, 1999).

75 Floyd-Wilson, *English Ethnicity and Race*, p. 1

76 Schoenfeldt, *Bodies and Selves*, pp. 3–4.

77 Philippe de Mornay, *The True Knowledge of a man's owne selfe*, trans. A[thony] M[unday], London, 1603, p. 18

78 Earlier accounts of humoral physiology do mention various forms of reading. Increased attention to the relationship between reading and the passions of the mind, though, seems to be connected to print culture. Henry Crosse, for instance, complains repeatedly about how printing is a technology that makes it possible for vain readers to find texts fit for their own humors and generally laments what he sees as the humoral decadence of the present age (*Vertues Common-Wealthe, or the Highway to Honour* [London, 1603], O2^r, O4^r, Q3^v; I3^r).

79 Th[omas] Wr[ight], *The Passions of the Minde* (London, 1601), pp. 7–8.

80 For two slightly different contemporary summaries of the three faculties of the brain, see Mornay, *True Knowledge*, pp. 110–12, 114–18 and André du

Laurens [Andreas Laurentius], "The Diseases of Melancholy," in *A Discourse of the Preservation of Sight* (London, 1599), pp. 75–79. This model was not, however, universally accepted: see Juan Huarte, *The Examination of Men's Wits*, trans. R[ichard] C[arew] (London, 1594), pp. 24–32, 52–56, for a four-ventricle model of the brain, which rejects the idea that the different ventricles are each dedicated to separate faculties of the brain. See further, Walter Pagel, "Medieval and Renaissance Contributions to Knowledge of the Brain and its Functions," in F. N. L. Poynter, ed., *History and Philosophy of Knowledge of the Brain* (Oxford: Blackwell, 1958), pp. 95–114; and Alberto Manguel, *A History of Reading* (New York: Viking, 1996), pp. 28–32.

81 Juan Huarte, for instance, metaphorically treats remembering as a form of reading (*Examination*, p. 79).

82 Katharine A. Craik, *Reading Sensations in Early Modern England* (New York: Palgrave, 2007), p. 17.

83 Francis Bacon, *Essayes* (London, 1597), 1$^\mathrm{v}$.

84 Hobbes, *Leviathan*, p. 170.

85 Crosse, *Vertues Common-Wealthe*, B1$^\mathrm{v}$, N4$^\mathrm{r-v}$.

86 Juan Luis Vives, *Education of a Christian Woman*, trans. and ed. Charles Fantazzi (University of Chicago Press, 2000), p. 73.

87 Vives, *Education*, p. 79.

88 John Milton, "Areopagitica," in Merritt Y. Hughes, *Complete Poems and Major Prose*, ed. Merritt Hughes (1957; New York: Macmillan, 1985), p. 727. Milton, notably, begins with a humoral model of the body in which the identity of a particular book as either meat or poison largely depends on the body of the reader, but he then turns to a Paracelsian model of the body when he begins discussing the view that foreign books are a "contagion" or "working minerals" through which poisons could be "tempered."

89 Renaissance attitudes toward the physical consequences of reading here differ notably from attitudes toward reading in the pre-codex period: Guglielmo Cavallo thus notes that Roman medical treatises included reading (aloud, from a scroll) among types of exercise that were physically healthful ("Between Volumen and Codex," in Cavallo *et al.*, eds., *A History of Reading*, p. 74).

90 "To Leonard Philaras," in Kerrigan, Rumrich, and Fallon, eds., *Complete Poetry*, p. 780; *Second Defense of the English People*, in Don M. Wolf, ed., *Complete Prose Works* (New Haven: Yale University Press, 1953–1982), IV: 587–88. On Milton's belief that he suffered from *gutta serena* and that his blindness was essentially the consequence of digestive failure, see Kerrigan, *Sacred Complex*, pp. 202–5.

91 Sean McDowell, "Author's Introduction" to "The View from the Interior."

92 Schoenfeldt, "Reading Bodies," in Sharpe and Zwicker, eds., *Reading, Society and Politics*, pp. 218, 220. Like Johns, Schoenfeldt is primarily concerned here with the largely post-Galenic character of seventeenth-century reading, which he sees less as mechanistic than as inflected by Paracelsian models of the body (p. 222).

93 On proposals by More and other humanists for controlling religious reading, see Brayman Hackel, *Reading Material*, pp. 82–83; on humanist attitudes toward reading, see Daniel Wakelin, *Humanism, Reading, and English Literature, 1430–1530* (Oxford University Press, 2007), pp. 128–34, 191–211; on dietaries as an attempt to either control or, in Schoenfeldt's terms, "manage" passion, see Ken Albala, *Eating Right in the Renaissance*, and Schoenfeldt, *Bodies and Selves*.

94 Wright, *Passions*, p. 13; B3^v; see also pp. 30, 101.

95 Lemnius Levinus, *The Touchstone of Complexions* (London, 1576), f. 36^r; my emphasis.

96 Craik, *Reading Sensations*, p. 3.

97 Medical writers try to distinguish complexionate melancholy, which is "natural" to both certain individuals and to people from certain regions of the world, from pathological melancholy, which is always a disease. Angus Gowland thus notes, "In medieval and early modern characterology, complexionate melancholy shared the core qualities of the disease of melancholy … Hence, one of the problems facing medical writers was the maintenance of an effective distinction between the emotional symptoms resulting from a normal melancholic complexion and those rooted in a melancholic disease" ("The Problem of Early Modern Melancholy," *Past and Present* 191 [2007], p. 191). In literary genres and cultural discourses, these distinctions between melancholy as a humor and complexion and melancholy as a disease are even harder to maintain than they are in the medical literature.

98 Schoenfeldt is primarily interested in identifying dietaries and other related texts that provide a "self control that authorized individuality," but he is also concerned more generally with texts and practices that confer and stabilize identity through the "productive function of discipline" (*Bodies and Selves*, pp. 11, 13); Craik similarly focuses on how reading certain kinds of texts became a practice for constituting "the bodies of English gentlemen" (*Reading Sensations*, p. 3).

99 Levinus, *Touchstone of Complexions*, 148^r.

100 The evidence for how romances might affect readers differently based on their religious faith is more complicated; see Chapter 3.

101 Teresa Scott Soufas, *Melancholy and the Secular Mind in Golden Age Spain* (Columbia, MO: University of Missouri Press, 1990), pp. 6–7; see also du Laurens, "Diseases of Melancholy," pp. 85–86.

102 See Vives, *Education*, trans. and ed. Fantazzi (University of Chicago Press, 2000), pp. 73–79; Jacques Amyot, *L'Histoire Aethiopique de Heliodorus* (Paris, 1549); François de La Noue, *The Politicke and Militarie Discourses of the Lord de la Noue*, trans. E. A. (London, 1587).

103 For more detailed accounts of the attacks on romance that began shortly after the publication of the first volumes of Amadis and continued through the mid-seventeenth century, see, among others, Ife, *Reading and Fiction*, pp. 12–36; Leonard, *Books of the Brave*, pp. 80–89; Marc Fumaroli, "Jacques

Amyot and the Clerical Polemic Against the Chivalric Novel," *Renaissance Quarterly* 38.1 (1985); 22–40; Alex Davis, *Chivalry and Romance in the English Renaissance* (D. S. Bewer, 2003), pp. 40–73. The attacks by Vives and La Noue were influential and widely cited among English readers. As late as 1631, well after the collapse of the furor over romance, for instance, Thomas Beard cites Vives' attack on *Amadis*, *Tristan*, and other romances as "unchaste and ribald bookes" in his *Theatre of God's judgments* (London, 1631), p. 438. La Noue's attack also seems to have been widely read: Crosse incorporates La Noue's critique directly into his own attack on dangerous books without acknowledging his source (*Vertue's Commonwealthe*, N4ᵛ); Richard Zouch refers to La Noue in his *The Dove: Or Passages Of Cosmography* ([London, 1613], E5ʳ⁻ᵛ); and several citations from the *Discourse* make it into Frances Meres' collection of commonplaces on reading in *Wits Commonwealth. The Second Part* ([London, 1634], pp. 592–93).

104 Writers often play on the differences or similarities between the "passions" of romances and those of religious texts. Sometimes secular romances are used as a warning to urge readers toward (the moral and physical) benefits of reading religious texts. (See, for example, Pierre du Moulin, *Theophilus, or Love Divine*, trans. Richard Goring [London, 1610], pp. 276–77: "the ridiculous Romanes and tales of *Amadis* do flie before the Bible ... all these pleasing and vaine readings which busied the spirit and tickled the imagination, do lesse their taste after this spiritual nourishment. Another kind of love is kindled.") In other cases, religious polemicists either metaphorically suggest that the religious texts that their opponents are using are no more substantial than romances or even, quite literally, that they are using romances to corrupt otherwise godly readers and propagate religious error. (See further, Chapter 3.) A notable example of the intersection between controversies surrounding religious reading and romance reading is the story of the conversion of Ignatius of Loyola, which suggested that his conversion to Christianity was essentially a conversion in his reading practices. Having once been a great reader of romances (and thus a depraved libertine), Ignatius was supposedly converted to Christianity as a result of reading the *Lives of the Saints*. In his *Enthusiasm of the Church of Rome Demonstrated* (1688), a response to the 1686 English translation of Dominque Bonhours' *Life*, the protestant Henry Wharton instead ironically suggests that reading saints' lives did not cure Ignatius, but rather compounded his illness: "*Don Quixote* began his Knight-Errantry with the reading of such romances, which even made him run Mad with ambition and desire of Glory: And as it happens most unluckily, *Ignatius* and *Don Quixot* were both inspired with reading the same Book, the Adventures of *Amadis de Gaul* ... But it was the reading the Legends of Saints, which finally compleated the Disease, and rendred it incurable" (*The Enthusiasm of the Church*, p. 22). Wharton's analysis of Ignatius' supposed "literary conversion" suggests that he was well aware of the humoral consequences of adust melancholy and its affect on both the body and the brain.

105 Crosse, *Vertues Commonwealthe*, R4ʳ. See also Wright, *Passions*, p. 31.
Romance's ability to arouse passion takes on a different valence in Restoration
England: Victoria Kahn, "Reinventing Romance, or the Surprising Effects
of Sympathy," *Renaissance Quarterly* 55.2 (2002), pp. 626–61, calls attention
to late seventeenth-century arguments that romance's ability to arouse passion made it a particularly good vehicle for creating political consensus, a
notable revision to the tradition that begins with Vives.

106 Wright, *Passions*, pp. 102–103.

107 Wright, *Passions*, p. 64.

108 I am using the term "image" here to refer to the text and mis-en-page.
These conclusions would arguably apply even more strongly to the illustrations included in many romances. Such illustrations were repeated at key
moments in the cycle and reused from one romance to another. A reader
who was reading about one of Amadis' brothers might find those pages
illustrated with an image of Amadis that had appeared earlier in the cycle
and that would be reused again later in a parallel context. Such readers
would thus literally be seeing the same image over and over again and usually at moments that emphasized the passions of the narrative. See further
Chapter 3.

109 Wright, *Passions*, p. 103.

110 Du Laurens, "Diseases of Melancholy," p. 97.

111 Wright, *Passions*, pp. 103, 127.

112 Huarte, *Examination*, p. 146.

113 Mornay, *True Knowledge*, pp. 30, 160.

114 Fr. Pedro Malón de Chaide, *La conversión de Magdelena* (1588); cited in Ife,
Reading and Fiction, pp. 34–35; Jacques Amyot, trans., *L'Histoire Aethiopique
de Heliodorus* (Paris, 1549), *iiiiiʳ.

115 Marion Wells, *The Secret Wound: Love-Melancholy and Early Modern
Romance* (Stanford University Press, 2007), p. 2. See Du Laurens, "Diseases
of Melancholy," pp. 91–96.

116 Laurence Brockless and Colin Jones, *The Medical World of Early Modern
France* (Oxford: Clarendon, 1997), pp. 287–88. Related versions of this
story – though usually featuring King Alonso – circulate both in humoral
treatises and in the (comparatively few) defenses of romance. These stories
turn on the curative powers of romance, but as a spoken text rather than
as a written one. See, for example, Wright, *Passions*, pp. 108–9; Anthony
Munday, trans., *Second part, of the no lesse rare, than excellent and stately
historie of the famous and fortunate princes Palmerin of English* in *The [first]
seconde part, of the no lesse rare, histories of Palmerine of England* (London,
1596), A3ʳ. See Chapter 3 for a further discussion of Munday.

117 Du Laurens, "Diseases of Melancholy," p. 105; see also, pp. 107, 111–12, 123.

118 Du Laurens, "Diseases of Melancholy," p. 107; see also Wells, *Secret Wound*,
pp. 33, 83–85; Smith, *The Accoustical World*, pp. 102–5.

119 Richard Braithwaite, *A Survey of History. Or a Nursery for Gentry* (London,
1638), p. 129.

120 Pagel, "Medieval and Renaissance Contributions," pp. 95–114; see also Alberto Manguel, *A History of Reading* (New York: Viking, 1996), pp. 28–32.
121 Wells, *Secret Wound*, pp. 40–43.
122 Wells, *Secret Wound*, pp. 19–59, 96.
123 Miguel de Cervantes, *Don Quixote*, trans. Edith Grossman and intro. Harold Bloom (New York: Harper Collins, 2003), p. 21.
124 Cervantes, *Don Quijote*, II: 997: más que medianamente moreno.
125 Du Laurens, "Diseases of Melancholy," p. 90; see also Timothy Bright, *A Treatise of Melancholy* (London, 1586), p. 125.
126 Cited in Leonard, *Books of the Brave*, p. 81; on attempts to control the sale, shipping, and possession of romances in the New World, see pp. 80–89.
127 R. F. Anthony Batt, trans., *A heavenly treasure of comfortable meditations and prayers* (London, 1624), p. 13.

1 GENEALOGY AND RACE AFTER THE FALL OF CONSTANTINOPLE

1 Fredric Jameson, "Magical Narratives: On the Dialectical Use of Genre Criticism," in *The Political Unconscious* (Ithaca: Cornell University Press, 1982), p. 118. See also his "Magical Narratives: Romance as Genre," *New Literary History* 7 (1975), pp. 135–63. See also Northrop Frye, *The Secular Scripture: A Study of the Structure of Romance* (Cambridge: Harvard University Press, 1976) and *Anatomy of Criticism: Four Essays* (Princeton University Press, 1957), pp. 186–205; and Erich Auerbach, "Odysseus' Scar," in *Mimesis: The Representation of Reality in Western Literature*, trans. Willard R. Trask (Princeton University Press, 1953), pp. 3–23. For a recent overview that stresses not just the form but the practice of romance, see Barbara Fuchs, *Romance: New Critical Idiom* (New York: Routledge, 2004). For two recent works that emphasize the centrality of racial discourse to the genre of romance, see Geraldine Heng, *Empire of Magic: Medieval Romance and the Politics of Cultural Fantasy* (New York: Columbia University Press, 2003), and Benedict S. Robinson, *Islam and early modern English literature: the politics of romance from Spenser to Milton* (New York, Palgrave Macmillan, 2007). For an introduction to the peninsular romances of chivalry, see Daniel Eisenberg, *Romances of Chivalry in the Spanish Golden Age* (Newark, Delaware: Juan de la Cuesta, 1982); Harry Sieber, "The Romance of Chivalry in Spain: From Rodríguez de Montalvo to Cervantes," in *Romance: Generic Transformation from Chrétien de Troyes to Cervantes* (Hanover: University Press of New England, 1985), pp. 202–19; and Henry Thomas, *Spanish and Portuguese Romances of Chivalry: The Revival of the Romance of Chivalry in the Spanish Peninsula* (Cambridge University Press, 1920).
2 See R. Howard Bloch, *Etymologies and Genealogies: A Literary Anthropology of the French Middle Ages* (University of Chicago Press, 1983), pp. 92–127, 198–227.

3 Bloch, *Etymologies and Genealogies*, p. 202.

4 Judith Perryman, "Introduction," in Perryman, ed., *The King of Tars* (Heidelberg: Carl Winter, 1980), pp. 42–49; all citations will be from this edition and cited parenthetically in the text. For sources and analogues, see Lilian Herlands Hornstein, "The Historical Background of *The King of Tars*," *Speculum* 16. 4 (1941), pp. 404–14.

5 Perryman, "Introduction," p. 46.

6 See Heng, *Empire of Magic*, pp. 211–39; Lisa Lampert, "Race, Periodicity, and the (Neo-)Middle Ages," *MLQ* 65.3 (2004), pp. 391–420; and Siobhain Bly Calkin, "Marking Religion on the Body: Saracens, Categorization, and *The King of Tars*," *JEGP* 104.2 (2005), pp. 219–38 and *Saracens and the Making of English Identity: The Auchinleck Manuscript* (New York: Routledge, 2009).

7 A third important issue, one that cannot truly be separated from these fictions of conversion and identity, is the question of imperial conquest. Recent scholarship has stressed how closely tied New World colonial activities, and the understandings of race that went with them, were to the European notions of *imperium* that emerged out of and against contacts in the Mediterranean. See especially, Fuchs, *Mimesis and Empire*, and the essays in Margaret R. Greer, Walter D. Mignolo and Maureen Quilligan, eds., *Rereading the Black Legend: The Discourses of Religion and Racial Difference in the Renaissance Empires* (University of Chicago Press, 2008) (on these questions, in particular, the editors' introduction as well as the essays by David Nirenberg, "Race and the Middle Ages: The Case of Spain," pp. 71–87; and Barbara Fuchs, "The Spanish Race," pp. 88–98). For the historical background, see Antony Pagden, *Lords of all the World: Ideologies of Empire in Spain, Britain and France, c. 1500–c. 1800* (New Haven: Yale University Press, 1995).

8 Robert the Monk's account of Pope Urban's speech at the Council of Clermont, 1095; in Dana C. Munro, "Urban and the Crusaders," *Translations and Reprints from the Original Sources of European History*, vol. 1 (Philadelphia: University of Pennsylvania Press, 1895), pp. 5–8.

9 Robert S. Burns, S.J., "Christian-Islamic Confrontation in the West: The Thirteenth-Century Dream of Conversion," *American Historical Review* 76.5 (1971), pp. 1386–434.

10 Judith A.Whitenack, "Conversion to Christianity in the Spanish Romances of Chivalry, 1490–1524," *Journal of Hispanic Philology* 13 (1988), p. 13.

11 For an overview of Church attitudes toward the relationship between crusade and conversion (from Innocent III, Honorius III, Gregory IX, to Innocent IV), see Burns, "Christian-Islamnic Conversion," pp. 1387, 1391–402.

12 Robert the Monk, in Munro, "Urban and the Crusaders," *Translations and Reprints*, pp. 5–8.

13 Jameson, "Magical Narratives," p. 118.

14 See Benzion Netanyahu, *The Origins of the Inquisition in Fifteenth Century Spain* (1995; New York: Random House, 2001); *Toward the Inquisition: Essays on Jewish and Converso History in Late Medieval Spain* (Ithaca: Cornell University Press, 1997); *The Marranos of Spain: from the Late 14th to the Early*

216 Notes to pages 50–53

16th Century, According to Contemporary Hebrew Sources (Ithaca: Cornell University Press, 1999). Netanyahu's arguments, though for some controversial, are certainly not unprecedented. Henry Charles Lea, for instance, concluded that "the hatred of old which had been merely a matter of religion had become a matter of race" (*History of the Spanish Inquisition*, 4 vols. [New York: Macmillan, 1906–7], 1:126). Netanyahu notes that the various terms for describing those who converted – New Christian, *converso*, and *marrano* – are problematic because they were introduced to articulate a prejudical distinction where one had not previously existed. Netanyahu adopts the term *"marrano"* when he discusses how religious Jews regarded recent converts; elsewhere he uses all three terms largely interchangeably. Except where a specific context demands something different, I am using the term *"converso"* because it emphasizes the pressure point that conversion becomes within the genre of romance.

15 Netanyahu takes as his starting point the failure of previous scholars of the Inquisition to recognize the import of racial categorization in having made the Inquisition possible: "It is strange that throughout this battle of opinions [in studies of the Inquisition from the eighteenth century onward], no importance was attached to a peculiar phenomenon that ... rendered the Spanish Inquisition distinct from all preceeding inquisitions. This was its adoption of the principale of *race* to discriminate against all *conversos*" (*Origins*, p. xviii).

16 Ivan Hannaford, *Race: The History of an Idea in the West* (Baltimore: Johns Hopkins University Press, 1996), p. 122.

17 Martín Gamero, *Historia de Toledo*, p. 1038; cited in Netanyahu, *Origins*, p. 381.

18 Netanyahu, *Origins*, pp. 995–98.

19 Netanyahu, *Origins*, p. 852.

20 Netanyahu gives a compelling account of Oropesa's arguments that the whole concept of race was inimical to Christianity (*Origins*, p. 879).

21 Netanyahu, *Origins*, pp. 1052–54; Netanyahu, *Marranos of Spain*, pp. 3–4.

22 Some of these laws pre-date the emergence of race-based arguments in the fifteenth century; others either appear or are only enforced later. The various kinds of racial sumptuary laws seem to originate in Morocco and were promolgated by the 4th Lateran Council in 1215 and repeatedly reasserted over the following three centuries (see, e.g., Netanyahu, *Origins*, pp. 185, 197, 194). One central issue here is how this legal practice contributed to attitudes toward the idea of "reading" identity in visual terms: see, for example, Fernán Díaz de Toledo's *Instruction* for the Bishop of Cuenca, the so-called *Libro verde*, or the *Tizón de la Nobleza de España*.

23 See David H. Rosenthal, "Foreward," in Joanot Martorell and Martí Joan de Galba, *Tirant lo Blanc*, ed. and trans. David H. Rosenthal (New York: Schocken Books, 1984), pp. viii–xi; Josep Guia and Curt Wittlin, "Nine Problem Areas Concerning *Tirant lo Blanc*," in Arthur Terry, ed., *Tirant lo Blanc: New Approaches* (London: Colección Támesis, 1999), pp. 109–11.

24 For recent collections of scholarship on *Tirant*, see Terry, *Tirant lo Blanc*, Institució de les Lletres Catalanes, *Actes del symposion Tirant lo Blanc* (Barcelona: Quaderns Crema, 1993), and *Tirant lo Blanc: Text and Context: Proceedings of the Second Catalan Symposium* (New York: Peter Lang; 1993). See also Mario Vargas Llosa's "Tirant lo Blanc, novela sin fronteras," *Letras Libres* 6.63 (2004), pp. 42–43.

25 For an assessment that disentangles some aspects of the authorship issues, see Joan Coromines, "Sobre l'estil i manera de Martí Joan de Galba i els de Joanot Martorell," in *Lleures i converses d'un filòleg* (Barcelona, 1971), pp. 363–78.

26 Martorell, *Tirant*, ed. and trans. Rosenthal, p. 39; Joanot Martorell and Martí Joan de Galba, *Tirant lo Blanc*, ed. Víctor Gómez, 3 vols. (Valencia: Edicions Alsons el Magnànim, 1990), I: 75: un gentilhom de llinatge antic e natural de Bretanya. Further citations are from these editions and cited in the text parenthetically and in the notes.

27 Martorell and Galba, *Tirant*, I: 78: jo rebí l'orde de cavalleria en les parts d'Àfrica, en una gran batalla de moros.

28 Martorell and Galba, *Tirant*, I: 76: puix a la santedat vostra plau tant saber mon nom, jo só molt content dir-lo-us. A mi dien Tirant lo Blanc, per ço com mon pare fon senyor de la marca de Tirània, la qual per la mar confronta ab Anglaterra; e ma mare fon filla del duc de Bretanya, e ha nom Blanca; e per ço volgueren que jo fos nomenat Tirant lo Blanc.

29 *Tirant* is unusual in this respect: as Eisenberg notes, "the protagonist of a romance of chivalry is always male and invariably of royal blood – a prince. His lineage is usually specified" (Eisenberg, *Romances of Chivalry*, p. 56).

30 Martorell and Galba, *Tirant*, II: 444: estrangers de mala fama; II: 445: un vil home estranger; II: 510: lo segon Judes.

31 Martorell and Galba, *Tirant*, II: 579: un diable de francés és vengut capità dels grecs, que totes les batalles los venç, lo qual dien que ha nom Tirant. Per ma fe, ell poria haver bons fets, així com dien, mas lo seu nom és lleig e vil, per ço com Tirant vol dir usurpador de béns o, més propi parlar, lladre.

32 Martorell and Galba, *Tirant*, I: 82: no penses que lo cavaller sia de més alt llinatge eixit que los altres, com tots naturalment siam eixits d'un pare e d'una mare.

33 Martorell and Galba, *Tirant*, I: 163: tots siam eguals germans e frares d'armes; I: 165: sens que no hi havia milloria neguna.

34 Martorell and Galba, *Tirant*, I: 168: notari per autoritat imperial, que fes acte públic com aquests són cavallers de quatre quarters, ço és a saber: de pare e de mare, d'avi e d'àvia; e negun senyor del món reprotxar no els pot per llinatge ni per títol negú.

35 Relator, cited in Henry Kamen, *The Spanish Inquisition: A Historical Revision* (New Haven: Yale University Press, 1988), pp. 32, 232; Villalobos, cited in Netanyahu, *Origins*, pp. 1070–71. See also Netanyahu, *Origins*, p. 416, for the relator's list of noble families with *converso* ancestry and strong warnings about the social upheaval that would bring so much of the heart of Spanish court and society under challenge.

36 Kamen, *Spanish Inquisition*, p. 239; Kamen, *The Phoenix and the Flame: Catalonia and the Counter Reformation* (New Haven: Yale University Press, 1993), p. 271. Kamen generally takes a more restrictive view, warning against overestimating the actual spread of *limpieza* statutes across Spain ("Limpieza and the Ghost of Americo Castro: Racism as a Tool of Literary Analysis," *Hispanic Review* 64.1 [1996], pp. 19–29). It is clear from Kamen's examples, though, that concern about blood purity was often most powerful in the symbolic register. In parts of Catalonia where there were no Jews, for instance, tribunals for the Inquisition nonetheless "had to sort out the quarrels of protagonists who insulted each other as 'Jews'" ("Limpieza," p. 24).

37 See Kamen, *Spanish Inquisition*, p. 242, for an account of the need to provide genealogical proofs for military and other posts, but notably not for membership in the nobility. This exclusion highlights the extraordinary nature of this episode.

38 Martorell and Galba, *Tirant*, I: 166 papafigos de vellut negre; I: 173: capells fets a modo de Turquia. Barbara Fuchs provides a good account of how the pure blood laws were a form of fictive ethnicity in which the demands for legibility were imposed on "deliberately unreadable" subjects (*Passing for Spain: Cervantes and the Fictions of Identity* [Urbana: University of Illinois Press, 2003], pp. 1–20).

39 Martorell and Galba, *Tirant*, I: 291: féu haver moltes peces de drap, e féu vestir a tots los catius de mantos, robes, gipons, calces, sabates e camises. E féu-los llevar les camises grogues que ells portaven e tramés-les en Bretanya, per ço que, com fos mort, fossen posades en la sua capella ab los quartre escuts dels quatre cavallers que vençuts havia.

40 Marc Shell, "The Wether and the Ewe: Verbal Usury in *The Merchant of Venice*," in *Money, Language, and Thought: Literary and Philosophic Economies from the Medieval to the Modern Era* (1982; Berkeley: University of California Press, 1993), pp. 47–83.

41 Daniel Vitkus, *Turning Turk: English Theater and the Multicultural Mediterrean* (New York: Palgrave), p. 109.

42 Lateran 4, Canon 68; see Shroeder, *Disciplinary Decrees*, p. 584.

43 Netanyahu, *Origins*, p. 197.

44 Martorell and Galba, *Tirant*, II: 834: eslau negre … moro per sa natura.

45 Martorell and Galba, *Tirant*, II: 836: que lo seu cos celestial posàs la sua bellea en llibertat d'un salvatge negre, e tothom coneixeria que la bellea de sa majestat seria miserable do per a qui virtuosament viure desija.

46 Martorell and Galba, *Tirant*, II: 876: Digues, donzella sens pietat, la mia disposició no era conforme als teus desigs més que del negre hortolà?

47 This portion of the book is the subject of the 2006 film, *Tirant lo Blanc*.

48 Martorell and Galba, *Tirant*, III: 923: E puix tant desiges saber lo meu nom, ab tota veritat, senyor, te dic que lo meu dret nom és Blanc. Although the hero's name comes from an earlier original, where it carries a different meaning, the authors emphasize the whiteness of Tirant. In the first portion of the

romance, the emphasis is on Tirant being a "foreign" knight and references to his denomination as "white" fit within this context.

49 Martorell and Galba, *Tirant*, III: 924: jo he nom Blanc, e la lluna és clara, blanca e bella ara en aquesta hora que só caigut, e la lluna restà endret del meu cap e dels braços senyalant lo camí que jo dec fer, e no és restada atràs ni al costat, e les mies mans són restades ubertes e esteses devers la lluna, per què demonstra que jo, ab ajuda de la divina Potència, tinc de conquistar tota la Barberia.

50 The romance prefigures this transformation of the narrative in another racially charged incident in which the Emperor's daughter, Princess Carmesina, captures "a little black boy" in the Saracen camp and announces that she will now "glory in my valiant knighthood, for I have boldly captured a Turk in the enemy camp" (282). This boy becomes a figure at the Emperor's court: his story mocks the "enslavement narratives" of courtly romance and critiques as a fantasy the notion that crusading and valiant knighthood will stand against the Turks.

51 Martorell and Galba, *Tirant*, III: 925: home fortíssim, tot negre e de molt desmesurada figura segons los altres hòmens, qui era rei molt ponderós.

52 Martorell and Galba, *Tirant*, I: 77: com la infanta bevia vi vermell, que la sua blancor és tan extrema que per la gola li veia passar lo vi, e tots quants hi eren n'estaven admirats.

53 Martorell and Galba, *Tirant*, III: 953: lo segon llinatge és d'aquells qui executaren l'acte.

54 Martorell and Galba, *Tirant*, III: 953–54: no em par que jo dega contaminar ne mesclar la noble sang ab aquella de perpetual dolor, e lo llinatge de mos fills fos menys cabat, que perdessen la successió de son dret llinatge.

55 The attitude that this Jew "from the race of David" expresses is a version of the attitude that anti-Marrano racists held about intermarriage between Old and New Christians. As Netanyahu makes clear, "from the racists' point of view, intermarriage between the groups – that is, between the Old and New Christians – confronted Christian Spain with a peril even greater than all the other threats posed by the conversos. For not only would intermarriage help the conversos take over Christian offices and possessions; it would also infect the Spanish people with a malady from which it might never recover. What they meant by this was that by marrying Old Christians, the conversos would 'contaminate' the latter's blood; and if this contamination became widespread, it would corrupt the Spanish character beyond repair and eventually cause its disappearance. Thus, from the standpoint of the anti-Marrano racists, their conflict with the conversos was infinitely more crucial than their struggle against the Jews; for while the Jews were opposed for what they *were*, the conversos were opposed for both what they *were* and what they wanted to *become* – namely, an integral, indistinguishable part of the Spanish people" (987). In making this argument, Netanyahu's key point is perhaps the final one: the real fear was that the Jews might become indistinguishable from the Christians.

56 Martorell and Galba, *Tirant*, II: 621: E com pots tu pensar que la mia real persona se pogués sotsmetre a un moro. This episode responds to the Ottoman empire's practice of allowing those in the lands that they conquered to continue in their own religions, a practice markedly at odds with what European Christians did when they conquered or reconquered various Islamic territories.

57 For an account of the sixteenth-century versions of the fantasies about Ethiopia that had been incited so powerfully by Mandeville, see David Quint, *Epic and Empire: Politics and Generic Form from Virgil to Milton* (Princeton University Press, 1993), pp. 234–47.

58 Martorell and Galba, *Tirant*, III: 1170: de blanques e de negres, car les blanques eren del regne de Tunis, e les negres d'Etiòpia.

59 Martorell and Galba, *Tirant*, III: 1169: era u dels grans senyors del món, exceptat lo Gran Can; III: 1015: aquests crestians batejats, los quals … no he vist de ma vida tan esforçada gent.

60 As will be the case in Montalvo's *Esplandián*, conversion drives the narrative and has its origin in Tirant. Emeraldine's passion for Tirant causes her to convert to Christianity. When Tirant remains true to his beloved, Emeraldine's conversion precipitates that of Escariano, her future husband (483), Escariano's men (486), and finally the entire country of Ethiopia (549).

61 Quint, *Epic and Empire*, p. 27.

62 Martorell and Galba, *Tirant*, III: 1282: de moltes nacions de gents.

63 Martorell and Galba, *Tirant*, III: 1273: los homenatges rebé d'aquells qui eren crestians o eren estats, e los qui renegat havien féu reduir a la santa fe catòlica.

64 William Thomas Little, "Introduction," in Garci Rodríguez de Montalvo, *The Labors of the Very Brave Knight Esplandián*, ed. and trans. William Thomas Little (Binghampton, New York, 1992), p. 3.

65 Montalvo, *Esplandián*, ed. and trans. Little, p. 209; Garci Rodríguez de Montalvo, *Sergas de Esplandián*, ed. Carlos Sainz de la Maza (Madrid: Clásicos Castalia, 2003), pp. 338–39: "osadía y temeroso accometimiento"; "que la diferencia que entre él y mí avrá será que las fuerças que Dios me diere serán empleadas contra los malos infieles, sus enemigos, lo que mi padre no fizo." Further references will be from these editions and cited parenthetically in the text and in the notes.

66 Garci Rodríguez de Montalvo, *Amadis of Gaul: a novel of chivalry of the 14th century presumably first written in Spanish*, ed. and trans. Edwin B. Place and Herbert C. Behm, 2 vols. (Lexington: University Press of Kentucky, 1974), II: 603; Garci Rodríguez de Montalvo, *Amadís de Gaula*, ed. Juan Manuel Cacho Blecua, 2 vols. (Madrid: Ediciones Cátedra, 1991), II: que nunca alcançó sino armas y cavallo. Both of these editions include the first four books, which were published together in the 1508 edition, and they will be cited in the text parenthetically and in the notes by the (modern) volume and page numbers; since the different books of the 1508 edition were

subsequently published and read individually, I will also indicate the original book number as well, when necessary.

67 Montalvo, *Sergas de Esplandián*, p. 546: ni dexasen esta sancta guerra que contra los infieles començada tienen.

68 See Chapter 3 for a discussion of these mysterious and only gradually legible letters with which the infant Esplandián is marked.

69 Montalvo, *Sergas de Esplandián*, p. 332: yo he passado mucho afán en buscar las cosas estrañas que por este mundo sembradas y derramadas son ... y el pensamiento mío que fasta aquí he tenido, que era ganar honra y fama en las cosas de la calidad passada, que todos las más de poco provecho an sido, es convertido y mudado en que siga aquello que, aventurando el cuerpo a la muerte, se gane la gloria y vida para el ánima.

70 Eisenberg, *Romances of Chivalry*, p. 83; see also Thomas, *Spanish and Portuguese Romances*.

71 See Chapter 3 for a discussion of Cervantes' family origins.

72 Eisenberg, *Romances of Chivalry*, p. 79; Little, "Introduction," p. 9.

73 Montalvo, *Amadís de Gaula*, I: 259: las más fermosa criatura que nunca fue vista.

74 Montalvo, *Amadís de Gaula*, I: 301 [él es muy niño, y tan fermoso que es maravilla de lo ver]; I: 317 [qué fermosura de cavallero]; I: 389 [Mucho se maravillavan todos de la gran fermosura deste Amadís].

75 Montalvo, *Amadís de Gaula*, I: 612: el más fermoso cavallero que nunca viera; y por cierto tal era en aquel tiempo, que no passava de veinte años y tenía el rostro manchado de las armas, mas considerando cuán bien empleadas en él aquellas manzillas eran, y cómo con ellas tan limpia y clara la su fama y honra hazía, mucho en su apostura y hermosura acrescentava.

76 Montalvo, *Amadís de Gaula*, I: 277: En el nombre de Dios, y Él mande que tan bien empleada en vos sea y tan crescida en honra como Él os creció en femosura.

77 Montalvo, *Amadís de Gaula*, I: 311: catávalo cómo era tan fermoso, y membrándose de sus fijos que havía perdido, viniéronle las lágrimas a los ojos. Assí que llorava por aquel que ante ella estava y no lo conoscía.

78 Montalvo, *Amadís de Gaula*, I: 337: más hermoso que nunca otro visto havía.

79 Montalvo, *Amadís de Gaula*, I: 528: sino que don Galaor era algo más blanco.

80 Montalvo, *Amadís de Gaula*, I: 748: mas no conoçieron a Florestán, pero que muy hermoso les paresció y, antes que llegassen, pos Amadís los tenían.

81 Marian Rothstein, "The Commemorative Images of Amadis de Gaule," in Martin Heusser *et al.*, ed., *The Pictured Word* (Amsterdam, Netherlands: Rodopi, 1998), pp. 99–107.

82 Montalvo, *Amadís de Gaula*, II: 1080: violo tan fermoso, que fue maravillado.

83 Montalvo, *Amadís de Gaula*, II: 1112: mucho maravilladas da la gran fermosura del donzel.

84 Montalvo, *Sergas de Esplandián*, p. 137: los que en ella biven todos son sus enemigos.

85 Montalvo, *Sergas de Esplandián*, p. 137: Mas mucho soy maravillado de vos, y más lo sería si yo creyesse que vos érades mortal, de lo que yo dudo según vuestra gran fermosura.

86 Montalvo, *Sergas de Esplandián*, p. 287: malo e fuerte cavallero; p. 299: mal hombre, que [entiendo] que en sólo lo que de mi señorío ha robado bastaría para hazer o desfazer dos reyes.

87 Montalvo, *Sergas de Esplandián*, p. 310: mala y perversa secta.

88 Montalvo, *Sergas de Esplandián*, p. 352: Frandalo, que lo mirava y lo veía tan fermoso y tan mesurado en su hablar, sabiendo ya las cosas maravillosas y muy estrañas que en armas avía fecho, bien creó verdaderamente que tal persona de hombre mortal no podía nacer ni de tal forma permanecer sino en la Ley de la verdad. E puesto caso que no fuera llegado a tal estrecho por dondé le convino prometer al emperador aquello que Esplandián le deman-dava, sola su vista y habla era bastante para que no tan solamente a él, mas a todo el paganismo convertir pudiesse.

89 Frandalo is a key figure in defeating the Persians precisely because of his knowledge of them: Esplandián and Frandalo, for instance, thus dress up "in Turkish style" (227) to infiltrate the enemy camp and try to drag the king over to their side; Esplandián avers that Frandalo's "advice and desire" con-stitute one of the principal tools for conquering this land of Turkey" (257); Frandalo knows the land well and is able to keep the Christian knights away from enemy strongholds (260), while Esplandián repeatedly asserts that they are strangers and must defer to Frandalo's knowledge (285).

90 Montalvo, *Sergas de Esplandián*, p. 643: todos los soldanes, califas, tamor-lanes y reyes, y a otros cualesquier grandes señores de la ley pagana de las partes de Oriente, así de la mano diestra como de la siniestra.

91 Montalvo, *Sergas de Esplandián*, p. 646: assí blancos como negros; p. 501: de los reyes bárbaros de naciones blancas y negras.

92 Montalvo, *Sergas de Esplandián*, p. 727: mugeres negras; mucho llegada a la parte del Paraíso terrenal; sin que algún varón entre ellas oviesse, que casi como las amazonas era su estilo de bivir.

93 Montalvo, *Sergas de Esplandián*, p. 729: desseando ver el mondo y sus dive[r]-sas generaciones.

94 Montalvo, *Sergas de Esplandián*, p. 756: todos son hermosos y bien armados; pero dígote, reina, que entrellos es aquel Cavallero Serpentino que nunca los pasados ni presentes, ni aun creo los por venir, otro tan hermoso y apuesto vieron, ni los que an de venir lo verán. ¡O reina! ¿Qué te diré, sino que si él en nuestra ley fuesse podríamos creer que nuestros dioses con sus manos lo avían hecho, poniendo en la tal obra todo su gran poder y mucho saber, sin que nada dello quedasse?

95 Montalvo, *Sergas de Esplandián*, p. 276: aquel que venía de parte de su madre de los más fuertes jayanes de todo el señorío de Persia, e de su padre de muy valientes y esforçados [cavalleros].

96 Montalvo, *Sergas de Esplandián*, p. 345: que oístes de su nacimiento fue pagano, y assí lo eran aquellos donde él decendía.

97 Montalvo, *Sergas de Esplandián*, p. 799: sin aver memoria del comienço, vengo de sangre real.

98 Montalvo, *Sergas de Esplandián*, p. 800: como si el rey, mi padre, entrambos nos engendrara; p. 800: un tal cavallero que muy más cumplido en virtud y linage tenga aquello que pides.

99 Montalvo, *Sergas de Esplandián*, p. 645: vosotros nacistes y que vos bien criastos todos, o los más, en la Gran Bretaña y en otras partes donde, aunque la diversidad de las tierras mucha fuesse, pero la ley toda era una.

2 THE FORM AND MATTER OF RACE

1 Recent and important critical assessments of the importance of the *Aethiopika* in the Renaissance include: Sujata Iyengar, *Shades of Difference: Mythologies of Skin Color in Early Modern England* (Philadelphia: University of Pennsylvania Press, 2005), pp. 19–43; Steve Mentz, *Romance for Sale in Early Modern England: The Rise of Prose Fiction* (Aldershot: Ashgate, 2006), pp. 1–71; Walter Stephens, "Tasso's Heliodorus and the World of Romance," in James Tatum, ed., *The Search for the Ancient Novel* (Baltimore: Johns Hopkins University Press, 1994), pp. 67–87; Alban K. Forcione, *Cervantes, Aristotle, and the "Persiles"* (Princeton University Press, 1970), pp. 49–87; Gerald N. Sandy, *Heliodorus* (Boston: Twayne, 1982), pp. 97–124; Wolfgang Stechow, "Heliodorus' *Aethiopica* in Art," *Journal of the Warburg and Courtauld Institutes* 16 (1953), pp. 144–52. For work on the *Aethiopika* and racial identity, see Tim Whitmarsh, "The Birth of a Prodigy: Heliodorus and the Genealogy of Hellenism," in *Studies in Heliodorus*, ed., R. L. Hunter (Cambridge Philological Society, 1998), pp. 93–124; Daniel L. Selden, "*Aithiopika* and Ethiopianism," in Richard Hunter, ed., *Studies in Heliodorus* (Cambridge University Press, 1998), pp. 182–214; Judith Perkins, "An Ancient 'Passing' Novel: Heliodorus' *Aithiopika, Arethusa* 32 (1999), pp. 197–214.

2 Jacques Amyot, *L'Histoire Aethiopique de Heliodorus* (Paris, 1547, 1549, 1553 [2], 1557, 1559 [4?], 1560, 1575, 1579, 1584, 1585, 1589, 1609, and 1616. Further citations are from the Newberry library copy of the 1549 edition, unless otherwise noted, and are included in the text. In cases where I am discussing *Aethiopika* in its own right rather than a particular early modern instance of it, I have used "Heliodorus: An Ethiopian Story," trans. J. R. Morgan, in B. P. Reardon, ed., *Collected Ancient Greek Novels* (Berkeley: University of California Press, 1989), pp. 349–588; further citations in the text. Scholars generally date the *Aethiopika* to the first half of the third century, but J. R. Morgan argues that it may be as late as AD 350. The 1557 edition included a re-editing of the text and a revised preface. Amyot notably deletes his treatment of the *sphragis*, the identity "signature" at the end of the *Aethiopika* (in which Heliodorus signs his text as "the work of a Phoenician from the city of Emesa, one of the clan of the Descendants of the Sun" [Morgan, 588]), as well as a discussion

of the discovery of a manuscript for the work in the Bibliotecha Corviniana (*vᵛ–viᵛ). The new preface thus replaces Amyot's speculations about the possible Arabic/Phoenician identity of Heliodorus with an account of his editorial work on a Vatican manuscript from which he revised his translation (1557, a4–5). Recent English-language scholarship on the *Aethiopika* has paid attention to other continental editions and translations, but not to the Amyot translation which was the major vehicle for transmission of this text during the sixteenth century. In addition to the many courtly readers that Amyot attracted, his translation was the basis for the first extant Spanish translation (Antwerp, 1554; cited in Forcione, *Cervantes, Aristotle, and the "Persiles,"* p. 49), and it was the base text used by Ambrosius Bosschaert [Ambroise Dubois], among others, to compose painting cycles of the Theagenes and Charikleia story. Antoine Fouquelin, *La Rhetorique françois* (Paris, 1555), drew examples from the Amyot translation to illustrate his commentary and adaptation of Pierre de la Ramée's [Petrus Ramus] *Dialectique*. Thomas Underdowne relied on Amyot's work in preparing his 1569 English translation of Heliodorus, and Josephine Roberts suggested that a number of the English writers, writing both before and after 1569, read the romance in Amyot's translation and adhered to his conception of the work in their rewritings of Heliodoran romance (*Architectonic Knowledge in the "New Arcadia" (1590): Sidney's Use of the Heroic Journey* [Salzburg Studies in English Literature, 1978]).

3 Daniel Javitch makes a persuasive case that Aristotle was a vehicle, rather than the impetus, for this change ("Assimilation of Aristotle's *Poetics*," in Norton, ed., *Cambridge History*, pp. 58–59). I have suggested here that the impact of Aristotle's *Poetics* was strengthened by its affiliations with a theory of "form" that was primarily understood to apply to living things. On the literary side, cross-over between discussions about literary genre and racial identity is intensified by the degree to which the Aristotelian model was understood as an explanation of creation, category, and identity in living beings. One indication of intensification in certain kinds of category thinking can be seen in a historic shift in how poets modeled themselves on their predecessors. Javitch suggests that, under a humanist model, writers tended to emulate a single writer (or at least present themselves as doing so); this "master author-centered poetics of Renaissance humanism" ("Assimilation," p. 62) began to break down in the sixteenth century. Poets increasingly tended to aggregate two or three or more authors into a collective model as a way of following Aristotelian arguments about the nature of category. This shift involves a modulation in the notion of imitation and, as a corollary, in that of identity.

4 Rosalie L. Colie, *The Resources of Kind: Genre-Theory in the Renaissance*, ed. Barbara K. Lewalski (Berkeley: University of California Press, 1973), p. 1. This relationship between the genealogies of literary kind and human kin is one that Gary Taylor also calls attention to when he introduces the phrase "'genres' of humanity" to emphasize the culturally, rather than biologically, created nature of certain groupings of peoples: "We do not have a word for such geotemporal population sets; I propose to call them 'genres' of humanity.

The word genre derives from the same Latin root as the biological term *genus*, but genres are cultural categories" (*Buying Whiteness: Race, Culture, and Identity from Columbus to Hip Hop* [New York: Palgrave MacMillan, 2005], p. 3). Aristotle is, as we shall see, aware of this distinction, but tends to move in the opposite direction.

5 Martin Lowry, "Aristotle's Poetics and the Rise of Vernacular Literary Theory," *Viator* 24 (1994), pp. 419, 423–25; Bernard Weinberg, *A History of Literary Criticism in the Italian Renaissance* (University of Chicago Press, 1961), vol. I, pp. 371–72; E. N. Tigerstedt, "Observations on the Reception of the Aristotelian *Poetics* in the Latin West," *Studies in the Renaissance* 15 (1968), pp. 20–21.

6 Daniel Javitch, "The Emergence of Poetic Genre Theory in the Sixteenth Century," in Glyn P. Norton, ed., *The Cambridge History of Literary Criticism* (vol. III: *The Renaissance*) (Cambridge University Press, 1999), pp. 139–43; Javitch, "Self-Justifying Norms in the Genre Theories of Italian Renaissance Poets," *Philological Quarterly* 67.2 (1988), pp. 195–97. Weinberg characterizes the discovery and incorporation of Aristotle's *Poetics* into the critical tradition as "the signal event" of the sixteenth century (*History of Literary Criticism*, p. 349). Weinberg carefully assesses the arguments and assumptions of the dozens of sixteenth-century works devoted to literary theory. Javitch, by contrast, emphasizes how proactive poets were in this intense genre debate: writers needed models that would authorize and legitimatize the new kinds of poems that they were writing, and he provides persuasive evidence that Aristotle was "used to justify modern [poetic] practice as often as to discredit it" ("Emergence," p. 143; "Pioneer Genre Theory and the Opening of the Humanist Canon," *Common Knowledge* 3.1 [1994], p. 54).

7 Weinberg, *History of Literary Criticism*, I: 371–72, 439, 444; II: 954–82; Javitch, "Self-Justifying Norms," p. 201; Javitch, "Italian Epic Theory," in Norton, ed., *Cambridge History*, pp. 209–11.

8 Javitch, "Italian Epic Theory," pp. 213–14; Javitch, "Self-Justifying Norms," p. 209; Weinberg, *History of Literary Criticism*, II: 983–1073.

9 Michel Balard, ed., *Fortunes de Jacques Amyot: Actes du colloque international* (A.-G. Nizet, 1986), pp. 5–7.

10 On the dating of Amyot's translation, see Laurence Plazenet, "Jacques Amyot and the Greek Novel: The Invention of the French Novel," in Gerald M. Sandy, ed., *The Classical Heritage in France* (Leiden: Brill, 2002), pp. 240–41.

11 Jacques Amyot, "Dedication and Preface to Plutarch's Lives," in Bernard Weinberg, ed. and trans., *Critical Prefaces of the French Renaissance* (Evanston, IL: Northwestern University Press, 1950), pp. 161–78.

12 Lowry, "Aristotle's Poetics," pp. 423–25.

13 Daniel L. Selden, "Genre of Genre," in Tatum, *Search for the Ancient Novel*, p. 40.

14 Norma E. Emerton, *The Scientific Reinterpretation of Form* (Ithaca: Cornell University Press, 1984), p. 48.

15 Emerton, *Scientific Reinterpretation*, p. 48. Maggie Günsberg (*Epic Rhetoric of Tasso: Theory and Practice* [Oxford: European Humanities Research Center, 1998]) provides a history of the *materia/forma* distinction in early modern rhetoric. For accounts of *hylomorphism* that suggest its pervasiveness as a structure of thought and cultural metaphor, see also Henry S. Turner, "Nashe's Red Herring: Epistemologies of the Commodity in *Lenten Stuff* (1599)," *ELH* 68 (2001), pp. 538–40; William N. West, "What's the Matter with Shakespeare? Physics, Identity, Playing," in *Shakespeare & Science*, ed. Carla Mazzio, *South Central Review* 26.2 (2009) 103–26, and J. M. Bernstein, "Wax, Brick, and Bread – Apotheoses of Matter and Meaning in Seventeenth Century Philosophy and Painting: Descartes and Pieter de Hooch," in *Against Voluptuous Bodies: Late Modernism and the Meaning of Painting* (Stanford University Press, 2006), pp. 19–46.

16 Colie, *Resources of Kind*, pp. 9, 2.

17 Aristotle, *Physics*, trans. R. P. Hardie and R. K. Gaye, in Jonathan Barnes, ed., *The Complete Works of Aristotle*, 2 vols. (Princeton University Press, 1984), 194a19–21. Further references will be from this edition and cited parenthetically in the text. See also William B. Hunter, "Milton's Power of Matter," *Journal of the History of Ideas* 13 (1952), pp. 56–57.

18 See also *Metaphysics* 983b 6–22.

19 Charles B. Schmitt, "Philosophy and Science in Sixteenth-Century Universities: Some Preliminary Comments," in John Emery Murdoch and Edith Dudley Sylla, eds., *The Cultural Context of Medieval Learning*, Boston Studies in the Philosophy of Science, vol. xxvi (Boston: D. Reidel Publishing, 1975), p. 493. For Schmitt's reassessment of the centrality of Aristotle to Renaissance thought, see *Aristotle and the Renaissance* (Cambridge: Harvard University Press, 1983), *John Case and Aristotelianism in Renaissance England* (Kingston, ON: McGill-Queen's University Press, 1983), and *The Aristotelian Tradition and Renaissance Universities* (London: Variorum Reprints, 1984).

20 See Weinberg, *History of Literary Criticism*, i: 48–50.

21 Weinberg, *History of Literary Criticism*, i: 113.

22 Torquato Tasso, "Discourses on the Art of Poetry," in Lawrence F. Rhu, intro. and trans., *The Genesis of Tasso's Narrative Theory: English Translations of the Early Poetics and a Comparative Study of their Significance* (Detroit: Wayne State University Press, 1993), p. 99. Further references in text as Tasso, 1587.

23 Filippo Sassetti similarly understands Aristotle's poetic theory as an extension of his natural philosophy, arguing that there are affiliations between natural and artificial creations because inventions, like poetry, arise out of the human mind, which imitates nature: "Just as the causes of natural things are four, which are composed of matter and of form and have the efficient cause which made them and the end for which they were made. [These will all be found in poems:] … Since these also have that element which, in proportion, corresponds to form … *These are causes which are in poetry just as matter and form are in natural things*" (cited in Weinberg, *History of Literary Criticism*, i: 577; my emphasis).

24 Günsberg, *Epic Rhetoric of Tasso*, p. 8.

25 Stephen M. Fallon, *Milton Among the Philosophers: Poetry and Materialism in Seventeenth-Century England* (Ithaca: Cornell University Press, 1991), p. 11.

26 Elizabeth Spiller, "The Physics and Physiology of Reading: Milton's Apple and the History of Reading," unpublished essay.

27 It is precisely because they involved an external cause that interrupted the general teleology of human creation that births that were thought to be the product of the maternal imagination were typically classified, from an Aristotelian perspective, as "monstrousities" (*Physics* 199b4).

28 "White" is often used by Aristotle as his key example of a quality (e.g., *Physics* 186a25–32), that which can be predicated of a thing, and whiteness is a mark of form. See also *Physics* 186b25, 187b7–9.

29 The publication context for Amyot's *Histoire* would also have contributed to readers' ability to recognize how Amyot was both affiliating his work with Amadisian romance, and also using that affiliation in order to attack the genre: Amyot's *Histoire* was published by the Parisian printer Estienne Groulleau. The preceeding year, Groulleau had supplanted Denis Janot, who had previously been the primary printer of Herberay's *Amadis* translations. From about 1547 to 1557, Groulleau was regularly publishing new editions of Amyot's Helidorus, hand in hand with new Amadis volumes. He even used a woodblock taken from his distinctive *Amadis* editions and reused it on the title page of Amyot's translation. See Chapter 3 for a discussion of the Grolleau editions.

30 Marc Fumaroli, "Jacques Amyot and the Clerical Polemic Against the Chivalric Novel," *Renaissance Quarterly* 38.1 (1985), p. 33.

31 Fumaroli, "Polemic," pp. 27–28.

32 Frederick Morgan Padelford, trans., *Select Translations from Scaliger's Poetics* (New York: H. Holt, 1905), p. 55.

33 Tasso, "Discourses on the Art of Poetry," in Rhu, ed. and trans., *Genesis of Tasso's Narrative Theory*, p. 109; further references in the text.

34 Abraham Fraunce, *The Countess of Pembrokes Yuchurch Conteining the affectionate life, and vnfortunate death of Phillis & Amyntas* (London, 1591).

35 Pierre Vallet, *Les Adventures amoureuse de Theagenes et Cariclee* (Paris, 1613).

36 Sir Philip Sidney, *The Defence of Poesy* in Katherine Duncan-Jones, ed., *Sir Philip Sidney* (New York: Oxford University Press, 1989), pp. 212–50.

37 Emerton, *Scientific Reinterpretation*, p. 49.

38 Amyot, *L'Histoire Aethiopique*, *iiii^v–v^r: Mais pourtant la disposition en est singuliere: car il commence au mylieu de son histoire, comme sont les Poëtes Heroïques. Ce qui cause de prime face un grand esbahissement aux lecteurs, & leur engendre un passioné desir d'entendre le commencement: & toutes fois il les tire si bien par l'ingemeuse liason de son conte, que l'on n'est point resolu de ce que l'on trouve tout au commencement du primier livre jusques à ce que l'on ayt leu la fin du cinquiesme. …. De sorte que tousjours l'entendement demeur suspendu, jusques à ce que l'on vienne à la conclusion, laquelle le lecteur satisfait, de la sorte que ce sont ceux qui à

la fin viennent à jouyr d'un bien ardemment desiré, & longement atendu. (Translation mine.)

39 Heliodorus, *An Ethiopian Story*, in Reardon, p. 409. Further references in the text.

40 Thomas Pavel, "Literary Genres as Norms and Good Habits," *New Literary History* 34 (2003), pp. 208–9.

41 Iyengar, *Shades of Difference*, p. 20.

42 Thomas Underdowne, trans., *An Aethiopian History* (London, 1569), M3ʳ; cited in Iyengar, *Shades of Difference*, p. 35.

43 In the *Heroikos*, the vinedresser conveys the hero Protesilaos' description of Achilles' physical appearance: "Achilles' hair is thick, lovelier than gold, and become no matter where and how either the wind or he himself may move it. His nose is not quite aquiline, but almost so; his brow is crescent-shaped. The spirit in his eyes, which are bluish-gray, casts off a certain eagerness" (Flavius Philostratus, *Heroikos*, ed. and trans. Jennifer K. Berenson Maclean and Ellen Bradshaw Aitken [Atlanta: Society of Biblical Literature, 2001], p. 143). See also Shadi Bartsch, *Decoding the Ancient Novel: The Reader and the Role of Description in Heliodorus and Achilles Tatius* (Princeton University Press, 1989), pp. 7–35 on the role of ekphrasis and rhetorical education in the second Sophistic.

44 Judith Perkins, "An Ancient 'Passing' Novel: Heliodorus' *Aithiopika*," *Arethusa* 32.2 (1999), p. 197.

45 Whitmarsh, "Birth of a Prodigy," pp. 95–97.

46 Indeed, while much of the narrative focuses on the search to claim Charikleia's identity, she is also clearly a figure for an abandonment of identity, for a process of becoming estranged from the identity you understand yourself to have. Theagenes and Charikleia make themselves exiles, "strangers in a strange land" (441), when they fall in love. The Tyrian merchant who tries to woo Charikleia in Book 5 is a lesser version of Theagenes but he, too, insists that he is "happy to adopt your nation and homeland as my own" (459).

47 Achilles Tatius, "Leucippe and Clitophon," trans. John J. Winkler, in Reardon, ed., *Collected Ancient Greek Novels*, p. 212. Ovid, who knows the details of Andromeda's descent and elsewhere imagines her as dark-skinned, equates the specifically aesthetic quality of her beauty with physical fairness when he sees her in the *Metamorphoses* as a marble statue ("marmoreum opus") (*Metamorphoses*, 4, 667–734). On Renaissance response to Ovid's dark-skinned Andromeda, see Elizabeth McGrath, "The Black Andromeda," *Journal of the Warburg and Courtauld Institutes* 55 (1992), pp. 1–16.

48 See David Quint, *Epic and Empire, Politics and Generic Form from Virgil to Milton* (Princeton University Press, 1993), pp. 234–47, on early modern desire for religious assimilation of Ethiopia.

49 Michael Neill, "'Mulattos,' 'Blacks,' and 'Indian' Moors: *Othello* and Early Modern Constructions of Human Difference," *Shakespeare Quarterly* 49 (1998), p. 367. See also, Ivan Hannaford, *Race: The History of an Idea in the West* (University of Chicago Press, 1992).

50 See, among others, Anthony Barthelemey, *Dark Race, Maligned Race: The Representation of Blacks in English Renaissance Drama* (Baton Rouge: Louisiana State University Press, 1987); Joyce Green MacDonald, ed., *Race, Ethnicity and Power in the Renaissance* (Madison: Farleigh Dickinson University Press, 1996); Imtiaz Habib, *Shakespeare and Race: Postcolonial Praxis in the Early Modern Period* (Lanham, MD: University Press of America, 2000); Catherine M. S. Alexander and Stanley Wells, eds., *Shakespeare and Race* (Cambridge University Press, 2000); and Dympna Callaghan, ed., *Shakespeare without Women: Representing Gender and Race on the Renaissance Stage* (New York: Routledge, 2000). On the geographical and ethnographic implications of humoral theory, see Mary Floyd-Wilson, *English Ethnicity and Race in Early Modern Drama* (Cambridge University Press, 2003), pp. 30, 46–47, 67–86.

51 Andrew Fichter, *Poets Historical: Dynastic Epic in the Renaissance* (New Haven: Yale University Press, 1982), pp. 113, 121.

52 Torquato Tasso, *Jerusalem Delivered* (Detroit: Wayne State University Press, 1987).

53 Valeria Finucci, "Maternal Imagination and Monstrous Birth: Tasso's *Gerusalemme liberata*," in *Generation and Degeneration: Tropes of Reproduction in Literature and History from Antiquity through Early Modern Europe*, eds. Valeria Finucci and Kevin Brownlee (Durham: Duke University Press, 2001), p. 47.

54 Stechow, "Heliodorus' *Aethiopica* in Art," p. 147; Boris Lossky, "Présence de Jacques Amyot dans le décor du château de Fontainebleau," in Michel Balard, ed., *Fortunes de Jacques Amyot* (Paris: A.-G. Nizet, 1986), pp. 345–53; Sandy, *Heliodorus*, pp. 120–21. The Salon de Louis XIII was renovated in 1757, and four of the paintings were relocated, although one of those four was later lost (Lossky, "Présence," p. 347). For reproductions, see Joconda: Catalogue des Collections des Musees de France, http://www.culture.gouv.fr/documentation/joconde/fr/pres.htm.

55 These include works and cycles by: Jean Mosnier (c. 1630–35), Chambre du Roi, Château de Cheverny; Abraham Bloemaert (c. 1626), Castle of Honselaersdijk (in Holland); Gerard Honthorst (c. 1634), and Kronberg Castle (near Copenhagen), as well as lost paintings done by Nicolas Knupfer (1649) for Copenhagen Castle (Stechow, "Heliodorus' *Aethiopica*," pp. 147–51.)

56 On early modern artistic responses to the Heliodorus story, see Peter Erickson, "Invisibility Speaks: Servants and Portraits in Early Modern Visual Culture," *Journal for Early Modern Cultural Studies* 9.1 (2009), pp. 41–45; and Jonathan Crewe, "Drawn in Color: *Aethiopika in European Painting*," *Word & Image* 25 (2009), pp. 128–42.

57 Lossky, "Présence de Jacques Amyot," pp. 345–54.

58 Stechow, "Heliodorus' *Aethiopica*," p. 147.

59 In the tenth painting from the cycle (which shows Charikleia on the pirate ship), for instance, Charikleia's skin tone is much whiter and bluer than

anyone else's. Some of this sculptural quality is also evident in the surviving studies for the cycle. This conception of Charikleia contrasts sharply with Van Mander's treatment.

60 Stechow, "Heliodorus' *Aethiopica*," pp. 151–52, pl. 19a–c; McGrath, "Black Andromeda," pp. 1–2.
61 Pierre Vallet, *Les Adventures amoureuse de Theagenes et Cariclee* (Paris, 1613), 1.
62 Vallet, *Les Adventures*, 11.
63 Pierre Vallet, *Le Jardin du Roy très Chrétien, Loys XIII* (Paris, 1623), p. 4
64 Lorraine Daston, "Marvelous Facts and Miraculous Evidence in Early Modern Europe," *Critical Inquiry* 18.1 (1991), pp. 93–124.
65 Ambrose Paré, *On Monsters and Marvels*, ed. and trans. Janis L. Pallister (University of Chicago Press, 1982), p. 38.
66 Andrew Willet, *Hexapla in Genesin* (Cambridge, 1605), p. 319.
67 Martin Luther, *Lectures on Genesis, Chapters 26–30*, in *Works*, ed. Jaroslav Pelikan, 55 vols. (St. Louis: Concordia, 1955), v: 380–81.

3 THE CONVERSION OF THE READER

1 Marian Rothstein, *Reading in the Renaissance: Amadis de Gaule and the Lessons of Memory* (Newark: University of Delaware Press, 1999), preface, n.p.
2 Winfried Schleiner, "Laughter and Challenges to the Other in the French *Amadis de Gaule*," *Sixteenth Century Journal* 32.1 (2001), p. 91.
3 See Simone Pinet ("The Knight, the Kings, and the Tapestries: The *Amadis* Series," *Revista Canadiense de Estudios Hispánicos* 30.3 [2006], p. 537) for the argument that the material realities of the Spanish book trade gave the *Amadís* cycle "certain formal features" that determined how the cycle was subsequently transmitted but that have been misconstrued by later critics.
4 On the material features of Janot's editions, see Rothstein, *Reading in the Renaissance*, pp. 32–34; Stephen A. Rawles, "The Earlier Editions of Herberay's Translation of *Amadis de Gaula*," *The Library*, 3rd series, 6.3 (1981), pp. 91–108; N. Cazauran, "*Amadis de Gaule* en 1540: un nouveau 'roman de chevalerie'?" in *Les Amadis en France au XVI ᵉ siècle* (Paris: Editions Rue d'Ulm, 2000), pp. 21–39. On Janot as a printer, see Rawles, "Denis Janot, Parisian Printer and Bookseller (fl. 1529–44): A Bibliographical Study" (Ph.D. dissertation, University of Warwick, 1976); Abby E. Zanger, "What is a Book? Repetition and its Compulsions in Sixteenth-Century French Book Illustration," Rutgers Seminar in the History of the Book (March 2007); and Annie Parent, *Les métiers du livre à Paris* (Geneva: Librarie Droz, 1974), pp. 107–9, 310–20. These two styles continue to coexist: English readers would have seen an elegant, Janot-like volume in Anthony Munday's *The Ancient, Famous and Honorable History of Amadis of Gaule* (1618–19) more or less alongside his old-fashioned, black-letter *Primaleon* (also 1619).
5 Virginia Krause, "Serializing the French Amadis in the 1540s," in Marian Rothstein, ed., *Charting Change in France around 1540* (Selinsgrove, PA: Susquehanna University Press, 2006), pp. 40, 50. For an account of romance reading in England that emphasizes the importance of serialization,

see Lori Humphrey Newcomb, *Reading Popular Romance in Early Modern England* (New York: Columbia University Press, 2002), pp. 21–129.

6 Rothstein, *Reading in the Renaissance*, p. 64.

7 Garci Rodríguez de Montalvo, *Amadis of Gaul: A Novel of Chivalry of the 14th Century Presumably First Written in Spanish*, ed. and trans. Edwin B. Place and Herbert C. Behm, 2 vols. (Lexington: University Press of Kentucky, 1974), II: 58; Garci Rodríguez de Montalvo, *Amadís de Gaula*, ed. Juan Manuel Cacho Blecua, 2 vols. (Madrid: Ediciones Cátedra, 1991), II: 1004 (Book 3, Chapter 66): vieron que tenía debaxo de la teta derccha unas letras tan blancas como la nieve, y so la teta isquierda siete letras tan coloradas como brasas bivas; pero ni las unas ni las otras supieron leer, ni qué dezían, porque las blancas eran de latín muy escuro, y las coloradas, en lenguaje griego muy cerrado. Further references are cited parenthetically in the text and in the notes. Montalvo's interest seems primarily to be in this physical text that can only be read by the right reader at the right moment. Contemporary translators provide their own interpretation of these letters: in *The third booke of Amadis de Gaule* (London, 1618), Anthony Munday, who is following the Herberay translation, instead describes these letters as being "as red as blood" (p. 29). Munday also confuses some of the details here ("all Greeke letters, composed in Latin words," p. 29) in ways that suggest he does not distinguish between the two different kinds of texts, or forms of identity, that Montalvo is inscribing into the body of his new Christian knight. Montalvo does not identify his red as a matter of genealogy; if anything, the red might present itself in textual terms, as a kind of corporeal version of a red-letter incipit, so it is notable to see other readers re-introducing precisely the concerns about bloodlines here that Montalvo was moving away from.

8 Montalvo, *Amadís de Gaula*, II: 1009: Y leyéndolas vio que dezían las blancas en latín: "Esplandián," y pensó que aquél devía ser su nombre, y assí jelo puso; pero las coloradas, ahunque mucho se trabajó, no las supo leer, ni entender que lo dezían.

9 Garci Rodríguez de Montalvo, *The Labors of the Very Brave Knight Esplandián*, trans. William Thomas Little (Binghampton, New York, 1992), p. 329; Garci Rodríguez de Montalvo, *Sergas de Esplandián*, ed. Carlos Sainz de la Maza (Madrid: Clásicos Castalia, 2003), p. 524: con la turbación no tuvo memoria de ver las letras que aquel cavallero en sus pechos tenía. Further references in text and in notes are to these editions.

10 Montalvo, *Sergas de Esplandián*, p. 795: dize una que en su diestra parte tiene su nombre y en la siniestra el de aquella que suya deve ser, las cuales letras por ella an de ser declaradas.

11 Montalvo, *Sergas de Esplandián*, p. 797: estas siete letras assí coloradas como aquí se muestran.

12 Montalvo, *Sergas de Esplandián*, p. 797: El emperador y todos aquellos señores las miraron y claramente vieron cómo en ninguna cosa discordavan de las que Esplandián tenía; y leyendo la declaración, dezía assí: "Aquel bienaventurado cavallero que la espada y el gran thesoro por mí encantado ganare terná en el su pecho su nombre y el de su amiga. E porque, según la

escuridad grande de las siete letras coloradas, ninguno sería tan sabio que su declaración alcançasse, quise que por mí sepan aquellos que dozientos años después de mí vernán cómo en ellas consiste el nombre de Leonorina, hija del grande emperador de Grecia."

13 Wolfram von Eschenbach, *Parzival*, ed. and trans. Cyril Edwards (Oxford University Press, 2006), p. 313.

14 Garci Rodríguez de Montalvo, *Amadis of Gaul,* p. 294 (Book 2, Chapter 52); Montalvo, *Amadís de Gaula*, ed. Cacho Blecua, 1: 741: tenía el rostro muy descarnado y negro, mucho más que si de gran dolencia agraviado fuera, assí que no avía persona que conoscerlo pudiesse.

15 Montalvo, *Amadís de Gaula*, ed. Cacho Blecua, 1: 741 (Book 2, Chapter 52): Los coraçones de los hombres … fazen las cosas buenas, que no el buen parescer.

16 Ludovico Ariosto, *Orlando Furioso*, trans. Barbara Reynolds, 2 vols. (New York: Penguin, 1977), 23.134.2; *Orlando Furioso*, ed. Lanfranco Caretti (Milan: R. Ricciardi, 1954): offuscato in ogni senso. Further references in text and notes.

17 Ariosto, *Orlando Furioso*, 24.13.8: con fiera voglia.

18 Ariosto, *Orlando Furioso*, 29.59:

> Che fosse Orlando, nulla le soviene:
> troppo è diverso da quel ch'esser suole.
> Da indi in qua che quel furor lo tiene,
> è sempre andato nudo all'ombra e al sole:
> se fosse nato all'aprica Siene,
> o dove Ammone il Garamante cole,
> o presso ai monti onde il gran Nilo spiccia,
> non dovrebbe la carne aver più arsiccia.

19 John Harington, trans., *Orlando furioso in English heroic verse* (London, 1591), 29.58.6, 7–8.

20 This surcoat is one that Orlando won by defeating Almonte, the son of Agolante. Almonte was one of Ruggiero's uncles, responsible in part for the deaths of Ruggiero's mother and father and representative of the African side of Ruggiero that this narrative is committed to overcoming. For evidence of Ariosto's attention to the black coat, see also 9.5 and 14.33.

21 See Marion Wells, *The Secret Wound: Love-Melancholy and Early Modern Romance* (Stanford University Press, 2007), pp. 24–30, for an account of the mind/body problem that melancholy raised. See also Chapter 4 for a discussion of how Philip Sidney and Lady Mary Wroth participate in this tradition at a later moment in the development of racial identity.

22 Ariosto, *Orlando Furioso*, 29.62.6–8:

> ma la pelle trovò dura come osso,
> anzi via più ch'acciar; ch'Orlando nato
> impenetrabile era et affato.

23 Ariosto, *Orlando Furioso*, 30.15.7–8:

fin che trovò, dove tendea sul lito,
di nera gente esercito infinito.

24 Ariosto, *Orlando Furioso*, 39.56.1–4:

Lo fa lavar Astolfo sette volte,
e sette volte sotto acqua l'attuffa;
sì che dal viso e da le membra stolte
leva la brutta rugine e la muffa.

Cf. Harington, trans., *Orlando Furioso*: "they saw his skin looke black as any soot" and so they wash him seven times to get "the scurfe from off his skin and face / With which his naked going had been bred" (39.53.6, 39.54.3–4).

25 For both Boiardo and Pulci, Orlando had functioned as a figure for conversion so Ariosto's reading of Montalvo is notable as a rethinking of what kind of figure of conversion Orlando will now be.

26 In Ariosto's version, the King of Senapo's people may be Ethiopian, Nubian, or perhaps Christian Arabs (38.46); the dream of a vast army that would defeat seven Africas does not represent the hope of triumph through conversion. Rather, Ariosto uses it to hold out the related (but not entirely compatible) fantasy that there was no need to rely on conversion because, as Mandeville had promised, out there, across the desert, there was a nation, already Christian and armed against Islam, waiting to reunite with Christian Europe. Even as his narrative depends on the Ethiopian rescue, Ariosto mocks its possibility as a fantasy. The Ethiopian army, for instance, stands as an almost frivolous parody of the very similar storyline in *Tirant lo Blanc*: insofar as whatever military help is brought by this army that depends on boats made from leaves and from stones that turn into horses, its power derives not from religious faith but through the (here more powerful) magic of literary invention.

27 Ariosto, *Orlando Furioso*, 33.102.7–9:

Gli è, s'io non piglio errore, in questo loco
ove al battesmo loro usano il fuoco.

28 Matteo Maria Boairdo, *Orlando Innamorato: Orlando in Love*, trans. Charles Stanley Ross (West Lafayette, IN: Parlor Press, 2004), II.12.11–15. Further citations are from this edition and noted parenthetically as OI.

29 For Ariosto's repeated emphasis on Orlando's enchanted skin, see *Orlando Furioso*, 12.49, 12,67, 34.62, 41.29.

30 Ariosto is rejecting Boiardo and Luigi Pulci's attitudes toward conversion as much as he is Montalvo's: in their accounts, Orlando is strongly associated with the conversion of pagans, and he converts the giant Morgante (*Morgante* [1483]), Agricane (OI 1.18.25–55, 1.19.1–20), and baptizes Brandimarte (OI 2.12.1–15) as well as Sansonetto (*Orlando Furioso*, 1.15.95, 97).

31 The subject of Ariosto's relationship to the genres of romance and epic, and particularly the sense of his shift toward epic, both later in his life and in the revisions to the different editions of *Orlando Furioso*, has been a subject of significant critical attention. See Sergio Zatti, "The *Furioso* between *Epos* and Romance," in *The Quest for Epic: From Ariosto to Tasso*, ed. Dennis

Looney and trans. Sally Hill with Dennis Looney (University of Toronto Press, 2006), pp. 13–59.

32 This strategy is notable because elsewhere race is rarely a dominant feature in Ariosto's fiction. The parade of the African and Spanish troops (14.11–27) does not employ the kind of language that dominates Boiardo's parade of the pagan troops, which is basically a catalogue of increasingly denigrating descriptions of the racially barbaric enemies (OI 2.22.1–32), from Sorridàno ("swarthy as his troops, / His lips were full, his eyes red, and / I tell you the man seemed mad," 2.22.6.4–6) to Brunello ("a swarthy little midget," 2.22.6).

33 Ariosto, *Orlando Furioso* 22.35.3–4:

> com'era stato il padre, e antiquament
> l'avolo e tutta la sua stirpe onesta.

34 Ariosto, *Orlando Furioso* 46.106.2:

> perché essendo cristian non pòi negarla.

35 Lady Mary Wroth, *The Second Part of the Countess of Montgomery's Urania*, Josephine A. Roberts, Suzanne Gossett, and Janel Mueller, eds. (Tempe, Arizona: Renaissance English Text Society, 1999), p. 43.

36 Much attention has been paid to Herberay's translations as a cultural phenomenon and print sensation. See, among others, John J. O'Connor, *Amadis de Gaule and its influence on Elizabethan literature* (New Brunswick, NJ: Rutgers University Press, 1970), pp. 43–83; Edwin B. Place, "El *Amadís* de Montalvo como manual de cortesanía en Francia," *Revista de Filologia Espagnola* 38 (1954), pp. 151–69; and Rawles, "The Earlier Editions." Assessments of the differences between the Spanish originals and French translations include O'Conner, *Amadis de Gaule*, pp. 133–46; Rothstein, *Reading in the Renaissance*, pp. 125–44.

37 Ivan Hannaford, *Race: The History of an Idea in the West* (Baltimore: Johns Hopkins University Press, 1996), p. 40.

38 Montalvo, *Sergas de Esplandián*, p. 310: mala e perversa secta.

39 Nicolas de Herberay, trans., *Le cinquiesme livre de Amadis de Gaule* (Paris, 1544), f. 40^{r-v}. Further citations in the text.

40 Montalvo, *Sergas de Esplandián*, p. 332: es convertido y mudado en que siga aquello que, aventurando el cuerpo a la muerte, se gane la gloria y vida para el ánima.

41 Montalvo, *Sergas de Esplandián*, p. 352: sola su vita y habla era bastante para que no tan solamente a él, mas a todo el paganismo convertir pudiesse.

42 Montalvo, *Sergas de Esplandián*, p. 756: si él en nuestra ley fuesse podríamos creer que nuestros dioses con sus manos lo avían hecho, poniendo en la tal obra todo su gran poder y mucho saber, sin que nan dello quedasse.

43 Montalvo, *Sergas de Esplandián*, p. 501: los reyes bárbaros de naciones blancas y negras.

44 Antony Munday, *The fifth book of the most pleasant and delectable historie of Amadis de Gaule* (London, 1598), Hh2^{v}.

45 See Donna B. Hamilton, *Anthony Munday and the Catholics, 1560–1633* (Aldershot: Ashgate, 2005), p. 74, on the fact that most translations were associated with Catholics and adaptations with Protestants; see also Brian C. Lockey, *Law and Empire in English Renaissance Literature* (Cambridge University Press, 2006), pp. 19–44. Munday's religious affiliations – somewhere between a pursuivant and a crypto-Catholic – have been the subject of controversy.

46 Hamilton, *Anthony Munday and the Catholics*, p. 77.

47 See the later polemic debate between Batt, a Benedictine, who published Augustinian apocrypha, and the religious controversialist Thomas Roger. In *A heavenly treasure* (London, 1624), Batt vehemently denied Roger's charge that Catholics were involved in "translating, and printinge of divers lewed legends of knights errants, as Amadis, Palmerin, and like" as a way "to pervert Protestants, whom they could not confute with disputations." To refute this charge, Batt insists that "the world knowes, the translators of those books to have been professed Protestants, and some of them Poursuivants, and damnable Apostates as Antony Munday, and the like, sworne officers, and helhoundes to hunt out poore afflicted Catholickes" (*A heavenly treasure of comfortable meditations* [1624], pp. 13–14). Batt does not deny that romances might be put to such uses but only denies that Munday was a Catholic.

48 François de La Noue, *The Politicke and Militarie Discourses of the Lord de la Noue*, trans. E. A. (London, 1587), p. 48. Further references in text.

49 Antony Munday, trans., *Second part, of the no lesse rare, than excellent and stately historie of the famous and fortunate princes Palmerin of English* in *The [first] seconde part, of the no lesse rare, histories of Palmerine of England* (London, 1596), A3^r.

50 Barbara Root, "Speaking Christian: Orthodoxy and Difference in Sixteenth-Century Spain," *Representations* 23 (1988), pp. 118–34.

51 Root, "Speaking Christian," pp. 129, 118, 132.

52 Fuchs, *Passing for Spain*, pp. 2, 7. Fuchs persuasively argues that this demand that subjects be "transparent and classifiable" in turn created a counter-culture dedicated to various acts of hiding, obscuring, or dissimulating identity – a culture of "performances of identity," of passing. See Introduction for my arguments about the dominance of performance-based models for understanding practices of identity and race.

53 Miguel de Cervantes, *Don Quixote*, intro. Harold Bloom and trans. Edith Grossman (New York: Harper Collins, 2003), p. 8; Miguel de Cervantes, *Don Quijote de la Mancha*, ed. Angel Basanta, 2 vols. (Plaza & Janés, 1985), I: 136: todo él es una invectiva contra los libros de caballerías. Further citations in the text and notes are from these editions.

54 Carlos Fuentes, "Introduction," in Miguel de Cervantes, *Don Quixote*, trans. Tobias Smollett (New York: Farrar Straus, 1986), p. xviii; Bloom, "Introduction," in *Don Quixote*, p. xxi.

55 Américo Castro, *Cervantes y los casticismos españoles* (Madrid, Alianza, 1974), p. 34; critics who agree that Cervantes probably came from a New Christian

background include, among others, Daniel Eisenberg, *A Study of Don Quixote*, trans. Isabel Veredaguer (Newark, DE: Juan de la Cuesta, 1987), p. 2; María Rosa Menocal, *The Ornament of the World: How Muslims, Jews and Christians Created a Culture of Tolerance in Medieval Spain* (Boston: Little Brown, 2002); Fuchs, *Passing for Spain*.

56 Norman Roth, *Conversos, Inquisition, and the Explusion of the Jews from Spain* (Madison: University of Wisconsin Press, 1995), p. 95; on the Inquisition and Fernán Díaz's own status as a *converso*, see Benzion Netanyahu, *The Origins of the Inquisition in Fifteenth Century Spain* (New York: Random House, 1995), pp. 385–96.

57 Michael McGaha, "Is there a hidden Jewish meaning in *Don Quixote?*" *Cervantes; Bulletin of the Cervantes Society of America* 24.1 (2004), p. 173. For an overview of the history of critical thinking in these issues, see also Leyla Rouhi, "Reading *Don Quixote* in a Time of War," in Simon R. Doubleday and David Coleman, eds., *In the Light of Medieval Spain: Islam, the West and the Revelance of the Past* (New York: Palgrave, 2008), pp. 53–66.

58 Cervantes, *Don Quijote*, II: 1346: renombre de *Bueno*.

59 Cervantes, *Don Quijote*, I: 181: que bien merecen ser abrasados, como si fuesen de herejes.

60 Cervantes, *Don Quijote*, I: 184: dogmatizador de una secta tan mala.

61 Cervantes, *Don Quijote*, I: 184: hijo legítimo de Amadís de Gaula; 184: dé principio al montón de la hoguera que se ha de hacer.

62 Thomas, *Spanish and Portuguese Romances of Chivalry*, p. 169; for several additional exceptions, see also Irving A. Leonard, *Books of the Brave: Being An Account of Books and of Men in the Spanish Conquest and Settlement of the Sixteenth-Century New World* (1949; Berkeley: University of California Press, 1992), pp. 112–13, p. 413 n. 1. For Leonard's account of royal decrees and other regulations, after 1541, that were designed to prevent the importation of romances into the New World, see *Books of the Brave*, pp. 77–90, 124–39.

63 Cervantes, *Don Quijote*, I: 335: Bien es verdad que yo soy hijodalgo de solar conocido, de posesión y propiedad y de devengar quinientos sueldos.

64 Cervantes, *Don Quijote*, II: 759: yo no sé, por cierto, quién le puso a él *don*, que no tuvieron sus padres ni sus agüelos.

65 Cervantes, *Don Quijote*, II: 997: más que medianamente moreno.

66 Cervantes, *Don Quijote*, I: 195: en él se resucitase la caballería andantesca.

67 Cervantes, *Don Quijote*, I: 131: padrasto; 132: ni eres su pariente ni su amigo.

68 Cervantes, *Don Quijote*, I: 133: y después los podéis bautizar y poner el nombre que quisiéredes, ahijándolos al Preste Juan de las Indias o al Emperador de Trapisonda.

69 Menocal, *Ornament of the World*, pp. 197, 223–4.

70 Cervantes, *Don Quijote*, I: 211: mejor y más antigua lengua.

71 Cervantes, *Don Quijote*, I: 212: por el claustro de la iglesia mayor, y roguéle me volviese aquellos cartapacios, todos los que trataban de don Quijote, en lengua castellana, sin quitarles ni añadirles nada.

72 Cervantes, *Don Quijote*, 1: 336: yo cristiano viejo soy, y para ser conde esto me basta.

73 Cervantes, *Don Quijote*, 1: 659: soy cristiano viejo … y debajo de ser hombre puedo venir a ser papa.

74 Cervantes, *Don Quijote*, 1: 335: no sé yo cómo se podía hallar que yo sea de linaje de reyes, o, por lo menos, primo segundo de emperador.

75 Cervantes, *Don Quijote*, 1: 179–80: Yo sé quién soy … y sé que puedo ser no sólo los que he dicho, sino todos los doce Pares de Francia, y aun todos los nueve de la Fama.

76 Cervantes, *Don Quijote*, 1: 245: el linaje, prosapia y alcurnia.

77 Cervantes, *Don Quijote*, 11: 1001: dice que era rubión; cosa que me hace dudar en la alteza de su linaje.

78 Cervantes, *Don Quijote*, 1: 388: Y para concluir con todo, yo imagino que todo lo que digo es así, sin que sobre ni falte nada, y píntola en mi imaginación como la deseo, así en la belleza como en la principalidad.

79 Cervantes, *Don Quijote*, 1: 388: en lo del linaje importa poco, que no han de ir a hacer la información dél para darle algún hábito.

80 For the sake of clarity here, I refer to the "ordinary gentleman" who becomes Don Quixote as "Alonso Quixano," but that is a clarity that the text does not ever give us.

81 A. S. Abulafia, "Christian Imagery," cited in Geraldine Heng, *Empires of Magic: Medieval Romance and the Politics of Cultural Fantasy* (New York: Columbia University Press, 2004), pp. 80–81; see also Jonathan Boyarin, *The Unconverted Self: Jews, Indians, and the Identity of Christian Europe* (University of Chicago Press, 2009), pp. 69–70, 99–102, for evidence of the persistence of these arguments in the early modern period and their application to native Americans as well as Jews.

82 In this respect, my argument differs from a line of argument that has emerged out of recent critical attention to Cervantes' religious ancestry. As McGaha points out, such attention has led some readers to an interpretive practice that ends up taking *Don Quixote* as a kind of Straussian allegory that hides a coded religious subtext. McGana notes, "Once the idea that Cervantes was of *converso* ancestry had won wide acceptance, some readers, not surprisingly, began to look for hidden Jewish messages in *Don Quixote*." Thus, Dulcinea symbolizes Shekhinah, the Glory of God; caballería refers covertly to the kabbala; the blowing of the horn at the inn when he is knighted points to the blowing of the shofar on the day of Redemption.

83 Cervantes, *Don Quijote*, 1: 148–49: y desvelábase por entenderlas y desentrañarles el sentido, que no se lo sacara ni las entendiera el mismo Aristóteles, si resucitara para solo ello.

84 It is at its heart an episode the emblematizes, however comically, how romance teaches its readers to "read" identity: Quixote is demonstrating a sophisticated ability to read and construe social identity in characters ("follow my fate"; "armors, colors, legends, devices," 128) and also following romance's injunction to apply the lessons of reading derived from the text and apply them to the social world.

85 Heng, *Empires of Magic*, pp. 181–238.

86 Cervantes, *Don Quijote*, I: 292: Quiérense mal … porque este Alifanfarón es un furibundo pagano, y está enamorado de la hija de Pentapolín, que es una muy fermosa y además agraciada señora, y es cristiana, y su padre no se la quiere entregar al rey pagano si no deja primero la ley de su falso profeta Mahoma y se vuelve a la suya.

87 Cervantes, *Don Quijote*, I: 291: diversas e innumerables gentes.

88 David Quint, *Epic and Empire, Politics and Generic Form from Virgil to Milton* (Princeton University Press, 1993), p. 27.

89 Cervantes, *Don Quijote*, I: 292: batallas, encantamentos, sucesos, desatinos, amores, desafíos.

90 Cervantes, *Don Quijote*, I: 174–175: Si os la mostrara … qué hiciérades vosotros en confesar una verdad tan notoria? La importancia está en que sin verla lo habéis de creer, confesar, afirmar, jurar y defender.

91 Cervantes, *Don Quijote*, I: 295: El miedo que tienes … te hace, Sancho, que ni veas ni oyas a derechas.

92 María Antonia Garcés, *Cervantes in Algiers: A Captive's Tale* (Nashville, TN: Vanderbilt University Press, 2002), p. 186. See also Luis Andrés Murillo, "El *Ur-Quijote*: Nueva hipótesis," *Cervantes* I (1981), pp. 43–50.

93 Cervantes, *Don Quijote*, I: 574–75: un soldado español llamado tal de Saavedra, el cual, con haber hecho cosas qu quedarán en la memoria de aquellas gentes por muchos años, y todas por alcanzar libertad.

94 Cervantes, *Don Quijote*, I: 422: dos pedazos de blanco cristal; suspendióles la blancura y belleza de los pies; de blanco alabastro parecía.

95 Sancho provides a comic recognition of the fact that conversion narratives produced not just racialism but also, ultimately, slavery. He initially is concerned that the Princess' kingdom was "in a land of blacks" (245). Ultimately, though, he decides that he need not worry if all his vassals are blacks: "All I have to do is put them on a ship and bring them to Spain, where I can sell them … No matter how black they are, I'll turn them white and yellow" (245). Sancho clearly has his own conversion narrative ready to deal with the racial conflicts.

96 Cervantes, *Don Quijote*, I: 576: una muy blanca mano.

97 Cervantes, *Don Quijote*, I: 425: sin mezcla de alguna raza mal sonante, y, como suele decirse, cristianos viejos ranciosos.

98 Cervantes, *Don Quijote*, I: 552: Mora es en el traje y en el cuerpo; pero en el alma es muy grande cristiana, porque tiene grandísimos deseos de serlo.

99 Cervantes, *Don Quijote*, I: 542: illustre sangre.

100 Cervantes, *Don Quijote*, II: 1186: quién te ha hecho franchote.

101 Cervantes, *Don Quijote*, II: 1186: el bando de Su Majestad, que con tanto rigor a los desdichados de mi nación amenazaba.

102 Cervantes, *Don Quijote*, II: 1274: mamé la fe católica en la leche.

103 Cervantes, *Don Quijote*, II: 1288: en ella hija tan cristiana y padre, al parecer, tan bien intencionado.

104 Richard Hitchcock, "Cervantes, Ricote and the Expulsion of the Moriscos," *Bulletin of Spanish Studies* 81.2 (2004), pp. 175–85.

105 Cervantes, *Don Quijote*, ii: 1190: yo sé cierto que la Ricota mi hija y Francisca Ricota mi mujer son católicas cristianas, y aunque yo no lo soy tanto, todavía tengo más de cristiano que de moro.

106 Cervantes, *Don Quijote*, ii: 1288–1289: que todo el cuerpo de nuestra nación está contaminado y podrido ... porque no se lo quede ni encubra ninguno de los nuestros, que como raíz escondida, que con el tiempo venga después a brotar, y a echar frutos venenosos en España, ya limpia, ya desembarazada de los temores en que nuestra muchedumbre la tenía.

4 PAMPHILIA'S BLACK HUMOR

1 Kim F. Hall, *Things of Darkness: Economies of Race and Gender in Early Modern England* (Ithaca: Cornell University Press, 1995), pp. 187, 129.

2 Dudley Carleton, Letter to John Chamberlain, January 7, 1605; cited in Maurice Lee, ed., *Dudley Carleton to John Chamberlain, 1603–1624, Jacobean Letters* (New Brunswick, NJ: Rutgers University Press, 1972), p. 68.

3 Carleton seems to have known, even when he saw the masque, that Jonson was in the process of publishing a description of it ("there is a pamphlet in press," 67). Josephine A. Roberts notes that Wroth is relying upon marginal commentary from printed versions of *The Masque of Blackness* (Jonson's notes about Aethiopians worshipping the moon, which Wroth refers to in 399.2–3) (Roberts, "Introduction," in *The First Part of The Countess of Montgomerie's Urania* [Binghampton, NY: Medieval and Renaissance Texts and Studies, 1995], p. xxxi). (Hereafter references to the text of the *Urania* will be from this volume and from Josephine A. Roberts, Suzanne Gossett, and Janel Mueller, eds., *The Second Part of the Countess of Montgomery's Urania* [Tempe, AZ: Renaissance English Text Society, 1999], by volume and page and will be included in the text.) That is, that even in the case of Wroth's direct responses to *The Masque of Blackness*, her representations of racial difference still involve responses to the texts that she read as well as to dramatic parts she "personated" (*The characters of Two royall Masques* [London, 1608], title page).

4 Michael G. Brennan and Noel J. Kinnamon, *A Sidney Chronology. 1554–1654* (New York: Palgrave, 2003), pp. 118–80; see also Margaret P. Hannay, *Domestic Politics and Family Absence: The Correspondence (1588–1621) of Robert Sidney, first Earl of Leicester and Barbara Gamage Sidney* (Burlington, VT: Ashgate Press, 2005).

5 Antony Wood, *The Life and Times of Anthony Wood, Antiquary, at Oxford, 1632–1695*, ed. Andrew Clark, 5 vols. (Oxford: Clarendon Press, 1891–1900), ii: 213; cited in Germaine Warkentin, "The World and the Book at Penshurst: The Second Earl of Leicester (1595–1677) and his Library," *Library* 20 (1998), p. 327. Warkentin and Joseph Black are currently editing a 1653–55 catalogue (De L'Isle/CKS U/475 Z 42/2) of the Penshurst Library. Many of the roughly five thousand separate volumes in this library were collected by Wroth's brother, Robert Sidney, but the core of the library dates before 1621.

6　John Aubrey, *Natural History of Wiltshire* (1685; New York: Kelle, 1969), cited in Margaret P. Hannay, *Philip's Phoenix: Mary Sidney, Countess of Pembroke* (Oxford University Press, 1990), p. 48. See also John Aubrey, *Brief Lives* (Oxford: Clarendon, 1989), 1: 311 and Thomas Herbert Pembroke, *Catalogue of a Selected Portion of the Renowned Library at Wilton House* (Dryden Press: Davy and Sons, 1914).

7　David McKitterick, "Women and their Books in Seventeenth-Century England: The Case of Elizabeth Puckering," *Library* 1.4 (2000), pp. 363–64; for Robert Wroth's will, see William Chapman Waller, *Loughton in Essex* (Epping: Alfred B. Davis, 1900), p. 24.

8　Brennan and Kinnamon, *Sidney Chronology*, p. 163.

9　Antony Munday, trans., *The Ancient, Famous and Honorable History of Amadis of Gaule* (London, 1618), A2^{r-v}. Munday had previously dedicated both *Zelauto* (1580) and *Palmerin d'Oliva* (1588) to Edward de Vere, Earl of Oxford.

10　Brennan and Kinnamon, *Sidney Chronology*, p. 163.

11　Richard T. Spence, *Lady Anne Clifford, Countess of Pembroke, Dorset and Montgomerie (1590–1676)* (Sutton: Indiana University Press, 1997), pp. 181–203.

12　For the important argument that Philip Sidney's extensive circulation of the *Old Arcadia* "may have changed the private character of manuscript circulation," see H. R. Woudhuyson, *Sir Philip Sidney and the Circulation of Manuscripts, 1558–1640* (Oxford University Press, 1996), p. 8. On the timing of the publication of the *Urania*, see Roberts, *The Poems*, p. 70 n. 15.

13　Roberts, "Introduction," in *Urania*, pp. xviii–xxxix.

14　Woudhuysen, *Sir Philip Sidney and the Circulation*, p. 9

15　Cyndia Susan Clegg, *Press Censorship in Jacobean England* (Cambridge University Press, 2001), pp. 184–85; Roberts, "Textual Introduction," in *Urania*, pp. cvii–cviii.

16　Roberts, "Textual Introduction," in *Urania*, pp. cv–cvi.

17　Roberts, "Introduction," in *Urania*, pp. xxii.

18　See Roberts, "Introduction," in *Urania*, pp. lxix–ciii; Mary Ellen Lamb, "The Biopolitics of Romance in Mary Wroth's *The Countess of Montgomery's Urania*," *ELR* 31.1 (2001), pp. 107–30; Jennifer Lee Carrell, "A pack of lies in a looking glass: Lady Mary Wroth's 'Urania' and the magic of romance," *SEL* (1994), pp. 79–107.

19　Jonathan Boyarin, *The Unconverted Self: Jews, Indians, and the Identity of Christian Europe* (University of Chicago Press, 2009), pp. 74, 97–104.

20　On the controversy generated by Wroth's fictional depiction of the scandals surrounding Denny, his daughter Honora, and her husband James Hay, see Roberts, *The Poems*, pp. 31–36; Roberts, "An Unpublished Literary Quarrel Concerning the Suppression of Mary Wroth's 'Urania' (1621)," *Notes and Queries* 24 (1977), pp. 532–35; Paul Salzman, "Contemporary References in Mary Wroth's *Urania*," *Review of English Studies* 29.114 (1978), pp. 178–81;

John J. O'Connor, "James Hay and 'The Countess of Montgomerie's Urania'," *Notes and Queries* 2 (1955), pp. 150–52.

21 *Historical Manuscripts Commission (HMC)*, Series 55, pt. 7: Manuscripts of Sir Hervy Juckes Lloyd Bruce; University of Nottingham Library, item C1 LM 85/1–5; cited in Roberts, ed., *Poems*, pp. 32–33. Versions are also extant in at least two contemporary commonplace books. See Roberts, *Poems*, p. 33, n. 83.

22 Lord Edward Denny to Lady Mary Wroth, February 26, 1621/2; *HMC*, Salisbury, xxii, 160–61; cited in Roberts, *Poems*, p. 238. See also Letter of John Chamberlain to Dudley Carleton, March 9, 1621/2; in Norman Egbert McClure, ed., *Letters of John Chamberlain*, 2 vols. (Philadelphia, 1939), ii: 427.

23 Letter of May 31, 1640, *HMC*, Rutland, Appendix iv, i, 520, rpt. in Roberts, ed., *Poems*, pp. 244–45.

24 Letter to Duke of Buckingham, December 15, 1621; Bodleian L Ms Add. D iii, ff. 173^{r-v}; cited in Roberts, ed., *Poems*, p. 236.

25 Letter to Sir Edward Denny, February 15, 1621/2; *HMC*, Salisbury, xxii, 160; cited in Roberts, *Poems*, p. 237; Letter to Sir Edward Denny, February 27, 1621/1622; *HMC*, Denbigh, v, 3; cited in Roberts, *Poems*, p. 240.

26 Victor Stater, "Herbert, William, third earl of Pembroke (1580–1630)," in *Oxford Dictionary of National Biography*, ed. H. C. G. Matthew and Brian Harrison (Oxford University Press, 2004); online edn., ed. Lawrence Goldman, January 2008, http://www.oxforddnb.com.proxy.lib.fsu.edu/view/article/13058 (accessed December 2, 2008).

27 Michael G. Brennan, *Literary Patronage in the English Renaissance: The Pembroke Family* (New York: Routledge, 1988), pp. 99–100, 103, 107, 117–22, 132–33, 141–45.

28 Brennan, *Literary Patronage*, p. 120.

29 Gonzalo de Céspedes y Meneses, *Gerardo, the unfortunate Spaniard*, trans. Leonard Digges (London, 1622), title page.

30 Roberts, *Poems*, pp. 217–18.

31 Mary Wroth, *The Secound Part of the Countesse of Montgomerie's Urania* (Newberry Library Case Ms fY 1565 W95), i, fol. 10^{r-v}.

32 Pierre Charron, *Of wisdome Three Books*, trans. Samson Lennard (London, c. 1608), p. 164.

33 Hall, *Things of Darkness*, p. 129.

34 On Pamphilia's constancy, see Naomi J. Miller, "'Not much to be marked': Narrative of the Woman's Part in Lady Mary Wroth's *Urania*," *SEL* 29 (1989), pp. 124, 129–30; Roberts, "Introduction," in *Urania*, pp. lix–lxii; Maureen Quilligan, "The Constant Subject: Instability and Female Authority in Wroth's *Urania* Poems," in Elizabeth D. Harvey and Katharine Eisaman Maus, eds., *Soliciting Interpretation: Literary Theory and Seventeenth-Century English Poetry* (University of Chicago Press, 1990), pp. 307–35; Elaine Beilin, "'The Onely Perfect Vertue': Constancy in Mary Wroth's

Pamphilia to Amphilanthus," *Spenser Studies* 2 (1981), pp. 229–45; Mary Ellen Lamb, *Gender and Authorship in the Sidney Circle* (Madison: University of Wisconsin Press, 1990), pp. 142–43; and Alexander Gavin, "Constant Works: A Framework for Reading Mary Wroth," *Sidney Newsletter and Journal* 14.2 (1996), pp. 5–32. On Wroth's attention to female authorship and her use of Pamphilia as a model, see Nona Fienberg, "Wroth and the Invention of Female Poetic Subjectivity," in Naomi J. Miller and Gary Waller, eds., *Reading Mary Wroth: Representing Alternatives in Early Modern England* (Knoxville: University of Tennessee Press, 1991), p. 180, and Barbara K. Lewalski, *Writing Women in Jacobean England* (Cambridge: Harvard University Press, 1994), pp. 243–307.

35 Gail Kern Paster, *Body Embarrassed: Drama and the Disciplines of Shame in Early Modern England* (Ithaca: Cornell University Press, 1993), p. 6. The classic survey of the history of melancholy in England is Lawrence Babb, *The Elizabethan Malady: A Study of Melancholia in English Literature from 1580–1642* (East Lansing, MI: Michigan State University Press, 1951); recent critical discussions of melancholy in the early part of the seventeenth century include: Douglas Trevor, *The Poetics of Melancholy in Early Modern England* (New York: Cambridge University Press, 2004); Lynn Enterline, *The Tears of Narcissus: Melancholia and Masculinity in Early Modern Writing* (Stanford University Press, 1995); Juliana Schiesari, *The Gendering of Melancholia: Feminism, Psychoanalysis and the Symbolics of Loss in Early Modern England* (Ithaca: Cornell University Press, 1992); Bridget Gellert Lyons, *Voices of Melancholy: Studies in Literary Treatments of Melancholy in Renaissance England* (London: Routledge, 1971).

36 For discussions of du Laurens, Huarte, and Charron, see the Introduction. For an account of the Spanish sources, see Teresa Scott Soufas, *Melancholy and the Secular Mind in Golden Age Spain* (Columbia: University of Missouri, 1990), pp. 1–36. See also Angus Gowland, "The Problem of Early Modern Melancholy," *Past and Present* 191 (2007), pp. 79–81, for a critique of the assumption that melancholy was a specifically "English" (or otherwise limitedly regional) phenomenon.

37 E.g., Roberts, "Introduction," in *Urania*, pp. xxv–xxvi; see also Mary Ellen Lamb, *Gender and Authorship in the Sidney Circle* (Madison: University of Wisconsin Press, 1990); Maureen Quilligan, "Lady Mary Wroth: Female Authority and the Family Romance," in George M. Logan and Gordon Teskey, eds., *Unfolded Tales: Essays on Renaissance Romance* (Ithaca: Cornell University Press, 1989), pp. 257–80; Wendy Wall, *The Imprint of Gender: Authorship and Publication in the English Renaissance* (Ithaca: Cornell University Press, 1993), pp. 336–38. For an argument that connects Wroth to other romances, see Helen Hackett, *Women and Romance Fiction in the English Renaissance* (Cambridge University Press, 2000), pp. 159–82.

38 Katherine Duncan-Jones, ed., *Sir Philip Sidney* (Oxford University Press, 1989), p. vii, xv–xvii.

39 Philip Sidney, *The Countess of Pembroke's Arcadia*, ed. Maurice Evans (New York: Penguin, 1977), p. 64. Further references in text.

40 pseudo-Aristotle, *The Problemes of Aristotle with other philosophers and phisitions* (Edinborough, 1595). For images that suggest this male gendering to the humors, see Raymond Klibansky, Erwin Panofsky, and Fritz Saxl, *Saturn and Melancholy: Studies in the History of Natural Philosophy, Religion, and Art* (New York: Basic Books, 1964), figs. 80, 81, and 82.

41 pseudo-Aristotle, *Problemes*, F7ʳ.

42 Gail Kern Paster, "The Unbearable Coldness of Female Being: Women's Imperfection and the Humoral Economy," *ELR* 28 (1998), p. 422.

43 There has been a great deal of recent work on the historical development and cultural meaning of the passions. For an overview, see Gail Kern Paster, Katherine Rowe, and Mary Floyd-Wilson, "Introduction," in their *Reading the Early Modern Passions: Essays in the Cultural History of Emotion* (Philadelphia: University of Pennsylvania Press, 2004), pp. 1–20; and Sean McDowell, "The View from the Interior: The New Body Scholarship in Renaissance/Early Modern Studies," *Literature Compass* 3/4 (2006), pp. 778–91, 10.1111/j.1741–4113.2006.00346.x. There have not been sustained critical discussions of female melancholy – either of women writers or of characters; melancholy has been understood to intersect with gender primarily on masculinity. Mark Breitenberg thus identifies melancholy as "a central discourse and performance of masculinity" in the early modern period (*Anxious Masculinity in Early Modern England* [Cambridge University Press, 1996], p. 40); see also Enterline, *Tears of Narcissus*, and Schiesari, *Gendering of Melancholia*, for different models for understanding how melancholy and the loss it implies is constitutive of masculine identity. Trevor, *Poetics of Melancholy*, pp. 21–22, comments on the absence of a critical history of melancholy and early women writers.

44 Gowland, "Problem of Early Modern Melancholy," p. 99.

45 Paster, "Unbearable," p. 429.

46 Pseudo-Aristotle, *Problemes*, F6ᵛ.

47 Panofsky, *Saturn and Melancholy*.

48 Panofsky, *Saturn and Melancholy*, pp. 3–13.

49 Mary Floyd-Wilson, *English Ethnicity and Race in Early Modern Drama* (Cambridge University Press, 2003), p. 49.

50 pseudo-Aristotle, *Problemes*, F7ʳ.

51 Panofsky, *Saturn and Melancholy*, p. 290.

52 Cited in Floyd-Wilson, *English Ethnicity*, p. 37. For an extended discussion of the humoral qualities of peoples from different regions, see Jean Bodin, *The six bookes of a common-weale*, tr. Richard Knolles (London, 1606), pp. 551–57.

53 Juan Huarte, *The Examination of Men's Wits*, trans. R[ichard] C[arew] (London, 1594), p. 74.

54 Sheila T. Cavanagh, *Cherished Torment: The Emotional Geography of Lady Mary Wroth's Urania* (Pittsburgh: Duquesne University Press, 2001), p. 20.

55 Cavanagh, *Cherished Torment*, p. 23.

56 Pierre d'Avity, *The estates, empires, & principallities of the world*, trans. Edward Grimstone (London, 1615), p. 939.

57 D'Avity, *Estates, empires, & principallities*, p. 1034.

58 Bernadette Andrea, "Pamphilia's Cabinet: Gendered Authorship and Empire in Lady Mary Wroth's *Urania*," *ELH* 68 (2001), p. 345. See also her *Women and Islam in Early Modern England* (Cambridge University Press, 2007), pp. 30–52.

59 The attempt by the King of Celicia to force Pamphilia to marry him (1.505–6) may be a fictional nod to the historical uniting of these two provinces as happened under contemporary Turkish rule. It is more likely, though, that Wroth would have been familiar with its classical antecedents: Pliny, for instance, notes that "All Cosmographers have joined Pamphilia to Cilicia" (*Historie of the world*, trans. Philemon Holland [London, 1601], p. 82).

60 Herodotus, *The Histories*, trans. Aubrey de Sélincourt (New York: Penguin, 1981), p. 472.

61 Acts 2: 9–11.

62 E.g., Hall, *Things of Darkness*, pp. 203–4.

63 On Antissia's writing, see Miller, *Changing the Subject*, pp. 174–76.

64 Roxann Wheeler, *The Complexion of Race: Categories of Difference in Eighteenth-Century British Culture* (Philadelphia: University of Pennsylvania Press, 2000), p. 11.

65 For examples, see Diego de San Pedro, *Castell of Love*, trans. John Bourchier (London, c. 1548), Nvᵛ; George Whetstone, *The rocke of regard* (London, 1576), pp. 94–95; Sidney, *Arcadia*, p. 496 (Amphialus); Thomas Lodge, *Rosalynde* (London, 1592), O4ᵛ.

66 Pietro Martire d' Anghiera, *The Decades of the New World of West India*, trans. Richard Eden (London, 1555), 311ʳ. The centrality of these claims – as well as the attention that they almost certainly got from contemporary readers – is confirmed by Eden's decision to foreground this mini-essay. Later editions and variations of this text move the "Color of the Indians" essay up to the front of the volume: see, for instance, *The history of Travayle in the West and East Indies* (London, 1577), 4ʳ, and *De novo orbe; or the historie of the west Indies* (London, 1612), pp. 4–5.

67 e.g., d'Avity, *Estates, empires and principallities*, p. 1143; Leo Africanus, *A Geographical Historie of Africa*, trans. John Pory (Cambridge, 1600), Book 1, pp. 36, 53; Book 2, pp. 63–64; Samuel Purchas, *Hakluytus posthumus, or, Purchas his pilgrimes* (London, 1625), pp. 67, 68, 151, 418, 419. d'Avity captures this sense of a skin color as change and degradation when he notes that on the island of Malta the heat of the summer sun "makes the inhabitants tawnie, and in a manner like in colour to the Moores of Africke" (*Estates, empires, & principalities*, p. 1143). In *A Geographical History*, Africanus tends to argue that climate is not the chief source of skin color (1.36), and the

term "tawny" is instead used to mark the transformation produced by inter-marriage. On the island of St. Thomas, for instance, "of the conjunction betweene the men of Europe and the Negro women are bred a generation of browne or tawnie people" (1.53), while among the inhabitants of the town of Tagauoust "their women are beautifull; but their men are of a tawnie and swart colour, by reason they are descended of blacke fathers and white mothers" (2.63–64). Notably, "tawny" is also gendered and used much more often to describe men, rather than women. Thus, Purchas includes a description of the men of Arabia as being "tawney," whereas the women "are some of them reasonable white, much like to a Sun-burnned countrey maid in *England*" (p. 150). Wroth's association of tawny with Pamphilia is thus even more distinctive.

68 Philippe de Mornay, seigneur du Plessis-Marly, *A woorke concerning the trewnesse of the Christian religion*, trans. Philip Sidney and Arthur Golding (London, 1587), pp. 21–22.

69 Hall (*Things of Darkness*, pp. 92–107) demonstrates how sunburn functions as a trope for moving from Africa to Europe.

70 Robert Garnier, *The Tragedie of Antonie*, trans. Mary Sidney Herbert (London, 1595), B8^r.

71 A literal example of how, despite Eden/Martyr, the "tawny" skin color of the Ameri-Indians quickly becomes entangled with notions of change and transformation can be found in Sir Walter Raleigh's account of special ber-ries, carnation and crimson, that are found in Guiana: extolling these berries for having the special property that "the more the skin is washed, the fairer the color appeareth," Raleigh concludes "even those browne and tawnie women spot themselves and color their cheekes" (*Discourse of the large, rich, and beautiful empire of Guiana in Richard Hakluyt, The Principal Navigations* [n.d.], p. 660). Here again, and specifically in a discussion of women, the skin color "tawny" is increasingly connected to the notions of change, trans-formation or self-transformation, that become explicit slightly later with the term "tanned."

72 More so than any other in Part 1, the Pastora story is ambiguously told in ways that suggest how autobiographically tense it is: it seems to be Pastora's story, but perhaps it is only a story that Pastora may be telling about a friend, which "might be taken as an Allegory" (1.420).

73 Miller, *Changing the Subject*, p. 173.

74 Miller, *Changing the Subject*, p. 173.

75 See also "Pamphilia to Amphilanthus," Song 1.

76 Jeff Masten, "'Shall I Turne Blabb?': Circulation, Gender, and Subjectivity in Mary Wroth's Sonnets," in *Reading Mary Wroth*, Miller and Waller, eds., p. 70. "Pamphilia to Amphilanthus" is cited from Roberts, ed., *Poems*, and included in the text.

77 Elizabeth Hanson, "Boredom and Whoredom: Reading Renaissance Women's Sonnet Sequences." *Yale Journal of Criticism* 10.1 (1997), p. 184; see also Lewalski, *Writing Jacobean Women*, p. 253.

78 Philip Sidney, "Astrophil and Stella," in Katherine Duncan-Jones, ed., *Sir Philip Sidney* (New York: Oxford University Press, 1989), 1.5; 47. 2–3; further citations in the text.
79 Masten, "Shall I turn blabb," p. 69.
80 Hall, *Things of Darkness*, p. 206.
81 Robert Burton, *Anatomy of Melancholy* (New York: Empire State Book Club, 1924); further references are to this edition and included in the text.
82 For similar claims about how melancholy is equally characteristic of both hot and cold climates, see also pp. 110, 156, 245, and 331.

Index